WOUNDED WARRIORS

Also by Mike Sager

NONFICTION
Scary Monsters and Super Freaks:
Stories of Sex, Drugs, Rock 'n' Roll, and Murder

Revenge of the Donut Boys:
True Stories of Lust, Fame, Survival, and Multiple Personality

FICTION
Deviant Behavior, A Novel

WOUNDED WARRIORS

Those for Whom the War Never Ends

MIKE SAGER

Da Capo Press
A Member of the Perseus Books Group

Design and production by Eclipse Publishing Services
Set in 11.5 point Centaur

Cataloging-in-Publication Data for this book is available from the
Library of Congress.

First edition 2008 by Da Capo Press, an imprint of Perseus Books Group

ISBN-13: 978-0-306-81735-9

Published by Da Capo Press
A Member of the Perseus Books Group
www.dacapopress.com

Da Capo Press books are available at special discounts for bulk purchase in the
U.S. by corporations, institutions, and other organizations. For more information,
please contact the Special Markets Department at the Perseus Books Group,
2300 Chestnut Street, Suite 200, Philadelphia, PA 19103, or call (800) 810-4145,
ext. 5000, or e-mail special.markets@perseusbooks.com.

1 2 3 4 5 6 7 8 9

For those who let me in

The business I am in is a strange one. I intrude into people's lives for an hour or a day or a week, and I scrape their lives for what I can, and then I display the scrapings to strangers. I get paid for this; whether it is a moral calling or not, I do not know, but I have no other craft.

Bob Greene
"American Beat," *Esquire*
September, 1981

Contents

#

9
The Sharpton Strategy / *183*

Oh no! Here he comes again, leading another protest—hair luffing, flesh roiling and slushing beneath the shiny nylon of his jogging suit, size XXL. He's got Martin Luther King's dream, James Brown's hairdo, and a date with political destiny. "I just haven't learned how to talk to white folks yet," he says. At home and on the road with the Reverend Al Sharpton.

10
Death in Venice / *201*

Back in the day, when gangs fought for turf and respect, V-13 ruled the streets of Venice, California—proud *vatos* in their Pendleton shirts and hair nets. They drove shiny low-riders and sold heroin to the *miatas*, the poor blacks across the street. Then crack arrived in the neighborhood and the tables turned. Life inside an L.A. gang.

11
Hunting Marlon Brando / *217*

At first it seemed like just another exotic assignment: Go to Tahiti and find Marlon Brando. But the worldwide search for the legendary Method actor, the star of *Apocalypse Now, On the Waterfront,* and *Mutiny on the Bounty,* soon became a quest, and finally an obsession. One man's journalistic coming of age.

Foreword

#

THESE STORIES ARE particularly dear to me. I consider them my milestones, the pieces that have defined and distinguished my work over some twenty-five years of magazine journalism—the adventures, high jinx, near-death moments, and wrenching intimate encounters that have helped to shape me as a journalist and as a man.

Facing life's trials, I have often found myself turning for guidance to the lessons I've learned in the company of my subjects, the many men (and women) I have lived with and listened to and written about. Fearless young marines irretrievably broken by the wars in Afghanistan and Iraq, recovering together in a barracks at Camp Lejeune, North Carolina. America's smartest men, carving out a life among the "norms." Members of a once-proud street gang, their fortunes lost in a cloud of crack smoke. Near-feral boys in the slums of Philadelphia fighting pit bull dogs to the death. Vietnam vets who moved to Thailand after the war, seeking a cheaper cost of living and plenty of unattached sex. The Reverend Al Sharpton—a man people love to hate. Blue collar tweekers smoking ice in Hawaii. Hip heroin addicts on the lower east side of Manhattan, searching for their muse in a bindle of white powder. A diverse group from every imaginable culture, an assortment of winners and losers and cautionary tales, they have served over time as my teachers, my village elders, my older brothers, my senior NCOs, my role models—both positive and negative.

When I think of the important men in my personal life, the list is much shorter. There is my father, 78, and my two grandfathers, gone now for many years. My maternal grandfather, Lee Rosenberg, sold shoes and other dry goods in a small store in rural Virginia. He had no apparent interests beyond his figures, his family, his evening constitutionals, his twice-daily prayers. My paternal grandfather, Harry H. Sager, a country lawyer, was hard of hearing. At family gatherings he'd often remove his hearing aid. He'd sit in the middle of everyone, lost in thought, his foot fiddling ceaselessly side to side, a near-blur. Though I remember passing pleasant times with both—Lee sharing his peppermint Chiclets; Harry sending me down the street on little errands, letting me keep the spare change, until my pockets bulged—I know precious little about them. I was too young to think to ask; they never volunteered.

As for my father, Marvin Miles Sager, ever since I can remember, I have talked and he has listened. He has loved, supported, and provided, though he has not always agreed or understood. One thing he has never done was volunteer much about his history or his inner life. When I think of my father, I think of his generosity, his erect bearing, the way he opened the doors for the ladies and always helped them on with their coats. And I think of his hugs, so strong and all-enveloping as to be nearly crushing, so pleasantly scented with his signature Old Spice aftershave. But never once do I remember him saying something like, "When I was a boy such and such happened and I felt so-and-so."

When I was in college—that four-year sleep-away camp where you stage the dress rehearsal for your later life—I wrote a letter to my Dad. "Tell me about yourself," I begged, with all the anguished torment of a senior about to be turned loose on the real world. "Who are you? Are you ever afraid? How did you become a man?"

His reply came in due course, his doctor's chicken scratch making it nearly impossible to read: "Do not try to dissect me, it cannot be done."

It was an interesting choice of words for a man who'd majored in biology. I never again tried.

As it happened, I have spent pretty much the rest of my life since dissecting people unrelated to me, the great majority of them men, looking into the deep recesses of their anecdotal souls. From Charlie Van Dyke, a fat man in a low-fat world, to Marlon Brando, the flawed model for today's sensitive male; from Lieutenant Colonel Tim Maxwell, who can't remember the word for "airport" but managed to start a whole program in the Marine Corps to benefit wounded marines, to NBA lightning rod Kobe Bryant, who has, through talent and relentless effort, lifted the craft of basketball into compelling art, the very model of perfection through sport that drove the Greek ideal . . . . these men have done the lion's share of making me the man I am today.

None of these stories are available in this form anywhere else on the Web or in print; all of them have been renovated, refined, re-edited, and, in some cases, subjected to healthy cuts. As I worked again on the pieces, sense memories came flooding back: The sounds of tires squealing and bullets splitting the air above my head, a drive-by shooting during my time with the Venice gang. The pitiful shriek emitted by one pit bull as it was mauled to death by another; the demonic howls of their teenage masters. Standing in the rain with the Reverend Al Sharpton and a small group of mourners, sobbing over the gravesite of Yusuf Hawkins, a young black man I had never met, senselessly killed after finding himself in all-Italian Bensonhurst, Brooklyn. The way Charlie, the 680-pound renaissance man, thoroughly consumed his potato au gratin soup and the big round loaf of hollowed-out bread that served as its bowl. At the conclusion of the meal, his plate was so clean it looked as if it had just come out of the dishwasher. The way Mark, a once-promising musician, took out another bindle of China White heroin and snorted greedily, back on the junk after another failed attempt at quitting, full of grandiose answers and pitiful rationalizations, not at all convincing to anyone, most especially himself.

"Thailand's Home for Wayward Vets" was my first magazine piece. It was commissioned during the summer of 1983, during a face-to-face meeting at *Rolling Stone*'s storied offices in Manhattan. There were iconic photos of rock stars on the walls, a bottle of Jack Daniels on the desk. Some kind of large and colorful talking bird occupied a cage on the window ledge, which commanded a view of Central Park. Then-managing editor David Rosenthal was so blown away by my idea—searching down American vets who were living in Thailand as expats after the Vietnam War—that he offered me $1,800 and no expenses to do the piece. (The story ran at a little over 5,000 words. You can figure out the pay rate if you want; I have made a commitment over the years not to drive myself crazy with that kind of math.)

One month later, having arranged a leave of absence from my job as a staff writer at the *Washington Post*, I was on a plane. In 1983, you could buy a ticket around the world for $2,000. You could go anywhere you wanted for as long as you wanted; you just had to keep traveling in the same general direction. And so I did, moving creatively eastward for the next three months.

Three months and one week later, I was sitting in the office of *Post* publisher Don Graham, saying goodbye to my career as a daily journalist. Everyone thought I'd gone insane.

On the other side of my journey thus far is "Wounded Warriors," the paint still drying as I type this—a wrenching piece based on my time at the U.S. Marine Corp's Wounded Warrior Barracks at Camp Lejeune. I am not sorry I am finished. It was brutal work. One snapshot: A veteran gunny sergeant kneels down to tie the boots of a twenty-five-year-old corporal, a former sheriff's deputy with an acrylic plate in his head, his left side paralyzed. For these men, there will never be an end to the wars in Afghanistan and Iraq; they are the best advertisement I know for peace— though I am certain my fond Devil Dogs will disagree with me on that. For the record, it is not their conduct of the war I question. In my mind, they are brave heroes, the best fighting men in the world, the righteousness of their cause notwithstanding.

Some interesting tidbits: I only met one marine who grew up in a two-parent household; most of the guys I interviewed said they didn't know their fathers very well. All the marines I spent time with felt *guilty* for being wounded—except Robert Wild. He lost both frontal lobes of his brain as a result of a rocket attack that sent him flying head-first into a wall. He says he realizes now that joining the military and going to war was foolish, that it solved nothing, in his life or in Iraq.

"Wounded Warriors" is an expansion of a piece I did for my beloved mother-ship of the past decade, *Esquire* magazine. I cannot thank enough editor-in-chief David Granger, and Deputy Editor Peter Griffin—my wonderful editorial collaborator—who have fostered and supported me and valued my work.

In one way or another, every one of us is a Wounded Warrior. All of us are engaged in wars, large or small, that may never end. Whether it's war against racism and misunderstanding like Reverend Sharpton's, or war against known personal limits like Kobe Bryant's, or war against pain and diminishment like the young marines', or war against genetics and societal standards like Charlie's, or war against crushing poverty and ignorance and disenfranchisement like Beo's and Zeke's, or war against the overwhelmingly potent call of the next hit of your drug of choice, like Mark's and Robert Li's and Sleeper's and the rest . . . all of these men have lived deeply and experienced in earnest the highs and lows that life can deal. Each of them has played his hand. To as great a degree as possible, their struggles and life lessons are rendered here, respectfully submitted for your entertainment, for your guidance, for your enrichment.

And perhaps to haunt you, as they will forever haunt me.

Mike Sager
April 21, 2008
La Jolla, California

Wounded Warriors

Wounded Warriors

Ringo and Wildman are kickin' it with Jo-Jo, Hazy, Sergeant D, and the rest of the Devil Dogs in the rec room at Maxwell Hall when who should come through the hatch but the old man himself, Lieutenant Colonel Tim Maxwell, the guy for whom the barracks was named.

Thick-shouldered and squared away, Maxwell is dressed in his digital cammies—the sleeves of his tunic rolled cleanly to his biceps, the trouser cuffs banded securely around the shanks of his sand-colored suede combat boots—the uniform of the day aboard Camp Lejeune, North Carolina. Forty-two years old with nineteen years in (twenty-three if you count ROTC), Maxwell did five deployments overseas without a scratch. Then one afternoon in 2004, three months into his sixth, in the southern Iraqi town of Kalsu, he decided to take a power nap—fifteen minutes after chow. He'd heard about it somewhere: Many leaders through history had done the same—a short pause to refresh.

Now he pauses just inside the door of Maxwell Hall and looks around, smiling his slightly crooked smile. The right side of his face still lags; it might come back or it might not—there is no way to predict. The room has been recently repainted, the windows replaced. The new carpet is due soon; the workmen have moved on to the fitness center next door. It is July. Outside, the temperature and the humidity are both in the high 90s.

Tree frogs bark, cicadas sing their familiar summer song in the lush and tangled undergrowth. In here it is air-conditioned, a cool 69 degrees. A couple dozen enlisted men and NCOs are hanging out—shooting eight ball, playing Call of Duty on the new Xbox 360, watching a cable movie on the big flat-screen TV. One group is huddled together on the doctor's-office-variety chairs, talking smack, scratching, waiting for pizzas to be delivered so they can eat their afternoon pain meds, which need to be taken with food. (The chow hall is just across the way. Nobody eats there, even though the cost of meals is deducted from their pay, which runs about $1,700 a month for a corporal, $1,300 for a private.) A couple of the guys are racked out on the new leather sofas. One kid with his mouth wide open is snoring loud enough to interrupt the dialog of the movie, *Risky Business*, about the hi-jinx of carefree high school boys in the affluent suburbs. Two more guys luxuriate in massage chairs, fancy models like something from Sharper Image, the hum of which is clearly audible beneath the raucous, clubhouse din generated by this assembly of young men, most of them in their late teens and early twenties, most of them damaged beyond full repair. In conversation, Maxwell fondly calls them "my marines." He has a thickish Southern drawl that he picked up from some mysterious recess of his brain when he began to recover his speech after the injury. In fact, he was born in Ohio.

Maxwell spots the guy he's looking for and moves in that direction, his gait powerful but uneven, like Chesty the bulldog with a limp. He has a strong jaw and piercing blue eyes; there is a large scar on the left side of his head, a ropey pink question mark that runs like concertina wire below the hedge line of his high and tight military flattop. He has trouble reading and taking instructions. His short-term memory is shot. It took him forever to build the little fort in the backyard for his son; he had to keep rereading each step of the directions over and over again. He tells his daughter to put refrigerator on her tuna sandwich. He refers to the airport as "the place where people come to fly," and to Somalia, where he once served, as "that country in Africa." His hernia, which he kept a painful secret so as not to miss his final deployment, is "that problem with your nuts." He calls the family's new dog Magic instead of Miracle (though he can remember perfectly the name of their old dog, Bella). His right arm and right leg are functional but "clumpy." He can still run several miles on a treadmill; he does three sets of ten bicep curls, thirty-five pounds each.

Though his IQ, his reflexes, his limb strength, all of his measurable functions are down from their "factory of original," as he likes to put it, he is still within what doctors tell him are "acceptable ranges." *Acceptable to whom?* Maxwell wonders. He will never be the same. He will never be as good. It weighs on him, you can tell. He is the type of man who has spent his whole life pushing and striving, trying to raise his score or to lower his time, a man who never took the easy path: As a high school kid, he wanted to play lineman in football, even though he weighed only 140 pounds. He took his undergrad degree in engineering and a masters in statistics, even though he struggled with math. He eats "morale" pills (he tried four varieties before settling on Effexor), anti-seizure pills (five varieties), more pills every day than he is capable of recalling. All the pills have side effects. Here is the list for Effexor: constipation, dizziness, dry mouth, insomnia, loss of appetite, nausea, nervousness, sexual side effects, sleepiness, sweating, and weakness. *Ask your doctor if Effexor may be right for you. Ooh-rah.* Sometimes, his brain starts to crash. That is his word for it. His speech becomes slurry; he gets this look on his face like a guy who has been up for several days doing alcohol and drugs. He just has to shut it all down and go to bed. It happened earlier this week, after he drove the six hours in his old green Land Rover to Quantico, Virginia, to meet his new boss. He is still on active duty. He's due to report to his new billet in one week.

Corporal Justin Kinnee is sitting on one of the sofas, staring at the flat-screen through a pair of dark Nike sport sunglasses, the kind issued to troops in Iraq. Several of the guys in the room are wearing them. Extreme sensitivity to light can be one of the symptoms of a traumatic brain injury (TBI). Dilated pupils, another cause of light sensitivity, can also be a side effect of some prescription drugs. In previous U.S. military conflicts, 14 to 20 percent of surviving casualties reportedly suffered TBIs. Of the twenty-eight thousand American troops injured so far in Iraq, anywhere from a quarter to a half are estimated to have suffered TBIs. Another statistic: The marines, which is the smallest of all the U.S. armed forces, has sustained nearly one-third of all the casualties in Iraq, due to assignments in sectors like the Anbar Province, the heart of the Sunni insurgency and the deadliest place in Iraq for U.S. troops thus far in the war. In bygone days, after you got whacked, the Marine Corps gave you a Purple Heart—the medal that no marine wants—and a discharge.

Then they sent you on your way to deal with the Veterans Administration for the rest of your life. Now, due to Maxwell's efforts, there is not only a barracks for wounded warriors aboard Camp Lejeune (and another aboard Camp Pendleton in California), but there is also a brand-new Wounded Warrior Regiment in the Marine Corps. That's why Maxwell is moving—he's joining the general staff as an advisor. Though none of the men know it yet, this is his last day in Maxwell Hall.

Before he enlisted, Kinnee was a sheriff's deputy in Cherokee County, Georgia. He'd been in Iraq three months when a piece of shrapnel ripped open his neck. He lost five of his six quarts of blood, stroked out, died in the dust. Somehow, they saved him. There is a precise-looking scar on his head, just right of center—running from the front hairline to the back, like a part scissored into his crew cut, which he has trimmed for seven dollars every Sunday after church—where they removed a portion of his skull to allow his brain to swell after the stroke. Now he has an acrylic plate and twenty screws—"five screws per manhole cover," he likes to say; you can feel where the plate starts. As a result of the stroke, his left arm doesn't work. He takes special meds to keep it from becoming palsied; at night, he sleeps with a brace on his hand. After he sits down, he will typically use his right hand to reach over and pick up his left arm by the wrist and place it on his lap, this inert thing attached to him that must be managed.

"How you doin', Kinnee?" Maxwell asks. He cops a lean on the arm of the sofa opposite and crosses his arms.

Kinnee looks up, groggy at first, uninterested. Then he realizes who's in front of him and snaps to a seated form of attention. Though he can't fully dress himself without help (the fussy rolled cuffs and trousers ties, the calf-high lace-up boots; "try putting on a sock with one hand," he says in his typical challenging tone, the result of personality changes and disinhibition caused by the death of the right hemisphere of his brain) he is one of the more motivated marines in Maxwell Hall, at least when it comes to doing chores and maintaining military discipline. Having joined later in life than most of the guys, Kinnee, twenty-six, is more serious. He made corporal in only two years. This was going to be a career for him.

"Fine and dandy, sir," Kinnee answers dryly. There is a cast to his face, a waxen awkwardness, as if the left side and the right side are expressing different emotions simultaneously. Think of your mouth after dental surgery. He always carries tissues or a napkin to mop up any moisture.

Kinnee's tongue is tricky, too, as is Maxwell's. The words come out with some difficulty.

"Did you start that morale pill we talked about?" Maxwell asks. "That shit is *intense.*"

A puzzled expression: "How so, sir?"

"How much did the doc give you per day?"

"I'm not sure. I told him what we talked about. How I was concerned, you know, about how my brother was saying I seemed to be more short-tempered than before. I got some concern that I don't wanna change too much or I'll push everybody away."

"Give yourself about two, three weeks," Maxwell advises. "After that, if you don't like the side effects, or if you think it's making you feel too weird or whatever, go back to that fuckin' doctor and get yourself another kind. I had to try a few different kinds before I got this one, I can't re-member the frickin' name—my wife told you, right? Temper is what they started giving it to me for a long time ago, actually. So give it a shot. But don't expect a miracle."

"I'll try, sir."

Maxwell regards him a moment, sizing him up the way a mother might take measure of her child at the end of a long school day. "Your morale seems better," he says. "That trip home musta did you good. Did you get that ball for your hand?"

"No, sir."

Maxwell thumps the corporal playfully on the shoulder. "Come on, *man.*" Before he was injured, Kinnee was bench-pressing 225 pounds. He carried heavy field radio equipment. He studies his boots.

"How much does it work?" Maxwell asks, his tone bright and encouraging.

Looking up: "What?"

"The arm. How much does it work? Does it have *some* utility?"

"I can squeeze the hand shut but I can't open it," Kinnee says. He doesn't bother to demonstrate.

"Fuckin' brain injuries," Maxwell says, shaking his head. "You know that, um—what's that chubby kid's name?"

"Reynolds?"

"Reynolds," Maxwell repeats, tapping the front of his broad fore-head with his fingertip. "Reynolds. Reynolds. Before I leave, I have to go around and get everyone's picture and label them. I can't remember *anyone's* frickin' name."

"I can only remember what I knew before, sir," Kinnee concurs.

"Anyway, *R-R-Reynolds*," Maxwell says, struggling with the name, his jaw working awkwardly on its hinge like a man with a bad stutter. "*R-Reynolds*' hand didn't work at all and his leg didn't work. But look at him now. He got a lot of it back."

"We'll see," Kinnee says, not at all convinced. In the images he's seen of his brain, the left side is entirely white, and the right side is entirely black. "That means it's dead," he'll explain later.

Maxwell searches the ceiling for a lighter topic. In earlier phases of his military career, he often found himself out among the troops, polling them, taking stock, reporting back to superiors. He likes to see himself as an idea man, as a guy who understands a little bit about what people need. Like the day he came across that young Devil Dog alone in his barracks, crying. The rest of his unit was still in Iraq. This boy was back at home, injured and alone, fighting his own fight, trying to recover. Wounds in combat are not like the ones in the movies. You hear about the amputees, the burn guys. But one bullet through the arm can turn a bone to sand. The nerve damage creates pain enough to make a junkie. The limb will never be right again. From day one in training, they teach a marine that there's no *I* in *team*. They teach him that he's only as good as the man on his left and the man on his right. They teach him to be a lean, mean, killing machine. What happens after the machine is broken?

So it was that Maxwell took his idea up the chain of command. He was assisted by his wife, Shannon, who had started a support group for marine families, and by Thomas Barraga, a former marine and a local legislator in Suffolk County, New York, who worked with Maxwell to write a proposal for a "medical rehabilitation platoon." Within fourteen months of Maxwell's injury, by order of Lieutenant General James F. Amos, then-commanding general of the 2nd Marine Expeditionary Force, there was a new central billet for injured marines. Maxwell Hall was open.

Maxwell checks his watch. His arm rotates awkwardly; he also took shrapnel to his left elbow. "A'ight," he drawls, "I gotta get going to the next item on my checkout list. I'm almost done. I gotta go to the C, uh"—he stumbles over the initials—"CSI."

"What's that, sir?"

Maxwell thinks a moment. "Oh. *CSI* is a movie. About cops."

"You mean, frickin', uh——" Kinnee gestures in the air with his hand, pointing generally to the west.

"*Yeah.* You know. The, uh——" an open palm, wrist rotating in the same direction.

Nodding conclusively: "Yeah."

"That's right."

"Okay, then. Catch you later."

#

I'M JUSTIN KINNEE, I'm twenty-six. This is my room in Maxwell Hall. It ain't nothin' special. It's where I live for right now. I was originally born in Pasadena, California. I stayed there until I was fourteen. We moved around a lot. My mother was a single mom with two boys. Eventually we ended up in Georgia, just north of Atlanta.

The right side of my brain doesn't work at all. You use your whole brain; I'm using half of mine. Stuff I knew before the injury, births and dates and stuff like that, I can still tell you. Everything after the injury is a little fuzzy. Like I can't remember names. The only way I can remember your first name is because it's my middle name. Justin Michael Kinnee. Your name is Michael, so I can remember it.

Memory is a game that's played every day. It's just a developing thing. I mean, I'm not speaking as well as I was a few months ago. By doing the exercises that I was taught, I'm trying to get better. The part of my brain that works the best is vision. Like, the medicines I take? I know which one to take because I know the color. I know that the white pill and the red-and-white pill are both my sleeping medicines. I know the yellow pill is for my seizures, and so on and so forth. After the injury that's how my brain works. I know the colors of the medicines but I don't know the names. I just know what they're for and what color they are. I take a lot of pills. Here they are in this box on my shelf. This is a pain pill, this is a pain pill, this is a pain pill. Sleeping, sleeping, sleeping, sleeping—oh sorry, this is a nerve pill, *that* one is for sleeping. Seizure medicine, multivitamin, tone medicine. T-O-N-E. Like muscle tone. See, since my left arm doesn't work, what happens is your body tends to kind of want to do this, you know, your fingers and your limbs want to curl up. You see it with paralyzed people all the time. The drug keeps it relaxed. Right now if I wasn't tak-ing the drug, my arm would be all curled up, which would put strain on the muscles and nerves and everything else. The medicine allows it to relax. Plus, I wear a brace at night that keeps my fingers straight, because night is the worst time for that to happen—night is when you grow and you heal; when your brain shuts down, your body reacts to that. So if I wasn't wearing that brace and I wasn't taking that medicine, then my hand, when it came back to its full use, would be like this (he makes a palsied claw with his good hand). That is, if it ever does come back.

In October of this year, it'll be two years. It has gotten a little better. My improvement has gone up, but it has also kind of hit a plateau. When I first got here I couldn't do a lot of shoulder movements. Now I can do some shrugs. And there's this exercise where I have to sit up on my elbows. I couldn't do that before—I couldn't hold it—but now I can. You have to understand: I was huge before I got hurt. I was about 160 pounds. I'm only five ten. I was just massive. In Iraq, I was benching 225 plus. When you're in my job, infantry, that's all you do. That's your whole job. You work out, you run, you tone up. If I'm not in shape and somebody gets shot or something, and I can't pick them up and carry them away, then I just killed that marine for no reason. I took it as a personal responsibility to make sure I was in the absolute best shape I could be in. That way I could handle everything. Plus, we were wearing, frickin', a hundred pounds of gear. And then I wore extra 'cause I was the radio guy, so I had the radio and the antenna and the batteries. It's a lot extra. Fifty pounds at least. Extra weight and extra responsibility. That's an important job. I'm not tootin' my own horn, but they don't just throw anybody on that.

I joined in August, 2004, when I was twenty-two. I'd been to junior college for two years. I'd been a cop for a year. I remember being an only child in the beginning, before my brother was born. There was no one to play with, so I always played with those little green plastic soldiers. I don't know why: being a marine was just something I've always wanted to do. By the time I joined, it was sorta like now or never. I was getting a little old. The war was going on in Iraq. I felt like I needed to do something to help. Now I been in almost three years. It's been incredible. I really love it.

The main thing is, I got in because I wanted to make a difference. That's why I picked the infantry. I didn't just wanna hear about the war from somewhere back in the rear, I wanted to be up front and be able to say 'This is what really happened.' I wanted to really be able to make a difference. I wanted to be the best marine I could be—one of the ones making the most difference. This was my first pump. I was in the Two/Six. I was only there for three months and one week; I was injured on the eighth day of October, 2005. That's what it says on my Purple Heart. We were in Fallujah, so we were right between Baghdad and the Syrian border, which is not such a great spot to be in, because everything and everybody comes in through the Syrian border to try to get to Baghdad. We were standing in between 'em. There was just constant stuff every day.

See, you got three units in the battalion. My unit was Fox Company— about 600 marines. My unit alone captured three Al Quaeda members off the FBI's blacklist. But you'll never hear that on TV, because that's a positive note of why we're there fighting and doing our jobs over there. On the news you only hear the crap—we got blown up, or somebody died, or we killed somebody. Another thing you never hear is, well . . . lemme tell you this story, see what you think.

One day I was on post. We'd occupied this house on a street somewhere and we were standing watch. That's really what we do a lot of there. We're like police. We hunt down wanted persons, answer to problems among the citizenry, watch for the enemy, patrol, stand post. And we have the Iraqi Army with us—we're supposed to be training them to do all those things. So I'm on post on this roof and I'm looking out. Over in the distance, we've got three lines—a green, a yellow, and a red line. Well, there's not exactly a line *per se*; there are these markers made of wood, set at intervals of one hundred meters, usually. The first is green, the second is yellow, the third is red—red being the one that gets you killed. If Joe Blow Muhammad Ali, whatever you wanna call him, crosses the green line, you sound a blow horn. If he passes the yellow line, maybe you set off a flash bang. If they cross the red line, you have to shoot 'em because at that point, if they do have an explosive device and they detonate it, everybody would die. So that's the scene. One day I was on post and there was this kid. He was playing with a ball. And he kept crossing the first two lines, the green and the yellow. When he did that, we had to blow the horn, we had to set off a flash bang. But he just kept going back and forth, playing with his ball, a basketball, bouncing it up and down, not even paying any attention to us. And the thing was, there was this bush, see. This bush by the side of a house. And sometimes the kid would go behind the bush, you know, disappear from my sight. I couldn't really see where he was going, because the bush was in the way.

Long story short: One time the ball came rolling out past all three lines, all the way to our barbed wire—*way* across the red line. This kid couldn't have been but six years old. Now like I said, I was a cop before I joined the Marine Corps. I'm thinking, *This is a little suspicious.* Before he was bouncing the ball but now, all of a sudden, at this point in time, the ball's rolling all the way to our wire. Why would the kid roll the ball all the way past the line? I gotta juggle all these things in my mind, and now I gotta think—I gotta make a split-second decision. If I kill this kid, I gotta live with that for the rest of my life. If I don't, I could possibly kill twenty marines.

Turned out, the kid was wired with a bomb. It was perfectly orchestrated. We called the QRF, which is quick reaction force. They come, and apparently, what I couldn't see, behind that bush was the kid's father. He was taking pictures of his child with a video camera. That bastard was just waiting for me to kill the kid, his own flesh and blood, so he could film it and to put it on their Muhammad Ali TV to make us look even worse over there in the A-rab world. And then they could sell that for money to CNN and all this crap, and we would just look like total shitheads. You'll never hear that shit on TV, you'll just hear what bastards we are over there. How we are murderers and all this shit. I mean, there wasn't no draft. We volunteered to do this job for not much pay. You know, we're not makin' a hundred grand a year over there. I'm making less than thirty and I'm twenty-six years old. Less than thirty grand to go over there and have my legs blown off, or die, or live on machines the rest of my life. I'm there to do a job. We're there to do a job. And we get nothing but bullshit on the TV news. That's something for you to think about.

The day before my injury we had a twelve-hour patrol. We have a twelve-man squad, and we patrol the city after curfew. We're on foot. I'm carrying 150 pounds, including the field radio. After twelve hours, we come back to post. We're exhausted as hell. We're sweating our asses off, which sucks because over there it's 130 degrees every day, but as soon as night hits it gets freezing-ass cold, and all of a sudden your balls are freezing, because you've been sweating all day, but now it's cold, and everything's wet at that point and then you're just frickin' miserable. After the patrol, we come back to stand post, which means another eight to ten hours when we're back in our FOB (forward operating base, pronounced like Bob) standing security, in case insurgents attack. So that's how our rotation works. After patrol we went to the post, and after the post we went to bed, which was great. Frickin' sleep. Oh God! That's the best sleep. 'Cause you don't have to think about sleepin', you know? As soon as you take off your clothes—I change into clean clothes because I didn't want to sleep wet—I change into clean clothes, and *boom*, I'm gone, I'm out like a light, that's all she wrote. Then you had to wake up like eight hours later and *boom*, you know, we get the call, we're back on patrol again.

That day was weird. That morning I'd gotten a modem mail from my fiancée at the time. Modem mail is like email. Your family or friends can send you email and it comes to you on paper, like a telegram. Like a letter, you know. So instead of waiting for a week for the mail, it's instant. It's really great. So I got a modem mail from my fiancée at the time. My ex-fiancée. We'd broke up before I left, but in this mail she said she wanted to get back together, so that was kind of a good thing. I put that modem mail in my pocket, grabbed my iPod, got dressed. Then we left.

We couldn't have gone but one hundred yards out of the FOB. We turned the corner to go down the alley, headed toward the city itself. I was in the middle of the formation because I had to stay with the squad leader—he's the one with the GPS (global positioning system, like those things you can get now for your cars, only a military version). One of my jobs is to walk with him and report our Pos Ref, position reference. He gives me the GPS coordinates and I call them into headquarters, and they put a pin where we are on the map, so if some shit went down, they would know where our last coordinates were. So we're walking, and the fire team ahead of us went past this open field. And then we came along. When you're at war, the two things that any military in the world will hit first are your com, your communications, and your machine gunner. And that's exactly what happened to me. The fire team was allowed to pass by the initial point where the IED, improvised explosive device, was hidden—this place in the open field. I remember, I had just did a Pos Ref, and then I hung up the radio. And then we came up on that point. And that's when it happened—*Boom!* It was two feet away from me on my right side.

I woke up on the ground. I was like, *Shit.* I felt like I'd got hit by a damn fucking truck. There was blood everywhere. My neck was ripped open. See here on my neck? My little happy face made out of scars? It wasn't that happy at that time. My whole neck was ripped open. I can't feel it to point it to you—I have no feeling in my neck anymore. But see right here? Right where my throat is? Below my Adams apple? There was a big hole there. All of the air in my lungs was coming out of it. The artery, the carotid artery—it's right in there, too. It was ripped open. Every time my heart would pump, it would pump the blood straight out of my body. The doctors said that everybody has six quarts of blood. I lost five. No blood. No air. *Boom*: You stroke out. You die. I have no idea how they saved my sorry ass. Those docs are the best in the world.

When you have a stroke, your brain swells. They had to cut this chunk out of my skull, so my brain would have somewhere to go. Now I have this acrylic plate. On a CAT scan, everybody's brain is supposed to look white. If you have a tumor or something, you'd have a black spot. The CAT scan of my brain shows one white half and one black half. By medical terms, half my brain is literally dead—it just doesn't work. Which is why this arm, my left, doesn't work, because the signals that come from that side of the brain aren't there. They're dead, they're gone, they're *fried*. Now, the left side of my brain, my right, has to take over. At first, I couldn't speak, I couldn't swallow, I couldn't talk. I still can't feel my face. It's like you've just been to the dentist, only it's permanent. When I eat I usually have a lot of napkins just to wipe. It's a habit now, because I'll have a piece of food hanging there if I don't watch it. Sometimes I drool. If I've got something on my face you need to tell me about it. Sometimes it gets all crazy over there.

I'm not mad or angry. I don't regret any of it. I am a little frustrated. I get frustrated easier now, for sure. My brother says I'm more short-tempered, but that's nothing I can control. Emotion is on the side of my brain that's dead. It's just something you have to work through every day, to try to get better. The biggest problem is there's not much I can do. Can't play pool or video games or fish, can't run, can't ride a bike, can't PT, can't do shit. I can watch a movie as long as the plot is not too involved. I can read. It's not so good, but I can read. I wear glasses—I lost vision in both eyes. I can see peripheral vision on my right, but I have none on my left. I had to go through a lot of classes to be able to be cleared to drive. I have to wear glasses, and I have to do a lot of scanning to make sure I see stuff coming on the left side. The reason I wear the sunglasses inside is because my brain doesn't know how to interpret the lighting inside. Like, the sun's okay—not too much of it, but it's okay, because it's a natural thing and my eyes are a natural thing, or so they tell me. But not the man-made light. Weird isn't it? You find out a lot of weird things about yourself in this process, weird quirks of the human body that you have absolutely no control over.

What plans do I have for the future? Well, in the immediate future there is another operation on my knee. I didn't tell you—in the IED explosion, my legs snapped, too, like a pencil. Since the IED was so close, I'm fortunate to still have the legs. See, you've got me with my 150 pounds of stuff on my back standing straight up like this, and gravity holding you down. And all of a sudden this massive force just hits you on the side. Snap, just like two pencils. But anyways, the future—after the surgery and all the therapy and that whole thing? To be honest with you, I'm looking at options. I'm a man of faith. The way I look at it is this: The Lord could have killed me. He coulda let me die right there. I mean, I did die. My heart stopped, I bled out almost all my blood. But he didn't take me. He let me live. So there's a reason why I'm here. There's a reason why I'm alive. I don't know what that reason is. I don't know what I'm doing. But he got me to this point so he's just gonna have to open the door for me when I get wherever it is that I'm going. I'm gonna do what I think is right, but as far as, like, going to law school or medical school or some other crazy shit, I don't really have a big plan. The Marine Corps was my Plan A. I didn't have no plan B. This was my Plan A, B, *and* C. This was it. But life doesn't always work out the way you want, you know what I'm sayin'? I'm like, 'Okay, I can do this, I can overcome.' I got no other choice.

#

TEN IN THE MORNING on the second floor of Maxwell Hall. Four guys are hanging out in somebody's room, call him LCpl. Romeo. It could be a college dorm, a double suite with connecting bath, each side eight by twelve with full cable hookup. You can pay extra for Internet.

Leeman and Ringo are on the sofa, using Romeo's laptop, YouTubing videos from Iraq of IED explosions and firefights; one of their favorites is set to the song "American Idiot." Cybula is on a folding chair, poking through the small fridge—nobody's had shit to eat today. You have to be up and dressed to report for formation at 7:00 a.m. Then . . . nothing.

A few guys have jobs or duties. These four do not. Romeo is on the queen-size bed, which faces a big-screen television. It has a built-in DVD player, standard issue in every room. On top of the TV are an Xbox and a PS2, two of the dozens of donated gaming systems floating around Maxwell Hall. All of the components fit snugly into a cherrywood armoire/entertainment center, also standard issue. Next to him on the bed is a beautiful young girl with flame-red hair and freckles, a rising senior at a high school twenty miles away. She says she's eighteen. Romeo met her a couple of weeks ago at a stoplight. Of all the marines in town—there would hardly be a reason for Jacksonville if there were no marines; they are everywhere in this franchise heaven of a city, looking as uniform in their civvies as they do in their uniforms: cargo shorts, Nikes, t-shirt, baseball cap optional—for some reason, she settled on him. She visits regularly, often in the evenings. If he asks, she'll bring a pizza. Once, in the middle of sex with her, his wife called. He picked up his cell phone and proceeded to have a conversation. At the moment, the redhead is transfixed on the TV screen, meanwhile pressing buttons on a toy guitar, a video game she is playing. Nobody pays her any mind.

"I miss Iraq *so* bad," Leeman says, clicking on another YouTube selection. Corporal Jeff Leeman is the ranking NCO in the room. He is tall and thin, twenty years old, from Lebanon, Tennessee. He talks low and fast and swallows his words like Boomhauer on *King of the Hill.*

"I know, man. *Fuck!* I just wanna kill some of those fuckin' people." This is Ringo, Lance Corporal Jeremy Dru Ringgold, twenty-two. He has big blue eyes and the gift of gab, an accent like the Marlboro man. He seems especially upbeat today, loud and expressive, a little bit hype.

"Watch this'n," Leeman mumbles. "Suicide bomber. Black car right thar. He's approachin' a checkpoint. Wait for it . . . ."

Boooooom!

The small extension speakers on the coffee table shake and rattle and hiss.

"Ohhhhh, shit!"

"Fuuuuuck!"

"That's *horrible,* dude."

"There's this one video I wish I could find," Ringo says, grabbing the keyboard away from Leeman. "It has this Iraqi. He's in his car, sitting next to all these 155 shells. He's fuckin', like, petting the fuckin' things. And then he drives down the road and blows himself up. I'm like, What the fuck, man? Why didn't you come to me and let me shoot you in the fuckin' face?"

A native of Augusta, Georgia, Ringo is charismatic, intelligent, and well liked. Lately, he has developed a potbelly from lack of exercise and too much beer, which he shouldn't be drinking anyway, due to his regular use of Percocet, which helps to mask the excruciating nerve pain in his arm. As a side effect of the drug, he is constantly rubbing his nose and sniffling—his behavior and the tone of his voice are very much reminiscent of a heroin addict. In fact, he says his brother was a heroin addict. His sister got pregnant and left home at fifteen. His other brother is a marine. Like every other marine in the room (and all but one of the marines I met at Maxwell Hall, including Maxwell himself), Ringo is a child of divorce. He didn't know his father very well. He does remember that his father gave him his first rifle, an AR-15, when he was nine. Until recently, to help pass the great stretches of unoccupied time as he endures the Middle Passage of the healing process, Ringo was working as a teacher's aide in a elementary school not far from base. Now that school is out, he says he's "bored outta my fuckin' mind." Back home, Ringo's wife, whom he calls Skinny (his screen name is *Skeremy*), is living in the house he recently bought for $90,000—his offer despite the asking price of $150,000. ("My wife and the agent thought I was crazy, but hey—that's all I could afford.") He has not yet slept there. She is a manager at a grocery store, pregnant with their first child, a little girl; he realizes he might end up having to shoot some guy someday for trying to get fresh—ha, ha, just kidding, he says.

Ringo did two tours in Iraq. During his first, he lost half his squad to a suicide car bomber. During his second, twenty-two days in, he got hit—trying to save a marine he'd never met before. He didn't even have to be on that patrol; for some crazy reason, he'd volunteered to sub in with another squad. At the top of the firefight, he got hit in the helmet—it went clear through but never touched his scalp. Then a second bullet found his forearm and turned it into chips and dust. He is convinced he was supposed to die that day. He doesn't know why he didn't. He feels guilty for getting injured. He was a team leader. After he left, some of his marines got whacked. Maybe if he had been there . . . .

Cybula burps loudly, causing everyone to laugh. Lance Corporal John Cybula, twenty-one, is a handsome guy from Sweetwater, Tennessee, raised by his grandparents. The top of his hair is a little longer than regulation; it's all gussied up with gel. He can sit at a table in a burger joint with two friends, and before he leaves, a cute little female marine, short-time to deployment, will give him her number. After he got whacked, Cybula ended up marrying his nurse from the hospital in Portsmouth, Virginia. She's still up there. She wants a divorce. He just discovered that she cleaned out his bank account. He has four one-dollar bills to his name—another explanation for his hunger. Reaching into a shelf, he pulls out a bag of Romeo's extra-spicy style Doritos. He rips it open, begins stuffing his face.

"I'll tell you something," Ringo says, standing up now, pacing the room energetically, two steps forward, turn, two steps back. "The first time I held a rifle in my hand and realized it made shit blow up, I was like, 'You know what? This is what life is all about right here.'"

"I heard *dat*," Leeman says, taking back the laptop. Almost all of the guys have deep caches of digital photos and homemade videos of themselves and their tours. Often, during a firefight, guys can be seen shooting videos. The most searing image I saw was a digital photo of the face of a suicide bomber a few moments *after* a blast—just the face, disembodied, lying abandoned in the street, as if the forehead and nose and mouth had been removed to be used as a Halloween mask.

Cybula burps again, theatrically, enjoying the attention of the group. He was on the roof of a building when a sniper bullet caught him in the back of his flak vest and knocked him through a hole. He fell three stories, broke his knee and pelvis. The marines are not convinced about the sniper part of the story; his Purple Heart has thus far been denied. Cybula is on morphine and Vicodin. He's also on meds to help him sleep and meds to block his dreams. He says he can't sleep without getting drunk, which he does many nights—beer and shots. His eyes are slits. His body itches all over from the morphine; he's constantly scratching. Back when he was on Demerol, only his stomach itched. Now it's everywhere, usually just out of reach. He has a sly smile, a sweet vibe that kills the ladies; you can tell there's a really nice guy buried somewhere inside all of that medication.

Ringo and Cybula used to be suitemates, but then Ringo was ordered to move to another barracks because of the overflow. He had been in Maxwell Hall for nearly six months. He hates his new barracks. It's a pog barracks, which stands for "person other than grunt," meaning someone who is not in the infantry. Pogs are lower than the skin on a snake's belly, lower than a hemorrhoid on a Haji's ass, etc. Leeman is a pog because he rides in a pussy LAV, a light-armored vehicle, instead of humping like the real men. Lucky for Leeman, they take pity on his pog self and let him hang around. As fate would have it, he outranks them. Presumably, pogs have more time to study for advancement exams. Ringo's pog barracks, which is full of administrative personnel—*super*pogs—is quiet and sterile. These weird big bugs from the marsh crawl under the door and into his room. There is no TV or pool table or Sharper Image massaging chair, and nobody else who has ever been in a firefight, much less been wounded in one. Lately he's been staying at Maxwell Hall, sleeping in the queen-size bed with Cybula.

"Did I tell you what happened last night?" Ringo asks, super-animated, still pacing.

"That was one helluva storm," Leeman says. "My dogs was goin' crazy."

Leeman was on his first tour when the eight-wheeled armored wagon he was driving hit a pressure-plate mine. They were only about five hundred meters outside the gate of their FOB. He was able to call in his own three-line injury report over the radio before everything went black, he explains with mumbled bravado. Because he doesn't have a fake ID, Leeman—who will not turn twenty-one for a couple more weeks—cannot drink a beer when he goes to Hooters, as the guys like to do, mostly for the wings and alcohol, partly for the hooters. The other day, in fact, the Hooters girls visited the barracks. People are always visiting Maxwell Hall. Often the wounded warriors are bused off base for field trips—a sailing regatta, a party at a local bar, even a trip to Washington, D.C., to speak to the kids attending the Presidential Classroom. The new guys really seem to enjoy all the fuss. It feels good to be called a hero. The guys who have been here a while enjoy the outings because it's something to do, but they don't like the attention. To a man, they will tell you they ain't no heroes. Heroes are people who fight, not people who get injured. When you're injured, you can't be a hero—other people become heroes saving your shot-up ass. Although the Hooters girls were wearing their tight little orange shorts when they came to visit the barracks, they didn't bring any wings. Who sends the Hooters girls to visit a bunch of young marines without any wings? The sense of disappointment in the rec room was palpable.

Leeman's wife is named Brandy. She is twenty-two. Sometimes, at a restaurant, she'll order a beer and give it to him. They live together in a small detached two-bedroom over in married housing; Leeman hangs out at the barracks all day, per orders. Like the other 115 men assigned to Maxwell Hall—some have been here as long as two years—Leeman's job is to attend his doctor's appointments (you pay up to eighty dollars out of pocket if you miss), to take his medicines, to follow doctors' orders . . . to get well and then to move on, either back to a unit or out of the corps and into a serviceable rest of his life. Brandy is a friendly and buxom redhead he met at church when he was a junior in high school. It was love at first sight, really. She just thought he was way cute. He is not allowed to say on tape which part of her first attracted him. She gives a hint by placing one hand, palm down, at the level of her shoulders, and the other hand, palm up, at her waist. Brandy used to work the overnight shift at Target, restocking shelves. That's where she was when he called her from the hospital in Al Asad, all doped up on morphine. "Honey, I have a little news." When you're injured, one of the first things they do is give you a phone card with nine hundred free minutes. Leeman doesn't remember whom he called or what he said. Brandy, whose screen name is *JeffreysWoman*, is hoping her husband will soon be well enough to get off LIM DU, limited duty, and start back with PFT, training for the physical-fitness test. She wants him to return to his unit. There is precious little for them to do back home in Lebanon. Not to mention the fact that the Hajis make the *best* blankets. They've gifted them to all their relatives; there are four in the spare bedroom right now. She wants him to send back a few more—and maybe a nice rug for the dining room?

"So me and this friend are watching TV," Ringo continues, "when all of a sudden there's this huge explosion: *crack!* And I thought, *Damn! Incoming!* Shit, man! I got down and covered up!"

"I fuckin' hate loud noises, man," Romeo concurs.

"No shit," says Cybula.

The high school girl, still holding the toy guitar, turns her head to listen.

"So who was this *friend*, anyways?" Leeman asks, a lascivious tone. His eyes are a little slitty; he's rubbing his nose, too. Though the nightmares have stopped, he still gets bad headaches. His elbow doesn't work the same anymore since the operation. In two days' time, he'll be walking down some steps and his knee will go out. He's on Percocet, too.

"She's just a friend that I worked with, okay? A *school*teacher. We were watching *television*. Can I just tell my story?"

"I ain't stoppin' ya," Leeman says.

"So I'm down and covered, and my friend screams, like, 'Eek! The house is on fire!' and I'm like, 'What?' and she's like, 'Look! The chimney's on fire!' And I get up from my covered position and I realize—" He stops in his tracks, and his eyes widen, and he thrusts both arms in the air, as if evoking the good Lord in heaven. "*A lightning bolt has just hit the fucking chimney!*"

"No shit!"

"Radical, man!"

"Ya damn skippy," says Ringo, pointing to his fellows like a huckster working the crowd. "See, a lighting bolt came down through the chimney and exploded the gas line in the fake fireplace. And the gas is like wooooooooosh—shooting out everywhere, hardcore. And I'm asking her, 'WHERE IS THE FUCKIN' FIRE EXTINGUISHER?' and she's like, 'I DON'T HAVE NO FUCKIN' FIRE EXTINGUISHER!' So I'm like, 'OH, SHIT!' I run outside the house and I find the garden hose, and jump the porch fence and run back inside and already my arm is like fuckin' killing me and I'm like—"

"Hey, Ringo," interrupts Corporal Leeman.

"I'm just gettin' to the *good* part, man."

A sober tone from the ranking marine in the room: "You took a lot of medication, didn't you?"

An impish expression, a sugar-drunk kid: "Why do you ask?"

"'Cause you all hype, tellin' that story. You taking extra?"

"Nah, man, I just didn't have nothin' to eat. I took the shit on an empty stomach."

Leeman stares him down a few long seconds, brother to brother. "Maybe we better go find us some chow," he suggests. "Who's drivin'?"

"Who's payin'?" Cybula asks, leaning way over, pretzeling one hand behind his back, trying in vain to reach an itch.

# # #

My name is Jeremy Dru Ringgold. I'm twenty-two, from Augusta, Georgia—the great state of Georgia. I spent two tours in Iraq so far. My first tour was 2005-2006. I got injured during my second tour, February 5, 2007.

The way it happened was this: We were at an OP, an observation post, at a water treatment plant on the Euphrates River. The whole area was real pretty—all these pine trees and shit. The first time I was in Iraq, the place I was in was barren desert. But this area was real nice—just a beautiful spot. Whenever we had to go to the water treatment plant, it was like we had the day off. Of course, there was always sporadic small-arms fire, or we'd get a mortar dropped on us, an RPG sent our way. But compared to the rest of the war, being out at this OP was great. It was like having a day off.

So we're sitting there, you know, doing our thing, when the battalion commander comes through. He says that he wants to go up to this spot on the river where we'd been in a firefight previously. It's not a good area. We know it's bad juju up that way. But the colonel's got his own idea. He wants to put a blocking force on the road that's coming from the river. And then he's gonna have a maneuver element sweep up the river and see if they can find any bad guys. For some reason, idiot that I am, I volunteer to go.

I'm part of the blocking force. We move up the road and this boot LT, this green-ass lieutenant, sets us in, puts us in positions. And I'm telling him, "Sir, we really need to find somewhere to put these Humvees in cover, 'cause right here we're exposed." He looks at me and he says, "We're good, lance corporal. If anything happens we'll be all right." And I'm like, *Yeah right, kiss my ass.* You know what I'm sayin?

Meanwhile, the colonel's detachment starts to maneuver up the river. All of a sudden, this convoy of cars appears on the road, coming our way fast. It's like a stampede coming from the direction we're facing. We set up a snap VCP, which is a real quick vehicle checkpoint. One thing I gotta say: I am terrified of searching cars.

During my first deployment, we had a suicide car bomb take out one of our squads. He killed the point man and took out nine other guys. They were just outside our base. Usually, you know, you go down a street and all these kids are playing—every street you go on, kids are playing. But then you go down another street and it's dead quiet. It's desolate. *Desolate.*

And you know something's gonna happen. It's like the movies. One guy says, "It's quiet out here." And the other guy says, "Too quiet." It's one of those situations.

The squad's on patrol on this quiet street when this vehicle pulls out of an alleyway. The driver spots the squad and he puts it into reverse real quick, backs back into the alleyway, which is kind of normal behavior, because if you're a citizen and you see a military patrol, your first instinct is to get the freak out of the way as fast as you can—at least, if you're a friendly and you value your life, which many of these Hajis do not. After the first part of the patrol passed the alleyway, the vehicle pulls out again into the street. The point man, Lance Corporal Anderson, screams, "Everybody get down!" He runs toward the vehicle and opens fire. Then the vehicle detonates. It was a God-awful huge explosion.

When we got there the world was on fire. I seen marines laying everywhere. It was just one of those things that sticks with ya, those marines laying everywhere. We had to search for Lance Corporal Anderson. We couldn't find him at first. And then we were like, "What's that big chunk of car layin' over there?" Well, it turns out it wasn't a big chunk of car after all. It was Anderson. He'd been blown to shit and charbroiled. The top of his head was missing, all kinds of nasty shit, whatever. It happens. It's warfare. But that was a rough day. The explosion caught the ground on fire. I remember when we got there, the ground was bubbling. And I was like, *Man, why is the ground bubbling?* Later I found out: When the vehicle detonated, the force of the explosion had broken a water main that was buried underground, so that all the water was bubbling up to the surface. And then there was gasoline floating on top of the water, burning, just floating down to the street in flames. It was one of those surreal things, like *holy shit*, you know what I'm sayin'? It was like some stuff out of a movie, you know, except it was real.

Ever since then, I have not liked searching cars. But here we are. We set up this snap VCP—on this frickin' patrol I volunteered for. And lo and behold, who do you think is assigned to search the frickin' cars?

This is the usual procedure: We stop them about 300 meters from our position. Then we bring them through, one car at a time. We have the male get out, or the driver, which is always a male in Iraq. Then you have him turn around, and you watch him closely, because if somebody's about to blow themselves up, they have this look about them. It's a nervous look—he's about to blow himself to smithereens. You watch them, you see their body language. You gotta figure there's gonna be a certain amount of nervousness to begin with, because they're up against these Americans with guns and shit. But if they're gonna blow themselves up they're usually sweaty and real fidgety. If they're gonna do something, you just know.

The first car pulls up. The guy gets out of the car. He's on the HVT list, high value target. So we PUCed (pronounced *pucked*) him, prisoner under control, meaning that we took him into custody. I strapped flexicuffs on him.

The second car comes through. And *that* guy's on our HVT list, too. And it's like, *Uh oh.* Alarm bells start going off in my head. We got like nine more cars lined up coming our way, and the first two are HVTs. The third car pulls through. We don't have anything on him, we send him on his way. The fourth car pulls through, nothing on him. By now, I'm starting to feel a little squirrelly. I said to the lieutenant, "Sir, I can't check no more cars today. I'm getting physically sick. I cannot do this." And he said, "Aw, Ringgold, nothing's gonna happen to you." After you check out the driver, you have him open up the car—the doors, the trunk, the hood. You're like, *ifta, ifta, ifta*, all around the car, which is Arabic for "open." After they open everything up, you have them come over to you, *tal, tal,* which is Arabic for "come." You search them good to make sure they're not holding some sort of trigger mechanism, you know, so that while I'm over there looking at the car he can't go *boom* and detonate a bomb. When you're satisfied he doesn't, you go check out the vehicle.

I start searching the engine compartment. Suddenly there's a huge explosion. *BOOM!* It's thunderous. My knees buckle. There's meat flying through the air. Big chunks of meat. I said to myself, *Oh man, I got a suicide fuckin' bomber.* And then I was like, *How did I miss that?*

Then this guy comes running out of the dust cloud, straight at me. He's one of the Iraqis we just pulled from his car, and he's running out of the dust cloud. And I'm like, *This motherfucker threw a hand grenade!* That was my thought, that maybe he wasn't a car bomber, that maybe he just threw a hand grenade and blew up some marines. So I kicked him as hard as I could in his knee and took him down to the ground. I put my rifle in the back of his head. I clicked off the safety, set it to "fire."

And right as I started to squeeze the trigger—he was looking up at me, just terrified. I could see it in his eyes, he was saying, "No," you know?

He was just wide-eyed. These bright brown eyes. Just the brightest, widest, brownest eyes. And right as I went to squeeze the trigger, I get knocked on my ass.

I'm down on the ground. I said to myself, *Man, what the fuck was that?* I thought it was shrapnel that hit me in the head. 'Cause it just hit me like a ton of bricks, just dropped me, I went right on my ass. It was a stunning blow. I was stunned. I took cover behind the guy that I'd just taken to the ground—I use him like a sandbag, you know, a human sandbag. His ass was toward me. His ass and his back. I get down as low as I can in the dirt behind this guy, and I pull my helmet off, and this is what I see: This here is the helmet I was wearing. See? The bullet went in the front, here, and came out in the back, there. But it didn't touch my head or nothing. Not a scratch. Have you ever seen the movie *Saving Private Ryan?* There's this scene where this dude gets hit in the helmet and he takes it off to look at it. And his buddy goes, "You're a lucky bastard." And then the guy smiles, you know, and then he gets shot in the head. That's the first thing I thought about. So I said *Fuck that.* I put on my helmet back on my head real quick.

I start putting rounds out across the river, in the direction the fire was coming from. It's the same place it had come from the other day, which is what I was trying to tell the frickin' lieutenant in the first place. My human sandbag was curled up into a fetal position; I had my rifle propped up on his side, on the meat of his hip area, just below the rib cage. I don't know if you've ever felt the overpressure of a barrel. As a round comes out, there's an extreme amount of overpressure; it's enough to make you feel like somebody's hitting you in the head with a hammer. My overpressure on this guy's midsection must've been intense. Meanwhile, I look over to my left and there's our interpreter. He's right near me, curled up in a ball. But he's still got his video camera going. And I remember thinking, *This is gonna be a cool video. I wonder if he got any video of me getting hit in the head?*

In a combat situation, my job is to get my team and to orient their fire—but I didn't have my team out there, remember. I had volunteered for this patrol. I was with a squad I didn't really know. So I start to look around to see what I need to do with this group. As I'm looking around, I see a marine layin face down on the ground, about fifty meters away. He's, like, convulsing. His body's twitching back and forth. He's facedown on the ground, and he's not trying to roll back over or anything, which is not a good sign. I said to myself, *Somebody has got to help this marine, he's in a bad spot.* And then I thought, *This is it. I'm gonna get hit.* I don't know why I thought that. I just did. It just came to me and I said it to myself, calm like that, I just had this feeling. I just knew that by the time I got over there to save that dude . . . See, when a bullet goes over your head it makes a cracking sound. When you're in a firefight it's like *crack, crack, crack, crack* everywhere. When a bullet is *real* close to you, it sounds more like a *zip.* This was like *crack, crack, crack, crack* and they were all over the place, a heavy volume of fire. It was not the worst firefight I've ever been in, but we were not in a good position. We were very exposed.

I ran over there as fast as I could, fifty meters, full combat gear, plus all those grenades for my 203, the grenade launcher attached to my M-16. I get to this marine. He's laying next to this Humvee, near the back passenger side, face down. Rounds are hitting the Humvee, like *ping, ping, ping.* I roll him over. He was already dead. I mean, his body—it was a direct hit with an RPG is what had happened. That's how they initiated the firefight. And he was blown to shit. His legs were pretty much blown off. The only reason they were even still there was because of his cammies, the cloth was holding them together.

I get up and I start putting rounds out to cover my movement, and as I start to move, the battalion gunner comes running up to help this guy. The battalion gunner is a chief warrant officer, the highest rank an enlisted man can attain. You gotta give them the utmost respect. I tell him, "Sir, he's already dead." But I guess he didn't hear me, 'cause he kneeled down anyway. Or maybe he did hear me; maybe he just wanted to see for himself. He probably knew this guy. So instead of me moving away, I stayed there to supply cover, I started putting rounds out. The gunner is like, no shit, he's kneeling down right in front of me, like almost underneath me, leaning over the dead marine. And I'm standing above him, putting rounds out, like *pow, pow, pow, pow,* puttin' rounds out across the river. I wish I had a picture of that, man. I would blow that shit up big and put it on my wall. They could made a statue or some shit outta that scene. Him kneeling over the dead marine, me standing over them both, putting rounds out, my M16 with its 203 attachment, badass shit.

All of a sudden my arm just, just—I could see it happening in slow motion—it just flew away from me and my weapon fell to the ground. And I was like, *Fuck! I just got hit.* I was more upset than anything. It was like, *Shit, shit, shit!* Like when you're really mad? A frustrated kind of mad. Disappointed. Like *Goddamshit!* I was just pissed to be hit. It didn't really hurt. It felt like somebody was standing on my arm, it just felt like so much pressure. I don't know who I was telling, but I was screaming, "I just got hit!" I was fuckin' screaming it. I picked up my rifle and I tried to use it again. As soon as I squeezed the trigger, that's when the pain really hit me. *Whoa.* It was intense. It was really, really, really—obviously, it was the worst pain I've ever felt, a bullet had just went through my body. It's like nothing I've ever felt before. Just intense pain. It hurt like shit.

I jumped into the front passenger side of the Humvee and yelled to the gunner, "I need a pressure bandage!" He throws me a tourniquet instead. I go, "No, you fucking idiot! I said a *pressure* bandage!" Because a tourniquet is fuckin' gonna cut off the blood and I don't wanna lose my arm. It's not that bad of a wound. And you know I was fuckin' out of my mind because the guy I was yelling at was the battalion gunner, a chief warrant officer. But I guess he realized what was what, because he doesn't say nothin'. He just throws me the pressure bandage. My arm was locked like this, turned down in a fist. My hand won't open, nothing. I can't move it. I can't even get to my own medical pack. That's why I had to get some- body else to hand me something in the first place—you know, we all carry our own first aid supplies. So I go to undo the blousing on my sleeve. It's all covered in blood. I pulled my sleeve down slowly. Some of the muscle was hanging out. And I was like, *Fuck!* But I was also, like, *Okay. I'm not gonna die.* There was this piece of red meat about the size of my pinkie, this dark red meat, and blood was just flowing out of the hole in my arm. It kind of looked like— You know when you drain the oil out of your car? How it just pours out? It's not like drip, drip, drip. Its more like glug, glug, glug. That's what it looked like. Pretty much like the oil draining out of a car.

I wrapped the pressure bandage around my arm. It's pretty much like an Ace bandage except it has a pad on it. You wrap it relatively tight, not tight enough to cut off the circulation, but tight enough. After I'm done I notice there's this guy standing behind me in the Humvee. He's on the 50-cal, this big machine gun mounted in the turret of the Humvee with armor all around it. But he's all tucked down. He's not shooting. He's obvi- ously boot, never been in combat. Right about this time the gunner looks into the Humvee and yells at the guy, "You better start fuckin' shooting!"

But the boot guy leans down and goes "I don't know what to shoot at!" I grab him by his pants leg and I yelled to him, "Look up at the fuckin' windows across the river and light them bitches up!" And he's like, "Roger *that*," and he starts firing his 50-cal, *jub, jub, jub, jub, jub*, just rockin' the Humvee. At that point I forgot all about my pain. I was feeling super motivated, you know, like *Fucking-a-right!* I wanted to blow somethin' up, you know what I'm sayin'? Fuck this injury shit. My boys were out there dyin'. So I go to get out of the Humvee and the gunner just like reaches over and throws me back in. And he's like, "You're not getting out of the fucking Humvee." And I was like, "Roger that, sir." So at that point it was game over for me.

Then it came time for evac. They put all the pieces of the marine who had been blown up—the guy I got hit trying to save—on the front hood of my Humvee. And they drove me and him down to the farmlands to where they were gonna land the bird to medivac us out. Like I said, I wasn't out with my squad that day. I was just subbing in with another squad for that patrol. And as I get out of the Humvee to go get on this bird—I'm walking, you know, I'm ambulatory—I see that my regular squad is there. It's *my* guys securing the area for the bird to land.

When they seen who it is was wounded, two of my best buds came running up. They was about to grab my arm to help me with it, but I said, "Don't touch, it fuckin' hurts." One was a guy named Orris, and the other one's a guy named Lance Corporal Dmitruk. On my first tour, Dmitruk's arm got blown in half. His bone was blown out. But they patched him up and now he was back in Iraq on his second tour with me. When Dmitruk was wounded, it was me and Orris who helped *him*. We put pressure on his arm so he didn't bleed out, we wrapped his arm up in a tourniquet, we put him on the bird. So it's kind of funny that Orris and Dmitruk met me and put me on the bird. That was the last time I got to see them—those guys, my squad, any of them. One thing that kind of gets lost is the real, like, the kind of brotherly bond that marines have. I can look at one of my marines and be like, *I love that guy*. I'll tell him, too. I'll tell him, "Hey man, I love ya." I learned that from my first tour. Because you can be sitting there one second with a buddy of yours and then the next second that bad boy's on a bird, all burned to shit, all blown to shit, what have you. So I have no problem telling my guys, "Hey dude: I love you." 'Cause you never know, he could go out on patrol, step on a bomb, and be done.

Then, I'm sittin' on the bird and we're being flown out of there. It's a CH-46 Sea Knight. I don't know if you've ever been on a 46. It's got the twin rotors. With both the rotors going, it actually shakes the whole helicopter like a damn washing machine. So I'm sittin' on the bird, shaking. And the marine who'd been killed was in there too. That was the first time I'd ever seen him. I'd never met the guy. He had real curly brown hair, and I was lookin' at him. And the corpsman was like, "Are you okay?" He kept getting in my face. "Are you okay? Are you okay?" And I said, "I'm good. I'm gonna live. I'm going home."

When we landed they tried to take me off the bird first. And I was like, "Nah, he's gettin' off first," meaning the dead marine. And they're like, "No, you're getting off first." And I said "You're gonna take him off first or I'm just going to sit in here and we're gonna have problems." So they took him off the bird and then I got off the bird.

When I got back to the States, I was at Andrews Air Force base. I had literally just landed, and I got a phone call from a staff sergeant back here at Camp Lejeune. And he's like, "Lance Corporal Van Perry's parents would like to speak to you." And I was like, "Who is that?" And he's like, "That's the marine that got killed when you got hit." He gave me their number, but it took me a little while for me to call them. I just had to prepare myself first, 'cause I didn't know what they were going to want to talk about, though I knew they were going to obviously want to know what happened. Finally I just called. It wasn't too bad. They asked how I was feeling and everything. They were obviously upset. They wanted to know how their son had died. So I told them. I said, you know, that he was hit with the first round, the opening salvo, so to speak. It was an RPG, a rocket propelled grenade. So it was a direct hit with an RPG. He was dead as soon as it hit him. I found out when the funeral was and I went up there to Arlington National Cemetery, in Virginia. I was obviously really, really sedated, because I'd only been hit ten days prior. My arm was jacked. I didn't wear a uniform. I just wore some civilian clothes. My wife took me up there. I never actually met the family before. They probably were like, "Who is this guy with his arm all taped to hisself?"

At Arlington there was four funerals going on at the same time. You could hear all of them going on at once. There was the funeral I was at, a funeral over here, a funeral up on the hill, and another funeral in the valley. All for guys who'd been killed in Iraq. It was about 3:00 in the afternoon. The sun was out. The snow was pretty thick. It was an awesome sight—the military honor guards, the marines in their dress blues, all those white crosses gleaming in the sun. It was beautiful.

People die in warfare. Warfare will always be. No matter what people think—world peace, whatever—warfare will always happen. If you take away all the guns in the world, I'm coming at you with a club. One thing I never realized until I went to war was that the guys who die in wars are so young. I mean, you just don't think about or realize how young they are. I was nineteen when I went on my first tour. I could have died at nineteen. There's so much more about life that I've learned from nineteen to twenty-two. These guys get mowed down in their prime. They never get to learn that shit. The vast majority of people killed in action, in any war, are young guys. So when I looked at those crosses lined up, I just thought, you know, of all those young lives.

#

Another morning, Corporal Kinnee is in the rec room. His tunic is half on and half off. He can't seem to get his left arm to go through the rolled-up sleeve. The roll is tight. The arm is rubbery. Think of a time when you woke up in the middle of the night and your arm was totally asleep, just dead meat. That's Kinnee's arm pretty much, except for the little bit he can squeeze his hand—the grip not as strong as a newborn baby's. His shoes are untied, his trouser bottoms are unsecured. He has asked one of the sergeants to help him finish dressing.

"When it gets past my elbow, I'm good," Kinnee explains.

"We'll git ya," the gunnery sergeant says reassuringly, meanwhile struggling a bit, trying to force the inanimate hand through the tight roll of cloth. Sometimes, Gunny's vision will all of a sudden flick off, like a shorted-out light bulb. It can last a minute or a day. So far, it has always returned.

They are standing in the far corner of the room, near the vibrating recliners. Devil Dogs watch the big screen, play pool, doze in chairs. There is a general morning heaviness in the air, the groggy feel of a hangover. Gunny is making scant progress. His lips are pursed and grim.

"Just cut it off," Kinnee says. "It might be easier. Shit. It don't even work."

"You might want it someday. Isn't there some indication it'll get better?"

"Yeah, there is. I'm just joking around. I don't want my arm cut off. I like it. I've had it for twenty-six years. I can't really see using some metal claw."

"How about we just loosen this sleeve a bit, take off one of the rolls."

"But it was lookin' *good*," Kinnee protests.

"It needs to be a little looser, pardner," Gunny says gently. He begins unrolling.

"Aw, *mannnnnn*," groans Kinnee.

"Don't worry. I won't make it look bad."

"Corporal Love usually does it for me. He makes 'em *tight*."

"You don't need 'em tight right now," says the gunny, a little annoyed. "Unless somebody's gonna be there to help you take them off, you'll be in trouble."

"I'm not *takin'* 'em off," Kinnee says, a tad petulant.

#

MY NAME IS JOHN CYBULA. I'm twenty-one, from Sweetwater, Tennessee. About the only thing famous there is this underground cave that has a waterfall and stuff. It's about two hours from Nashville—depends on how you drive. I lived there with my grandparents most of my life. I never knew my dad 'till I was seventeen. My grandpa is retired from the Marine Corps. He owns three Sonics—the fast food restaurants. He used to work me some crazy hours. He's one of those guys, like, when you work for him— I remember this one time I got in a car accident and he still made me go to work. I used to get up at three in the morning to go do the early prep and stuff like that. I'd be doing hours that weren't even counted on the clock, but I mean, it's a family thing, you know? He always took care of me, so it's the least I owed him. He was the one that pushed me in the direction of the Marine Corps. It surprised the heck out of my family when I joined, because I was the guy that wasn't supposed to do anything with my life. I wasn't really a mess-up in high school, I was just one of the dumb jocks. Like, I was the guy that didn't do my work, but I passed because I was the quarterback. I played for Mid-County High School. I was pretty good. I wasn't no college material, I'll tell you, but I was good for the high school level, I guess you'd say. You know the scene: the cheerleaders, the babes, the crowd, stuff like that. It's kinda funny now that I think about it. Seems like a long time ago.

When I was a freshman in high school I weighed 86 pounds. I had the bowl cut going on—my mom used to cut my hair herself. She really used a bowl. When I was younger I had this crew cut. I used to get the Batman logo cut into the back of my head. I thought that was the stuff, back in the day. Or then another time I had the Nike swoosh. It was like the trademark thing to do. It was trendy. Eventually, my mom and I lived separate. We had some family issues and stuff like that. Not child abuse, but my step dad and me used to get into it pretty bad. I was a real mess back then, totally white like a ghost—I looked anorexic. Then I moved in with my grandparents for good. I went up to 150 my sophomore year, and then by my senior year I bumped up to 5 foot 11, 200. So I was getting healthy and stuff like that. It was cool. When I came back to high school that fall, the girls were like, "Wow, who are you?" And I was like, "Hey, it's me, John." And they were like, "Oh, my God!"

My first tour I went to Afghanistan. That was a pushover. We didn't do much. My second tour I went to Iraq. When we first got there it was calm; it was relatively nice. I don't mean *nice*, but all you'd hear usually was sporadic fire—nothing towards us. Then it got bad. They turned the war up a few notches, I guess you can say. I remember the first time I shot somebody. That's probably my favorite combat story.

I remember it was night. We were doing house checks to search for weapons and stuff like that. We go to this one house. It was right behind the big blue mosque in Fallujah. Me and my squad, we go up on this roof, and there's chickens all over, so we start kicking 'em off the roof and laughing about it, just laughing and kicking these chickens off the roof. I don't know why we was doing it. Just something to pass the time, something for laughs, you know. That's how guys are.

Then we go back downstairs. We're in the courtyard. Every house is built like that, with a courtyard and a front gate. We noticed a group of men outside the gate, in the street, all congregated together. And what happened was, I had this squad leader named Sergeant Beach. He went out the front gate and I followed. He noticed that one of the men had a grenade in his hands and was going to throw it. After giving the proper warning, he shot one round. I shot three rounds and killed the dude—

double tapped him in the chest and hit him once in the artery in the leg. He was dead instantly, I think. And I remember when I first did it, right after I shot the guy, right after I saw him land on the ground. I don't know why, but I turned around to the SAW gunner, his name was Lance Corporal Pugh, and I said, "I just killed that guy." And Pugh was like, "Yes, you did." And we was all laughing about it, you know, because I must of had this expression on my face, this look like, *Wow, look what I just did.* 'Cause it didn't really hit me. It was all, like, muscle memory. It was automatic. You see somebody posing a threat to you, you're gonna raise your weapon and shoot. You don't think about it. That's what they train us to do. So that's basically what happened. And that's my all-time favorite combat story. It's not action-packed or nothing like that, but most of my other combat stories deal with losing somebody. In this one, nobody I know gets hurt. Maybe that's why it's my favorite.

I lost two good friends over there. One was Corporal Snyder. He got shot in the back of the head by a sniper on post. And it just so happened I was his medivac. I was in the Humvee with him, holding his head on the way to Fallujah Surgical. He died in my arms right there. That hurt me real bad. And then we had a Corporal Albert Gettings. He was like the best squad leader I ever had. The way he got hit, the way he conducted himself—it was just heroic. He got shot by this sniper and fell to the ground. But then he got right back up and started returning fire—even though he had this bad stomach wound. Then another guy behind him got hit; he dragged that guy to safety and was *still* returning fire. Finally we got him to lay down. By then he'd lost too much blood. They couldn't get enough blood back into him in time, so he passed away. That was the worst ever, right there.

As far as myself, I'm okay. I'm in a lot of pain right now, like my hip really hurts bad—when I fell off that roof I broke my pelvis in three pieces. It's been about eighteen months now since my injury. I'm on a lot of meds. I just have to deal with it. People don't realize: Yeah, we get hurt and stuff like that, but you don't always go back to perfect. That's my case right now. I'd like to go back to my unit. I'd like to get back to Iraq. What they're probably gonna do is put me on a PEB, which is a physical evaluation board. They will say if I'm well enough to go back to my duties. Seeing how my hip's pretty bad busted, they're gonna probably end up pushing me out.

At first, the initial thought after the injury was, "Hey, this guy's hip is gonna heal back together, he's gonna be fine, he's going to return back to full duty." And that's what I did at first. I healed up, I rejoined my unit. But then, about the second day back I hurt it again. I had this bad limp for like six months. That's the whole mentality of a grunt, you know. *Suck it up, it'll be okay, you'll get over it.* And I dealt with it for a long time. But it started getting worser and worser and worser. Finally it was to the point where I couldn't even ride in a car and hit a bump, that's how bad it got. And I mean, don't get me wrong, the first surgery I had after that, it helped me a little bit. They did a hip scope basically, and scraped off all the bad cartilage. And, like, my bone had overgrown when it repaired itself, so it was popping out of the socket. They had to shave off some of that stuff, trying to get it to quit doing that. They told me I'd probably have complications, but at least I can walk now without a bad limp. That's the only good part. I used to limp bad. Like it used to be so bad I couldn't even walk down stairs.

Right now I'm waiting to see if I can get another surgery to make me better. But they're kind of like, "No, you just need to get out of the Marine Corps." I'll tell you one thing: I'm not gonna do no desk job. I didn't join the Marine Corps to do no desk job. I don't sign papers; I make papers get signed. That's just how I feel about things. I'd rather be shooting at shit. It's just my mentality. I'm 03-11 Infantry. A rifleman. I didn't pass the knowledge test, or I'd be a machine gunner. To be honest with you, rifleman was my main choice anyway, because basically, I wanna be right there, kickin' doors in, stuff like that. I'm not saying it fascinates me; it's just what I like to do. I love the whole mentality—I love to be in firefights, I love the adrenaline rush, I love everything about it. I mean, it has its bads, you know. You lose friends, you lose a lot of people and stuff like that. It blows big-time. But you just gotta suck it up and deal with what you got. Freedom isn't free. You know what I mean?

Right now, I'm not regretting anything. Like, I'm not regretting anything that I did. I don't regret going. I don't regret getting shot and falling through that hole in the roof. I don't regret not getting my Purple Heart. I don't regret killing nobody. Not really. I did what I did because I feel like this: I'm keeping *them* over *there.* I'm keeping them from coming back over here and doing another 9/11. There's a lot of people who got lost in 9/11. That's one of the big reasons I joined. I remember sitting in the classroom and seeing that on TV, and I was like, "Yeah! I'm joining the military!" I was a sophomore in high school. I was sitting in the science classroom. And I remember they turned the TVs on, and like at first, everybody thought, *This is something from Hollywood. Somebody is messing with us. This is some kind of bull crap.* But then it set in that it really happened. And you kind of felt, like, *Wow, we just got hit on our home shores. Somebody brought the fight to us.* I wish I coulda joined up that minute. I woulda went right then if I could have, but I was too young. So that's how it is. That's my motivation. Honestly, I'm not doing this for the money—ha ha, right? The main reason I went into the Marine Corps was because I was so pissed off at what happened on 9/11. I'm not sayin' I went over there for revenge. I just went over there to keep them over there.

When I first got back, there were a lot of bad things happening to me. Like, that's what happened with my marriage. My wife—my soon-to-be-ex-wife—she was a psych tech, a navy chick from Albany, New York. We fell in love very fast. I mean, once you know you love somebody, you know. We just knew it. We had our fallouts, we had our fights and stuff like that, but something always brought us back together. Finally we were like, "Hey, let's get married," so we got married. I'm glad I tied the knot. I love her to death—or at least I did, until she cleaned out my bank account, the bitch, pardon my French. I don't know why she had to go and do that for. It's funny sometimes what people do. Not funny, *ha ha*, you know. Funny *strange*. Fucked up, you know? But I have to give her one thing: She helped me get through some stuff. There were times when I first got back that I didn't know what I'd do without her. She took care of me and everything, 'cause, like, I had a lot of bad things going on—the nightmares, the recurrences, stuff like that. For the first six months I was back, I dreamed about falling off that building. I dreamed constantly about that. Or not every night. It would alternate between falling off a building and seeing Corporal Gettings get shot. And then seeing the kids that we shot—that we had to shoot because they had grenades. Every time I went to sleep, I'd see all the recurrences of all the bad times, you know, stuff that made an impact on your mind.

Basically, what happens is you're sleeping and you re-enact what happened. Those are your dreams. It seems pretty real. You wake up either in a cold sweat, or sometimes I'd wake up swinging. It just depends. Thank God I never did that to my wife. I think the reason I didn't was because when she was around, I had that closeness. Like in the Marine Corps, when you go to sleep at an OP or something, all your buddies are all around you, making sure you're safe, and you feel better. But when you're alone, you're just like . . . . You feel like you're in a corner, you know? So I think that my wife, when she was with me and stuff, well, I just slept better knowing there was someone there with me. I feel safer, basically.

You try to forget about things and you try to put them out of your mind, but the dreams just bring them back. It opens that wound back up. Sometimes it makes you cry. Sometimes it makes you sweat. Sometimes it makes you scared. It just depends on what you dream about. If I see Corporal Gettings, I get really sad. I have trouble sleeping at night because I don't wanna dream about that crap. I really don't wanna go through it again. I'm going to appointments and stuff for it now, so it should be getting better. I go to talk therapy; they help you out with meds, too, like they give you stuff to make you go to sleep. One major drug they put you on is this stuff that blocks you from dreaming. It keeps you from going into REM sleep or something. You don't dream. Either that or you don't remember what you dream, I forget which.

The worst thing about all of this is leaving the guys. Ever since I got whacked, the only thing that really hurt me the whole time was like—I really wanted to be back with my guys. When you're with your unit, you're like a family. You're a big family. That's your brothers around you. And leaving your family always sucks. You don't wanna leave your brothers. It's like, they have your back, and you have theirs. You're willing to give up your life for the guy on your left and the guy on your right, and they're willing to give up their lives for you. So it's like trying to take a little kid from his mom. It ain't gonna happen. You're going to scream and kick and do all you can do to stay back. That's just basically how it is.

#

MASTER SERGEANT KEN BARNES is the second in command of Maxwell Hall—at least for the time being, until they get a replacement for Lieutenant Colonel Maxwell. Born in Montana, raised all over, he joined the marines at seventeen. Now he's got twenty years in. He served with Maxwell in Iraq in the 24th MEU (pronounced *mew*, Marine Expeditionary Unit), a fighting force of about 1,200, deployed to trouble spots around the world via navy fleet, the historic mission of marines dating back to ancient Greece. From the day Maxwell briefed him on his idea for a Wounded Warrior Barracks, Barnes worked hard to help get the concept off the ground. Sometimes, he muses, it felt like they were running a three-legged race—two guys all shot to shit, diminished, they pooled their resources, made things happen despite all odds.

Hard and sardonic, at once a cynic and a true believer, Barnes is your textbook senior noncom, noncommissioned officer. He's exchanged live fire in Liberia, in Somalia, in George Bush senior's Desert Storm, in George junior's post-Saddam Iraq. As it happened, Barnes joined the 24th only six days before it left for Iraq. He was a gunnery sergeant at the time, assigned to lead the personal security detachment of the MEU commander, Colonel Ronald Johnson (since promoted to brigadier general). As a kid, Barnes had dreamed of becoming an Air Force pilot. After he started wearing glasses at age eleven, he settled on wanting to be an Air Force MP, military policeman. When he discovered you had to be 21 to carry a gun in the Air Force, he opted for the marines, following in the footsteps of his stepfather, who had gone on to make a small fortune in concrete. "I was a good grunt all the way through," Barnes says, "but what I really liked was working security detachments. It's that MP thing come back again to haunt me, I guess. The best way to describe it is like the secret service guarding the president. The colonel was our president. You're on the road all the time, you're moving all the time, you're in the middle of shit all the time. It's like leading your own platoon. The only officer that is really in charge of you is the guy you're protecting. When this billet came open, I was teaching machine gunnery at the School of Infantry. You better believe I jumped at the chance."

As Colonel Johnson's security man, Barnes worked closely with Johnson's Ops O, his operations officer, Lieutenant Colonel Maxwell. "First thing I could tell about Maxwell was that he was smart as hell," Barnes remembers. "You could tell that operationally, he had his finger on that entire MEU—all 1,200 men. There was just no bullshit about him. And when you get a guy like that, you know, whether he's chewing your ass or he's giving an order or just sitting around and shootin' the shit, that's what it is. It's no bullshit. He's not gonna hide anything from you. He's gonna give it to you straight whether you like it or not; he's not gonna dance around the issues. He was firm but fair. On some occasions when I was pissed off or whatever, I could go in his office and shut the door and rant and rave. Maxwell would sit back and he'd be like, "Alright, Guns (he was a gunnery sergeant at the time), get you a cup of coffee—go ahead and vent, buddy." I'd get it off my chest and I'd be good.

"See, any time Colonel Johnson left that FOB for anything, whether it was to go up to Baghdad or to Ramadi, or to visit somebody, or to check on something—anytime he moved one inch off the base, I had to arrange all the travel and security. Colonel Johnson was not one to shy away from a fight. If shit was blowing up and people were shooting, he felt like he needed to be there. Working for him, you knew that going in. You couldn't be a candy ass, because we were there to keep him alive. He relied on us every second of the day to make sure that if he did get into a shit sandwich that we got him out. So it was just a great job. I had a great relationship with the colonel. He's like one of those big uncle kind of guys that you could really get along with—though on occasion he'd piss me the fuck off, which is when I'd go into Max's office and rant and rave.

"The day was November 2, 2004. For some reason, we were escorting a British convoy of minesweepers. I never understood that mission, because they had more armor than we did. The minesweepers themselves were escorted by M113s, which are armored personnel carriers, so they have more armor than my Humvees do—they're just a tad bit slower. But it was a push from division. That was what they wanted us to do. The colonel even tried to wave it off, but then the next thing I knew he was calling me back into his office and telling me, 'We're doing this mission.' And I was like, 'Roger that, sir,' 'cause that's my job, to do what the Colonel tells me even if I thought it was crazy.

"I was riding in the turret of the Humvee. That was usual for me. We didn't have the full shield back then, it was just the front gunner shield. To me, riding in that position was just the easiest way to control a lot of stuff. If we were running in a convoy, I had to be able to see everything. I certainly couldn't see from *inside* the Humvee. I always rode in the command vehicle. I had the colonel in one seat, I had a shooter in another seat, and I had my driver. And then I needed a seat for the sergeant major, because he liked to ride with the colonel too. I had to be able to see all the vehicles behind me, and I had to be able to see all the vehicles in front of me. When you run a hundred meters of dispersion on fast roads, when you're runnin' 65, 70 miles an hour, with one hundred meters between each of the five vehicles, well, that's a long way if the front vehicle gets hit. That's a long way if the back vehicle gets hit. Somebody's got to be able to see all that stuff to control it. Having been a machine gunner before, I know how to use the machine gun better than anybody in my section; I *instructed* it for three years. Who better to have on the gun on the move? Now, when the colonel got *out* of the vehicle, we had to have somebody from the dismount truck come back and man that machine gun for me, because I would always accompany the colonel, which kind of made it a little bit awkward, but it doesn't really matter—that's just how we ran it. The colonel was totally cool with it. He was like, 'Do it how you think you ought to, Guns.'

"When you're on patrol, when you're driving places, when you're on foot patrol, when you're going anywhere, you have to constantly be aware of everything. Every person, every car, every piece of trash. In Iraq, the ground is covered with trash. Literally. Everywhere you go, there is a carpet of trash. A landscaping of trash. There's all kinds of shit. There's dead animals. There's dead people. And they put IEDs in everything. They don't give a shit, they will put them in a dead body, anything. So you gotta keep super-aware when you're over there. Anytime you go anywhere, your eyes are peeled. But you can't see everything. You can only suspect everything. It hardly matters. Sooner or later, it's your turn."

Without warning, a thousand-pound IED, planted by the side of the road, was detonated. Barnes remembers a bright flash, intense pain, his hand going numb. He thought he'd lost the hand. He looked down at the end of his arm where it used to be and there was just a big hole that was bleeding everywhere. The tendons of the first two fingers were severed, the thumb tendon was severed, the artery was severed. The wrist was shattered into little itty-bitty pieces. The shrapnel went clean through the wrist bone. The doctor told him that if it hadn't been for the way he wore his watch, facedown, the hand would have been completely detached.

Now he's behind this desk, in an office near the rec room of Maxwell Hall, his feet up like an executive, fiddling in midair with a golf club the way men do. A bunch of the more senior Wounded Warriors are being treated to golf this coming weekend at a resort in Myrtle Beach. His grip is totally fucked. He plays anyway. As physical injuries go, his is permanent and annoying. The top half of the hand—his thumb and first two fingers—has no feeling at all. The bottom two fingers and the base tingle all the time, pins and needles. The hand is constantly in pain. It is constantly an inconvenience—try pulling down your fly without using your thumb—but it is not life threatening, he's quick to point out. Sometimes he pays no attention; sometimes it bugs him. On some days it's really bad. At one point, he talked to his doctors about amputation because he was seeing guys do more with prosthetics than he could do with what remained of his real hand. He was on meds for nine or ten months. Pain meds. Sleep meds. Anxiety meds. There was a nerve drug to calm the pain. "The problem was, it didn't just target one nerve in the body, it targeted every single one. I felt like I was trying to walk through mud." Finally, he said to himself, *I'm not takin' this shit no more.*

"I'm glad I got off the pain meds," he says, worrying his grip, searching evermore for a solution, for the ultimate one-and-a-half-handed grip. The acoustic tile ceiling above his head has been partially removed. There is a leak in the roof, white shit all over the shelves and the floor. The contractor has promised to get to it. "Do I hurt? Yep. Does it bug me? Yeah. Do I still have bad dreams? Yeah. Do I still have anxiety attacks? Yeah. I get all that stuff. But to me, it's better to feel like shit than to feel like I'm drowning or like I'm trying to get through a puddle of mud. If I don't sleep, I don't sleep. That's it. I'll get up, play on the computer, watch some TV, stand out in the yard at 2:00 in the morning and swing a golf club. It just doesn't matter. If I can't sleep, I can't sleep. If my hand hurts, my hand hurts. You rub it, you pay attention to it, you don't bump it—eventually, it settles itself down. As far as bad dreams, I've had bad dreams since I was, you know—everybody has nightmares. When you were a kid, you had nightmares. So, to me, it's the same thing. You wake up startled and sweating and holy shit, what was that, and then you take a deep breath, you go get a glass of water, you look under the bed like Mom told you—there's no bogeyman. Then you either go to sleep or you don't.

"To me, the worst dreams are the ones when you're awake," he continues. "It's almost like an anxiety attack. Something triggers it and you start to drift off mentally and kinda disconnect from where you're at, which is a little dangerous, especially when you're driving. That's when a lot of 'em tend to happen to me. It's different for everybody. In time, you start to recognize what's happening. I still have a hard time driving past a parked vehicle. You know, you're driving down the road here in the United States, it's not uncommon to see a vehicle parked on the side of the road. Maybe somebody's car broke down, maybe it's out of gas, what have you. If I'm driving on a two-lane road, seeing a car like that will send me almost over the edge. Still today. It really—I still grip the steering wheel. I consider the possibility—what if? What if that car is loaded with explosives? What if it's going to blow up any second? You start going through that and then it triggers *other* things, and before you know it, you're off and running. Then you really have to get a grip on yourself, you just have to pull off to the side of the road. You're like, *All right, asshole. Settle down. You're okay. Ain't nothin' but a car beside the road, some piece of shit that broke down.*

"It's like this TBI business. At first I just thought I was just tired. I thought maybe it was the pain medication. But when I came off the medication, I realized. It's still really hard to remember stuff that's happening fast. It's like, if stuff is going on, you know, if things at work are going *boom, boom, boom, boom,* you have to deal with the things that come up one at a time, in rapid succession. And I'll do that. But then I'll be doing something else, and all of a sudden I will think, like, 'What in the hell did I just do?' Or somebody will come in the next day and say, 'You ordered me to do such and such.' And I'll be like, 'Why would I tell you to do that?'

"Focus is another thing. It's very hard. I used to be able to focus on four or five different things at once, and keep everything on track. I used to be able to have two or three different missions running, you know, things happening around you all of the time, *bang, bang, bang, bang, bang.* Now, now it's really hard to focus on anything. I used to love to read books. I grew up reading books. That's what you did in your spare time when you're on the float, long months at sea on navy transports. I'd read four, five, six novels while I was overseas. But I can't read books anymore because I don't have the focus to keep track. You read a chapter, you know, and by the time you hit the second chapter, you're like, 'What the fuck happened in the first chapter?' What's funny," he says, raising his hands to indicate the bookshelves in his office, and those as well that line the rec room, "is we have so many books around here. Look at all those bookshelves. My kids and my wife are all like 'God, you don't read anymore.' And they're right. I *don't* read anymore. I tell 'em I don't have time to read. I used to love it. Just can't do it anymore. You move on, you know? Even stuff like hunting is affected. Like, I used to absolutely love to hunt. Now it's very hard for me to get the patience level to stay out in a tree stand now and wait for a deer. I just can't focus for that long.

"Sometimes you get frustrated, of course. You ask yourself: *What the fuck?* You know what I mean? You ask yourself, *Why did I get blown up?* What I try to do is look at it in the way that, well, if I *hadn't* had got blown up, then Maxwell wouldn't have had somebody he knew that he could go to, somebody who was strong enough at the time to help get all of this started. And I damn sure know he'd never have found anybody to run it for the first year like we ran it. So, you know, it's just one of those things where I say if I had *not* gotten hurt, we woulda never started this barracks. Or maybe somebody would have started it, but it wouldn't be what it is. It's a huge fuckin' deal to me to watch this happen. Because when we first got hurt, this kind of barracks wasn't available. You look all the way back to Vietnam, to Korea, to WWII. Those guys spent all this time in the hospital, but then they were discharged. There was nobody to look after 'em. Nobody who could really understand. It's like, back during the Civil War—"

"Excuse me . . . Master Sergeant? You sent for me?"

A young grunt, call him Lance Corporal Mario, is knocking on the frame of the open door. A good-looking kid, a little on the short side. Plucky, you can tell, like the Italian-from-Queens guy in one of the old black-and-white movies about soldiers in World War II. His mouth is a little crooked, making it appear as if he is talking out of the side of his face like Popeye.

Barnes points his golf club accusingly: "You got a drug problem, marine?"

Taken aback: "What?"

"Do . . . you . . . have . . . a . . . drug . . . problem?"

Indignant: "I *wish.*"

"Why aren't you taking them?" Barnes asks.

"I took 'em," Mario protests. "You can prove it with the blood test."

"That's the problem. The blood test is saying that you *don't* have the drugs in your system."

"I do. I *do.* They just keep telling me to put more and more poison inside myself."

"Well," says Barnes, practicing his golf stroke again from his seated position, "they're obviously not gonna tell you to take something that's gonna kill you."

"I took ten milligrams."

"Well, that's not enough. You have to take what they tell you. They want you on that much because you have a potential for blood clots."

"They're just feeding me rat poison."

"Look, I take the same shit they use to make nuclear weapons, and I still stick it in my mouth every day."

In walks Sergeant D, a six-six string bean with a tattoo for every year he's been in the Corps. He gapes at Barnes with mock horror. "You stick what in your mouth every day? Maybe you gentlemen need to be left alone."

#

MY NAME IS CORPORAL BOBBY JOSEPH. I got no middle name. I've done five deployments in all: Iraq three times, Afghanistan once. The other time I was on a MEU. Tomorrow's my birthday. I'll be twenty five.

I was born in Smithfield, North Carolina, but I was raised in Naples, Florida. You can call me Bobby or you can call me Joseph or you can call me Jo-Jo, everyone does. Or you can call me Ruthless—I got that name after my deployment in 2003. That Jason mask hanging from the rearview mirror of my Chevy Avalanche? That's Jason from the horror movies. I got that mask to sort of commemorate the name, 'cause I'm a killer. In 2005 I got the name Darkness. As you can see, I'm pretty dark. That was always the big joke in my family, how I was so dark and how my parents were so white—my adoptive parents. At nighttime it's hard to find me. I creep up on people. I take their weapons. I'm all up in their shit. But I also got a lighter side. That's the side I have when I'm back in the States. Most people only see that—my sunny disposition. I'm known for keeping up the morale. I'm gonna get a tattoo soon. It's gonna say "333" because I'm only *half* evil.

Right now I'm just laying up in my room. Yesterday I got my Purple Heart. They had this guy who came to give it to me. He won the Congressional Medal of Honor. He told his whole story. There was this battle in Vietnam, and it was his first patrol, and they were being attacked on three sides; this was back in the day, 1965, I think he said. Then he pinned on my Purple Heart. The day before that, I got my NAM, my Navy and Marine Corps Achievement Metal. That's it over there on my desk. The narrative part talks about how I lead this assault on an enemy position. You can read it for yourself. It's all in there. It's been a big week for me, I guess.

Right now, I'm just lyin' up in the room, on the couch. My leg is sore. I took some pain meds. I got Cartoon Network on the big TV. Got my boy Al Pacino on the wall over there. You ain't gangsta if you don't have your *Scarface* memorabilia. And hanging up there on the other wall is my Dress Blues. When you have that stack on there, the ribbon rack over the pocket, they call it the Dress Blue Bravos. If you put your medals on there, they would be Dress Blue Alfas. That reminds me, I gotta get over to the PX and get me another ribbon rack. It's easier to get around now that I'm off crutches. You should have seen me when I was in the wheelchair. I was a stone demon in that chair. We had these fancy electric ones that got donated. Fingertip control. At least now I'm down to the cane and this walking boot. It stabilizes the ankle and the foot. I asked them to put me upstairs so I would have to climb up and down. It's a bitch, but ain't nobody gonna help me get better but me. I can use the extra PT, physical therapy.

There's nothin' like being in pain for a long time. My shrink is like, "Are you frustrated? Are you getting mad? Are you feeling short tempered?" And I'm like, "NO! I'm *not* fuckin' mad! What do you fuckin' think?" Everybody has to go to the shrink. Mandatory. I don't go anymore. I told 'em I'm not crazy. I told 'em, "Every time you schedule me an appointment to come to you guys, the more pissed I get. Because I'm not crazy. There's no point in me coming to you. I'm not gonna kill myself or whatever." But yes, I am pissed off that I got blown up. And I'm pissed off that I can't play basketball or run around with my sons or you know, something like that, the normal things, the simple things. I'm stayin' in here rotting away, just waiting for some procedures and appointments that I have to do just to get out the military. It's gonna be a while. I have to have patience. And I do, for the most part. It's just that at some points, you know, you get sick of it. I try to maintain the attitude. I try to keep myself busy. It's like the tattoo idea. When you bored you come up with the weirdest things. I mean, all we have is time. Fuckin' time. You know what I mean?

I joined on September 17, 2001. The recruiters had been trying to get me in high school, but I kept dodging away. I was like, "No, I'm not joining the military, you guys are crazy." I was like, "I'm gonna go to college and move on." I was probably going to get a business management degree and open a business. I didn't know exactly what I wanted to do. I had two choices. One, go to college. Or two, work for my dad doing land-scaping, because I was really good at it, and it's really good money down in Florida. He does landscape maintenance. He does the whole thing: sprinkler systems, once a week service, edging, mowing, fertilizing, mulching, planting sod. I mean, you won't believe the houses he does on Marco Island—half-million dollar houses. He does 'em for maybe $1,700 a month. Good money.

My parents have been taking care of me for a while. I'm adopted. It was a little weird, growing up. I would see my skin color and then I'd look at theirs, and I was like, "What's wrong with me?" In Naples, where I grew up, they had a ghetto. It's called Golden Gate. Everybody calls it Ghetto Gate. There's black people in there. But where I grew up, it was downtown. There were nothing but rich white people. I was the only black person there. Everybody knew me. Then we moved to Golden Gate because the traffic in downtown Naples was horrible. My parents bought a house— four bedrooms, three baths, two living rooms, a swimming pool, all that. You could live pretty good there if you had some money. When I was about seven or eight years old, I met my real parents. Now they live in Golden Gate too. So me going home is a pain in the butt, because both of them wanna see me. Everybody wants me to come over and eat. Before, I had no parents. Now, I got too many parents. Life is weird like that. It's like a pain in the butt. So I just stay at my girlfriend's house—there I have no drama. All in all I had a pretty good upbringing. They called me a spoiled brat.

Then 9/11 happened. I was pissed off. I had friends and family up there in New York. And I was like, "You know what? Let's see what I can do to help." So I went and talked to a recruiter. And he was like, "What do you want to do?" And I said, "I want to be a fireman in the Marine Corps." And he's like, "Okay." So I signed on the dotted line. Sometime between boot camp and school training, the whole thing changed. They sent me to SOI, the School of Infantry, to train as a grunt. From then on, I was straight infantry. I never did get to go to firefighting school. I don't know what I thought. I thought my orders got changed somehow. Later I found out that my recruiter did some bad things. Like some people who couldn't pass the aptitude test? He had people to take it for them. He made some fake high school diplomas for some guys to join. It took the Marine Corps a while to figure that out. Finally they caught him. He's out now. But what happened with me was, after I was in for three years—I'd been to Spain, Iraq, Afghanistan—they gave me a choice: Either you can get out of the marines, or you can continue staying in. If I wanted to stay in, I would have to stay infantry. I was like, "You know what? Lemme switch jobs, 'cause I already did enough infantry jobs. Let me become a fireman like he promised in the first place." But they were like, "Nah, you don't get that choice. Either you stay infantry or you get out." If I got out, see, it would be like they'd erase my name from the books, like I was never in the military at all. I wouldn't even be a veteran. All record of my service would be gone. I had worked way too hard for that. It had to do with the fact that my contract was forged or something, or because it was made under illegal circumstances or whatever. So I was like, okay, I got two years left, I'll just stay in.

The first time I ever got shot at was my first deployment to Iraq. This was 2003. We were in Nazarea. We'd cleared out the town, everything was fine. We were just waiting to go over the bridge—at the time, it was Saddam's regime over there across the river. We were dug in and waiting for a command to move. We had already put some vehicles over there, some tanks, and we were just waiting for the go ahead, getting ready to fire, getting ready to take over the city because it was gonna be a big battle, a big pain in the butt.

I was in my hole, you know, we were dug in, we had to dig a hole with our own little shovel. There was a sniper somewhere. Probably across the river. And he took a shot and it hit the tree behind me, it hit the bark, it just barely missed me. I heard the crack in the wind, just like this *craaaaack*, unmistakable, and then I heard it hit the tree right behind me. It must have gone, I don't know, like one inch over my head. If it had been one inch lower, or maybe two inches lower, I could have been dead. I have to tell you: I was boot. I was pretty scared. I stayed down on the ground for like thirty minutes. I didn't want to get up. I was shocked. I was like *Wow*, you know? Because the second that bullet whizzed over my head, it was like this moment for me, this moment where things came into sharp focus. Like Snap!, you know? The first thing that went through my mind was the fact that my wife was pregnant. *My wife's pregnant! I gotta get down because I'm coming home alive. I am coming home alive.* And then it was like, *Wow, I could have been dead just now. If I'd made the wrong movement and was in the path of the bullet, I could have been dead. If I had reached back to scratch my ass at that moment, and raised my head just a little bit while I was doing it, I could have been frickin' dead.* I was thinking all kinds of weird stuff like that. But then, at the same time, you still got that Marine Corps mentality in you. After all that, I got mad. I wanted to shoot this guy who was shooting at me, this guy who was fucking up my whole life, putting my life in danger. I wanted to kill this guy, because marines don't retreat. They're not wussies, period. That's the reason why they call us Devil Dogs.

After our sniper took out their sniper, they called on the radio to say everything's clear. I got back up, and from then on, I was never standing still. I was always moving, walking in a square, moving around, never standing still so a sniper could shoot me. The Gunny was like, "*What* are you doing?" And I was like, "I don't wanna get shot, sir. My wife is six months pregnant."

That was my second deployment, January to May 2003. Then, four months later, I went to Afghanistan—August 2003 until February 2004. Then I went on a MEU—Saudi Arabia, Israel, Jordan, Kuwait, Iraq, Malta, Greece, Italy, Spain. That was July 2005 until January 2006. Then I reenlisted and I went to DI school. I wanted to be a drill instructor. Unfortunately, I hurt my wrist in DI school and had to quit. I went back to Iraq in July 2006—as a grunt.

When I got back to Iraq, it was weird. Everything had totally changed. Nothing compared to this deployment, everything had gone to shit. It's horrible there. It's one hundred times worse. The Iraqi soldiers we're supposed to be working with? They get behind a wall and they hold their weapons up over their heads and they fire over the wall. They don't even aim. How the fuck do they expect to kill the enemy like that? They act like they're working with you, but they're just stabbing you in the back. They know who the bad guys are, but they're not helping us out. You can't trust them, so you just teach them the bare minimum. I don't teach them everything I know. No fuckin' way. Because they're gonna turn around one day and use it against you. You know how, in *our* military, you have to sign a contract for three or four years or whatever? If you're in the military, you're in for four years. No matter what. That's us. If we don't do what we're supposed to do, we go to jail and do hard time. But over there, if an Iraqi signs a contract, he can quit any time he wants. Like, when you're training these guys, if you piss someone off, guess what you just did? You just made a terrorist. You just created a terrorist. And then they'll go right to their terrorist buddies and they'll be like, "Guess what? The marines train like this, they do that, this is what they do." That's the reason we don't teach them everything we know. We just teach them the basics so they can learn to take care of their country so we can leave.

That's what I was doing when I was hit. I was training Iraqis. November 11, 2006, 1400 hours, also known as 2:00 p.m. I was walking in the street in a city called Anah. It was me and my squad. We had the 2nd LAR with us, light armor reconnaissance. We were teaching the Iraqis an exercise where I basically show them what to do and what not to do on patrol. And see, always, before I go out on patrol, I like to do what I call my "research." You have to understand: When I'm over there, I'm a non-stop person. They call me Lightswitch. That's another of my nicknames. Lightswitch. I'm either on or I'm off. I'm off when I'm in the States. But if it's time to train, or if I'm in Iraq, the switch is on. and when that switch is on, it stays on until I leave that nasty place over there. So I'm always on guard. I'm always on the move. I'm always doing something, always keeping my guys busy, keeping 'em motivated. If there's a patrol, before we go, I'll go talk to the squad leader who just came in. I'll be like, "How did your patrol go? What did you guys find? What did you guys see? Anything suspicious? I'm always taking four or five steps before everybody takes a step. I'm always ahead of everybody. I'm always that person to be like, *All right, what can I do to make this better? What can I do to make it safer for my men?* See, when I'm over there, I'm always thinking. You have to be. Because these people, these Iraqis, they don't care. They'll do anything to hurt you. They'll put a bomb in a dog or a cow, whatever. They'll put a bomb in their cousin's body. They do that, you know, boobie trap dead bodies. They say it's all about religion over there. What kind of religion is it if it's okay to blow up your cousin's dead body? One minute you're just walking along on the street. The next minute, you're dead. Or you're hurt. That's how nasty those people are. You gotta learn to think like a terrorist. So that's what I do. If you can't beat 'em, join 'em, you know? You got to think like 'em. That's what I always tried to do.

So we're on patrol, we're walking down the street in Anah, and all of a sudden I spot this hole on the side of the street—something I didn't remember being there before. I was looking through my ACOG, advanced combat optical gun sight, which is like a sniper scope. It's mounted on the weapon. So I got my weapon pointed at this hole, where it's obvious that someone's been digging. And as I'm looking though the scope, just as I was about to yell out and say that I'd spotted this suspicious hole, before I even said the first two words, there was this huge *BOOM.*

Everything shook. Black smoke everywhere. I was still standing on my feet. I looked to my right and Sergeant Holizinger was on the ground fifteen feet away from where he'd been one second ago. I was like, "Oh my goodness." I tried to walk toward him, but I took one step and fell to the ground. I couldn't feel anything from my waist down. And then, like within about thirty or forty seconds, I started feeling this burning sensation in my legs. I was like *Ahhhhhhhhhh!* I mean, I done a lot of damage to myself over time. I've been in a lot of pain. I broke stuff. Once I dislocated a finger playing basketball, and I popped it back into place myself. But this pain . . . I'd never felt anything like it. I kinda yelled. I definitely yelled. I yelled, "FUCK! SHIT!" I was cussin'.

Then I looked down. There was blood everywhere. I was like, "You motherfuckers got me, but you know what? You can't stop me!" And I'm laying there, still pointing my weapon out, holding it with one arm, looking for the bad guys, because they could be anywhere. But I couldn't shoot, you know, because you gotta have positive identification of a target to shoot.

My corpsman pulled me out of the road. I was still conscious, but I had a terrible headache. My head was just pounding, pounding, pounding, and then my ears were just ringing. My head hurt all over. Like, the vibration of that blast, it felt like my stomach was turned inside out. I wanted to piss and shit at the same time. I'm lucky I didn't piss and shit myself. Sometimes a blast will make you do that. Doc says to me, "You're going home, buddy." And I was like, "Can I look?" And he was like, "Don't look, trust me, you don't want to see." Because there was a big chunk of metal stuck in my shin of my left leg. It fractured the bone, the tibia, the fibia. I had a fractured femur also, and a torn femoral artery. There was shrapnel all over my body: my left ankle, my knee, my upper thigh, my right calf, my lower knee, my upper body. I was peppered, peppered meaning hit by a bunch of shrapnel. It just went everywhere. So I took his advice and didn't look down. The only thing I saw was this gash in my arm. I was like, *That is freakin' huge.* I could see my muscles moving inside. Blood was squirting into my face. I was like, *Ahhhhh!* You know? It was *nasty*. The corpsman was like, "Do you want morphine?" But I was like, "No, man. That shit makes my penis soft." That kind of made him laugh. I was trying to keep up the morale, you know. I was the squad leader. It was like, "I'll be okay. You guys gotta carry on."

Right now I have a lot of nerve pain, that's the worst part. But the most *annoying* part is all the shrapnel. I can't sleep with sheets because the shit comes out of me while I'm sleeping. It gets snagged on the sheets and then of course it hurts. I have to have a space heater. I heat the air in the room real warm to counteract the air conditioning. I can't put a sheet or a blanket on myself. They call it migrating. The shrapnel migrates out of your body. It travels, it comes through the skin, like little tiny pebbles coming out. Or really, there's a variety of shapes and sizes. What you can do is you can be your own surgeon if you want. You can get a magnet and stick it next to your skin—if the magnet's strong enough, it'll pull it out. Once I put a magnet on my leg and it stuck to the shrapnel inside my body. It'll just stick right there. Everybody says it's pretty funny. A while back I flew home to Florida. I set off all the metal detectors. Luckily they'd already called ahead and said I was coming. Everybody knew I was a wounded vet, so they treated me pretty well.

My morale has always been high. That's what I've always been known for. Being motivated. Being upbeat. That's one reason why I wanted to be a DI. I've always been a motivated guy. But lately, you know, there are days . . . . I guess everybody has their days, right? If I'm having one of my days, I just stay away from everybody. Because my morale's not good, my attitude's not good, I'm in a bad mood. I'm infectious in a bad way. I don't know what it is. Maybe after I got bombed, I got more short-fused. Like I barely have enough patience for anything. I'm just so darn short-fused. Sometimes I go to Wal-Mart. I go shopping and everything, I pick out what I want. But then, I get to the line and it's ridiculously long. And standing there waiting, I just lose my patience. I get pissed, you know? I can't stand there anymore. So I'll just drop everything and go walk outside and drive somewhere else. And then of course I'll have to shop all over again. That's one thing that happens to me. Or sometimes I get these random headaches. Once I have the random headache, I will not be downstairs at all—I will be sleeping in the bed the whole day. These are worse than migraines. It just pounds and pounds everywhere around the head.

You don't want to do anything. You don't want to answer the door, you don't want to hear nobody knocking, you don't want to hear nobody at all. You don't want to be near nobody.

Basically, my contract says I get out on October 17, 2009. But I plan on getting out within the next year. The doctor says first I have to do about six months of therapy, which I have to wait a while to do, because basically the nerve damage is screwing me, and my legs are not healing the way we want them to heal, and they don't want to do any more operations because they could cause even more nerve damage. So far I've had three operations. So we're really just waiting to see if the nerves are gonna calm down a bit. I'm on a couple different medications to help that out.

There's this dream I have. It's the same dream over and over. It's me walking down the street in Anah before I got blown up. And as I'm walking, as I'm looking through my ACOG, trying to get a closer look at that suspicious hole in the ground, I'm waiting for the boom to come. I know it's coming. I'm aware that I'm dreaming. I know that I'm in a dream. I keep telling myself, *Wake up. Wake up! Wake up before the bomb goes off!* Because every time I have this dream, the bomb goes off, and I get scared shitless and I wake up in this cold sweat. But it's always too late. I can't get myself to wake up. The bomb always goes off. *BOOOM!*

And then I wake up in a cold sweat, and there's this feeling inside of me. I say I'm scared shitless but really, it's not fear because I'm not scared of anything. It's more like anger. First comes the anger. Because we're over there in Iraq trying to help these people, but they don't wanna be helped. They're not telling us everything. They're screwing us over. They want us to die and get hurt. That's the first thing—anger. And then the second thing would be . . . well, my kids. I want to be around to help them grow up.

#

FRIDAY AFTERNOON FORMATION. A lot of the guys haven't bothered to show up. Sergeant D has sent a fire team, three guys, to scout the dorm—to bang on doors and rouse the Devil Dogs from their naps or jerking off or whatever the fuck they're doing when they're supposed to be here.

Ringo, Cybula, and Leeman are here on time, sitting together on the doctor's-office chairs in their usual spot in the back of the room.

"The hardest thing to deal with when I got back," Ringo is saying, "was the fact that my guys were still over there. I've been with my guys coming up on three years now. I know when their bowel movements are. I know 'em that well. I know what foods give 'em gas. Or why this guy is all of a sudden really angry for some reason. When you know people like that, and then suddenly you're gone, it's really tough."

"I think a lot of people think we come back and we're real happy we're home," Cybula says. "Yeah, we're glad we're alive. We're not stupid. But they don't see the other side of it."

"My thing is, it's warfare. People die. People you *know*," Ringo says. "The hardest thing I've ever done was at my buddy's memorial service. You put the helmet on top of the rifle, the boots in front. It was the hardest goddamn thing I've ever done in my life."

"I had no illusions about it goin' in," Cybula says. "I still don't."

"I don't complain about it, but it upsets me," says Ringo. "'Cause I got hit and had to leave my boys. Now I been six months with this thing, and I got no feeling in my hand."

"Ain't that good for jerkin' off?"

"Yeah, like it's somebody else with a weak grip."

"No matter how much you train to deal with stuff like that, it's still gonna be hard."

"People always think it'll happen to someone else," Leeman mumbles. He is not a man of many words, but when he says something, and you can understand it, it usually has the air of folksy wisdom.

"When that round went through my helmet," Ringo says, "I thought, *This was supposed to be the one that killed me.*"

"Well, it didn't, man," Leeman says conclusively.

"What do you know about that?" Ringo sings.

"It gets so bad over there," Cybula says. "At first you're all, like, alert and lookin'. Scared shit, even though nobody admits it. By the time you get to that third month, it's like you actually *like* it. You get to that point where you need that adrenaline rush. And then you come back here and everything is so damn slow. You're still lookin' for that rush. You come back here and you try to fit back into your life, but it don't work. Your relationships with everybody suck. They don't understand how you feel."

"I came back and my wife was like, 'I'm not sure you've dealt with your issues,'" Ringo says, doing an impression of an Oprah-influenced female. "And I'm like, 'Yeah, no *shit*. I lost half my platoon when I was over there. I didn't really have no time to deal with it. I think I was a little busy, doing my job, *trying to keep my boys alive*. I waited until I got home to deal with shit.'"

"The women just want you to come home and take care of their problems," Leeman says.

"Big daddy's home," Ringo sings, another tune.

"Everybody here helps everybody else out," Cybula says. "We're here with other people who share the same problems with you. You're not alone. If me and him were back in our unit, you know, on LIM DU, whatever, the whole grunt mentality is like 'Oh yea, you're a wuss, you're not doing your job, you're just sitting around the barracks fakin' like you're hurt.' So they send us here, and it's like a fair mentality. Everybody else is hurt too. Your job is to get better."

"Here's something you can record," Ringo says. "After I went to that funeral in Arlington—for the young marine I tried to help? Me and my younger brother, who is also a marine, we go to the Marine Corps Museum. We're standing there looking at these photos of the landing on Iwo Jima, and these two ladies are there also. The pictures are pretty graphic. You see marines jumping off the side of the boat and people getting hit. And the ladies, they're like 'Man, it takes a lot of courage to do what you guys do.' And when she said that, I don't know, something just hit me real quick, and I'm like, 'No ma'am, it ain't courage. It's love.' That's what I told her. Because it ain't courage. What we do is not courage. It's love. It's love for the guys. Like I always say, this is as close as you can be to a man without being gay. There's no such thing as courage in the corps, it's all about love."

"I would *love* to be in a firefight *right now*," Cybula says. "I would absolutely love *that*. It would make my day. Remember the kill house we found in Fallujah? They were like, takin' people's eyeballs out, torturing people every way they could, fuckin' stretching 'em out and stuff like that. These were Iraqis doing it to their own Iraqi people. Remember that, Ringo?"

Ringo cuts his eyes toward his former suitemate. "I never been to Fallujah, bro."

#

SERGEANT D is really pissed. It's 3:30 p.m. He's still here. He could have dismissed these guys an hour ago if they'd shown up. It's Friday, true, and all the senior guys have left for Myrtle Beach to play golf, but where the fuck is the military discipline? They are still marines. He scratches his head. His skull is caved in slightly on the right front, above his eyebrow.

Jack Durgala, Jr. is thirty-one, from Birmingham, New York. He actually met his father for the first time courtesy of the U.S. Marines. His buddy was working as a recruiter. He was on a call at a family's house to talk to their son, who wanted in. He noticed the name of the father, Jack Durgala, and asked if he know his buddy, Sergeant D. The guy was like, "I've been looking for him for years."

Sergeant D was also training Iraqi soldiers when he got hit—a suspicious rice bag two hundred feet down the road turned out to be an IED. His left leg was broken. His left foot got spun around. A piece of shrapnel hit the lower part of his right leg and took a big hunk out of it. Another piece ruptured his intestines. A piece of iron rebar embedded itself into his helmet. Luckily, he had one of the new-model helmets. Whoever designed it did a great job. The rebar hit the helmet and stuck, but it didn't go through. The force of the blow, however, was enough to split open his skull.

Like the others, Sergeant D's life was saved by quick work in the field and by quick evacuation. Combat mortality rates have fallen from 24 percent in Vietnam to 10 percent in Iraq and Afghanistan. Most troops are in Germany within a few days of their injury. They're back stateside within a week, two tops. Sergeant D has less intestine now than he used to. "Food goes through me a little bit faster," he laughs. He has nerve damage in his right leg; it causes something called drop foot. His left leg has metal plates and screws holding the foot to the ankle. He has very mild TBI, mostly a short-term-memory problem. Sometimes he'll tell his marines to do the same thing five times, because he doesn't remember the other four. The worst for him is the nerve problem. "You know how when your leg falls asleep and you get the pins? Well," he says dryly, "I have the pins. Now dump gasoline on it, light it on fire, have a midget come over with a sledgehammer and start slamming on your foot, and then you add one deranged person with an ice pick trying to put the fire out, and then somebody coming by with water, ice-cold water, and dumping it on your leg. All that within a second. It just gets very frustrating, to say the least. And now they've diagnosed me with a crack in one of my vertebras from getting thrown by the blast. Every time I go to the doctor, it's something else. I'm happy that they found the problem, but I would like to move on with my life already.

"More or less, Maxwell Hall is kind of—" He searches for the right word. "A holding pen is the best way to put it. Some of the marines refer to it as purgatory. A lot of the injuries they don't know how to fix. They don't know *what* to do. The gear is better now than before. If I was wearing, like, Vietnam-era gear, I wouldn't be alive right now. Today, more people are getting injured and living, and the doctors don't know how to solve a lot of the problems, especially the brain problems. Or like myself: nerve damage. Before, it was like, okay, the leg got ripped off, give him a prosthetic. Now they reattach it. But how do you fix a nerve problem? Obviously, they don't know how."

Finally, some stragglers arrive in the rec room. Their numbers are obviously down from the morning formation. The place has the feel of a ghost town. It's something they're constantly struggling with in Maxwell Hall: how appropriate it is to still play the game.

"Every one of you in here should be frickin' pissed off at the guys that aren't at formation," Sergeant D. tells them, pacing the floor in front of them. "'Cause you been waiting around for an extra hour while we're trying to track everybody down. Simple shit. You know it's Friday. You know we're gonna get the hell outta here as early as I can get us outta here, right? So get your frickin' buddies, your roommates, whatever, get 'em to start doing what you're supposed to be doing. It's simple. All you gotta do is show up. Nobody's making you frickin' fill sandbags or anything like that. Nobody's being abused. As far I'm concerned, this is the best barracks I've ever seen. Yes, it sucks, the reason why you came here, I ain't arguing that. Just do what the fuck you gotta do to get yourself better to go back to your unit, to medically retire, to get your money every month, or whatever.

"I mean, I walked through the barracks today, and let me put it this way: I'm embarrassed as fuck about the whole fuckin' barracks. Some of those rooms I walked in . . . . If Sergeant Simms wasn't standing there next to me at the door, restraining me—just about physically restraining me, that was what it was coming down to—I would have dumped every piece of shit in those rooms. *Everything* would have been on the floor. You would be lost in laundry like fuckin' Hurricane Katrina. Only this would have been Hurricane D. Don't let me find your fuckin' rooms like I found them today. Vacuum your damn floors. Pick up your goddam dirty laundry. I don't care if you gotta do a goddam sniff test, you do it. If it stinks, throw it in the wash. Get yourself a laundry hamper or something. Get a laundry bag. Put your shit away. You got food and shit in your room, fuckin' put it in the goddam fridge. Don't just leave it sittin' the fuck out. We had a real bad problem with ants last year. Let's not give the ants any fuckin' reason to come in. Tupperware works pretty goddam good, gentlemen. You just stick it in your microwave. And the fuckin' toilets. Holy fuck! Holy FUCK! A disaster within itself. Gentlemen: They sell this thing at Wal-Mart for like 99 cents. This little scrubby thing? Buy one. Rub it around in there. It's an amazing piece of technology. You should look into it. If you don't wanna do that, you can fuckin' stick your hand down there like a fuckin' ape and scrub away. Whatever. I DO NOT WANT TO SEE THE TOILETS LOOKING THAT WAY ANYMORE.

"Let's get out there and start doing what we're supposed to do. It's simple. Get a haircut. Wash your uniform once in a while. Some of y'all stink, all right? I got a girlfriend. She washes my shit. If you can't get a girlfriend, then get a boyfriend and have him wash your shit, all right? Wash your uniform, get a haircut, clean out your room. Clean the frickin' toilets. Take care of yourself. If you got a problem, don't wait until it becomes a huge problem to let somebody know about it. If you don't feel comfortable talking to a squad leader, come talk to me. If you don't wanna talk to me, go talk to Master Sergeant Barnes. Go talk to the doc. Tell me you wanna see your chaplain. *Whatever*. If you're having sad thoughts or bad thoughts or family problems or something, everybody in here's got something going on in their head—whether you realize it yet or not, something's going on up there. And if you've got other problems, that's just gonna escalate things. So talk to somebody, okay?

"Besides all that, do all the right things for the right reasons this weekend. No drinkin' and drivin'. If it ain't eighteen, don't fuck it. If it is, wear a condom."

"Errrr," the Devil Dogs chorus.

#

BRANDY AND JEFF LEEMAN are sitting side by side on the floral couch in their little two-bedroom house, about ten minutes across base from Maxwell Hall. Presently off duty, Corporal Leeman is wearing civvies—tee shirt and blue jeans. In this getup he looks a lot less like a grizzled marine veteran and a lot more like what he also is—one year out of his teenage years, the same age as most college juniors. The furnishings in the house have a newlywed feel: the DVD collection, the shot glass and beer mug collection, the framed certificate from the "Before I Do" Marriage Foundation Workshop. There is a computer desk at one end of the living room, an entertainment center on the other. Brandy bought the latter with her employee discount at Target while her husband was in Iraq. She assembled it herself. It took six hours.

On Leeman's lap sits Gunner, their miniature Doberman pincher. Gunner has a lame leg like his master—his right hind. He was born that way. He'll sit on Leeman's lap all day long if he's allowed. Gunner has this weird thing where he doesn't want anyone to be in the bathroom without him. If you go in to poop and you close the door, Brandy explains, Gunner will put up this huge ruckus until he's let in—turns out he just wants to sit there and observe. Brandy is wearing a red tee-shirt with the word Marines in yellow script across the area of her body we're not allowed to mention on tape. In her lap she holds Lucky, a shepherd mutt they found in a ditch on the side of the road, starving and full of fleas. Lucky indeed. This is their little family.

"All they do is show the bad shit," Leeman is saying. He is talking about the press, the nightly news, the impressions people have of the war in Iraq. "They don't show how we help the little kids. How we give them food and stuff, even though some of them might be wired up with IEDs—did Kinnee ever tell you his story about the kid? The press doesn't show the kind of stuff we see. They don't show how all the Iraqis get their water out of the Euphrates River—where they put all their waste. They take a dump in there, they put all their pollution in there, and then they go and get the same water to drink. You don't see reports on how we're building up the water treatment plants over there so that the people aren't nasty and disgusting all the time. And how we're giving them actual food instead of them having to go out and catch fish and grow stuff. The press shows us doing bad things. But what they don't show is, like, say we accidentally kick in the wrong door or something like that? Say we're on a patrol or we're looking for bad guys and we kick in the wrong door. I bet you didn't know that the U.S. government will pay to have that door fixed. We will *pay* to have it fixed. They don't show that. They show us kicking it in and the Iraqis getting mad about it, but they don't show us paying to fix it."

"If I was over there, I'd keep my happy little butt in the tent," Brandy says. She is fair and freckled, with long, straight, naturally red hair. When her husband was in Iraq, she sent him packages several times a week. At the FOB, he slept on an Aero Bed until it mysteriously got stabbed. He ate so much junk food he gained twenty pounds. Her packages continue to arrive since his return, rerouted back from Iraq—there were some crumbled homemade cookies in the last box. What Leeman really missed while he was over there (besides his favorite unmentionables, of course) was Brandy's lasagna. Whenever she makes it for dinner, his buddies from Maxwell Hall start showing up.

"When you're over there," Leeman explains, "you do what you're *told.*"

"That's what you signed up for, right?"

"Is *that* what I signed up for?" he laughs. "Why *did* I sign up, anyways?"

"Because you didn't want to go to college?"

"Where I probably would have just flunked out and wasted a bunch of time and money."

"And because it was a way to keep you out of trouble back home."

"Most of my buddies from back then are working on a farm now. Or they're in the military. Ninety percent of my class went into the military."

"Or they went to jail."

"There's that. I wasn't ever in no trouble with the law, but maybe I woulda been."

"Lebanon, Tennessee," Brandy says. As if the name is explanation enough.

"And now I want to go back."

"Back to Lebanon?"

"Back to Iraq."

"Back to Iraq," she repeats. There is an odd tone in her voice, neither upbeat nor down.

"When I got hit, I didn't want to go home. I didn't want them to send me home."

"You were kind of excited about coming home, but at the same time you were upset. The first couple of weeks, you were like 'Man, I wish I was back over there.' And I was like, 'Why would you want to go back over there?' And you're like, 'My friends are still over there and I want to help them.'"

"I'm still trying to get back to active duty," Leeman says. "My old captain? He's moved over to H&S Company. He's pretty much telling me he can get me back and I can be on light duty till I get out. That means I can go to Iraq and *everything*."

"What do you mean, 'till you get out?'"

"Well, I get out next November, so if I stay on light duty until—"

"I don't want you to get out. I want you to re-enlist."

"I do too, babe."

She looks at him. "It's job security, right? It would be rough if you get out and neither of us has a job and neither of us has been to college. And then we'll have to move back home and I'll have to give up my job here at the dealership and you won't have a job. I guess you could probably go home and work on the police force like your stepdad."

"The marines is job security," Leeman agrees, nodding with all the sagacity of someone who has experienced life on this earth for nearly two decades. When he was growing up, his mom was always working. She used to be a nurse; now she sells construction equipment. His dad was a landscaper. They were divorced when he was twelve or thirteen. His stepdad used to sell medical equipment; now he's on the police force, working as a guard at the jail. Brandy's dad used to work for Nissan, building cars at a plant in Smyrna, Tennessee; her stepmom is a registered nurse. (There is a big nursing school at a nearby college.) Brandy's bio-mom only recently came back into her life. She works as a cashier at a gas station–convenience store. Her stepdad works in a pencil factory.

Brandy scratches Lucky vigorously behind the ears. The first time she saw Leeman at church, she thought he was hot, but there was *no way* she was going to talk to him. She was just standing there, like *Wow*, you know? But she wasn't going to say anything to anybody because she didn't want anybody to tell him. It was, after all, a very small church in a very small town. Three pews, an aisle down the middle. Everybody knew everybody's business. Leeman was new. Brandy was like *Oh God, this is gonna be horrible. He's not gonna like me.* And then her stepbrother gets this big smirk on his face. "You can't go out with *him*," he tells her. And she was like, "Who said I wanted to go out with *him*?" but secretly she was thinking, *Oh God! He knows! How does he know? Is it that obvious?* That was almost three years ago now.

"Of course, if you stay in, I'll be worried the whole time that you'll get hurt again," Brandy says. "After *hurt*, there's only one more thing that can happen."

Leeman cocks an eyebrow, devil-may-care. "If I was gonna be dead, wouldn't I be dead already?"

"When you called me from the hospital—"

"I was high as a kite on morphine."

"It was ten in the morning. I had just got home from working all night at Target. We were getting the Christmas stuff done, like we had to put all the display trees together, and we had to re-do the toy section. I had just got home and I was getting ready to lay down, and I think I was eating because I remember I was starving, and then my phone rings and I look at the display and I'm like, *Okay, it's a weird number, it's gotta be him.* So I answer and I'm like, 'Hey, how you doing?' And you're like—"

"I don't even remember what I said." His lips curl, a rakish smile. He plays tom-tom with his fingertips on Gunner's smooth belly.

"I *remember*," Brandy says. "You said you was in the hospital at Al Asad. And I was like, 'WHAT ARE YOU DOING IN THE HOSPITAL AT AL ASAD!!!!?'"

"When you're over there, you can't think about getting injured, or you're not gonna be doing your job," Leeman says. "If you're worrying, you're letting your guy to the left and right down. You're going to get them hurt or yourself hurt. When somebody gets hurt in Iraq, you say, 'That sucks.' But you can't really think about it—on patrols and stuff you can't really think about it. Otherwise, you're gonna screw yourself and everybody else. It gets infectious. It's ju ju. The deployment's gonna be miserable."

"Aren't you afraid to get . . ." She searches for the right words. "Hurt again?"

He shrugs. His face rearranges itself into a somewhat abashed expression, maybe something like a fraternity brother who is about to tell his fiancée some of the secrets. "Everybody is afraid. A little. But they'd rather just go over there and deal with it instead of worrying about it the rest of their lives. You know how they say—shoulda, coulda, woulda. You don't wanna have that."

Brandy nods seriously, taking it in.

"And besides," Leeman continues, "going back over there a second time—it's gotta be different. It's like doing anything the second time. I've already been hurt. I know what to do. I know the drill. I know what the processes are now, so it won't be as bad if I'm hurt again."

He looks at her. She looks at him. Neither seems convinced.

ON SUNDAY AFTERNOON the old man is wearing cargo shorts. His feet are bare—the ghosts of socks meet the tan-lines on his rock-solid calves. The founder of Maxwell Hall is sitting in a cheap plastic patio chair—three for five dollars at the CVS—on the narrow front porch of his house, in a well-laid-out development behind the strip malls of greater Jacksonville. There is a man-made lake with a fountain, a rec area with fields and courts, a water tower presiding over rows and cul-de-sacs of cute little houses made of siding and stucco in several styles.

On that fateful day three years ago, Lieutenant Colonel Tim Maxwell—Max to his friends, a graduate of Texas A&M, father of two, triathlete, career leatherneck on his sixth deployment, operations officer for the 24th Marine Expeditionary Unit—walked back to his tent in the seemingly secure command compound after lunch at the chow hall and prepared to take a fifteen-minute power nap. He took off his flak vest and his helmet. He left his boots on. He was dirty and dusty, so he lay down on the wooden floor of the tent (or maybe he lay down on his bed; another thing he can't remember clearly). It is interesting how fast you can crash out, he says, snapping his fingers. Comfort is irrelevant when you're exhausted. You just lie down and turn it off.

He was in a secure area, the command base. His tent was secured all around with, with—that stuff in the bag. What's the word? Not concrete . . . you fill them up . . . they're heavy . . . *sandbags*. There were sandbags leading out the door of the tent, an alley of sandbags, like a tunnel without a roof, two feet wide, six feet high. The alley ran for about three feet, then turned a hard left, continued on for a bit. He hadn't been asleep for more than five minutes, ten at most, when enemy mortars hit the compound. There would be about fifteen in all. The first one landed right in the middle of Maxwell's sandbag alley, just outside the flap of his tent.

Two pieces of shrapnel entered his brain through his left cheek near the zygomatic arch. The fragments damaged the central and temporal areas of his brain on the left, and also the optic radiation on the left. Specifically, the Broca and Wernicke's areas and possibly the conduction bundle between them were affected. This is where the language center of the brain is located. Because of the damage, Maxwell has expressive aphasia (trouble getting words out, problems with names and labels) and some receptive aphasia (trouble processing complex speech). The optic radiation damage left Maxwell with a right peripheral cut in both eyes, meaning that he can see to the left with both eyes but not to the right, despite having 20/25 vision. The shrapnel also damaged the motor portion of his brain, resulting in weakness and loss of control on the right side of his body, including his leg, arm, and face. Two mortar fragments are still embedded inside his brain, too deep to risk extraction. For three months, to allow his brain to heal, part of his skull was removed and placed inside his gut for safe keeping. More recently, surgeons have begun using acrylic to replace portions of the skull, cutting down the incidence of infection. For the most part, Maxwell's health and function have continued to improve, though he's had some problems during the past year with seizures. And then there are the pesky "crashes," as he likes to call them, when his brain gets overworked and overstimulated and shuts down. The doctors have been adjusting his meds. They'll just have to wait and see.

From the backyard can be heard shrieks and laughter, a small tenth birthday party for Maxwell's son, Eric, who always wears cammie cargo shorts and wants to be a marine when he grows up. He was six when his dad came home wearing a crash helmet to protect his injured brain where the piece of skull had been removed; he still worries that his dad might die unexpectedly in the middle of the night. Eric's best friend Collin is here, as is his thirteen year-old sister, Alexis, and a contingent of rugrats, all of them cousins and neighbor kids, the children of Shannon Maxwell's sister and her two best friends, who together have formed their own little marine wives support group, *Sex and the City* meets *Semper Fi*. Inside the planked fence, the yard is a patchwork quilt of mismatched sod—a large square of fescue here, Bermuda grass there, and over by the deck, an irregular, weedy-looking rectangle of God-knows-what that Shannon picked up on sale at Home Depot while he was in Iraq. In one corner is a largish jumpy with a basketball hoop. In typical fashion, Shannon transported, dragged, and inflated it herself.

The daughter of an Air Force pilot who left active service when she was five, the former Shannon Grothues grew up in San Antonio, Texas, romanticizing about travel. "I hated not being the typical military brat," she says. As it happened, in twenty years as a marine wife, she has never had the opportunity to live outside the continental United States, either. The couple met in College Station, Texas, when both were students at Texas A&M. He was an ROTC cadet; she was a business administration major, with an emphasis on marketing and advertising. The setting was a dive bar called the Dixie Chicken, an Aggie hangout. Shannon was nursing a beer, watching TV while her roommate and another friend were playing pool with some of Maxwell's friends. Then Max walked in. Another pool table was open. He challenged her to a game. His eyes are very big and very blue.

Shannon liked his confidence. She liked his broad shoulders. She liked—well, she doesn't know how to put it into words without sounding like the kind of woman she's not. Bottom line, he's probably a lot like her father. A very strong individual, but also an individual who listens and respects her opinions and her ideas. Maxwell graduated in May, 1989; they were married in July. She graduated the following June, after only three years. Maxwell took five years to graduate—let's just say his freshman year wasn't all about academics. He likes to joke that between them, they averaged four years a degree. For the record, each took two years to earn their masters.

As Maxwell pursued his career as a first lieutenant at Camp Pendleton, Shannon worked as a junior executive at an ad agency in Orange County. Most of his friends were not married; Shannon was the only wife in the group. They had a great time going to bars and picking out women for the boys. They'd do Thanksgiving dinners at their house, that was fun too. They purposely didn't live on base—Shannon didn't feel like she had a lot in common with the other marine wives. They were all very much into their husbands' careers; they had kind of taken their husbands' identities. Shannon saw her marriage as a collaboration between two strong people with bright futures ahead. When Tim was gone on deployment, though she missed him, it kind of worked in her favor. She stayed late at the office. Ten p.m. was not unusual. Her bosses loved her. After their two children were born, Shannon quit working full time. Over the years, she has earned a first-degree black belt in Tae Kwon Do, taught martial arts to four and five year olds, created and supervised a practice for a popular psychiatrist, earned a master's degree in international management and marketing, run the Marine Corps Marathon. More recently, she started Hope for the Warriors with her good friend Robin Kelleher, which helps spouses and families of wounded marines, providing everything from food, groceries, and fishing rods to rental cars for moms and dads and lodging for "morale visits" from spouses. Last spring, in a White House ceremony, President Bush presented Shannon with an award for her efforts.

"I don't think, when I was twenty years old, I really comprehended what was at stake, what he was really going to be doing for a living," Shannon says. "As I got older and he started commanding marines, I started understanding the magnitude of it all, the huge responsibility that was resting on his shoulders. The fact that he's got to be responsible for the lives of these young men—that they're going to be in harm's way and that he's responsible for them—that is a huge thing, a huge responsibility, to have people's lives in your hands. It's not until you're a parent that you really understand. Each one of these Devil Dogs is somebody's baby.

"When your husband goes to war, you worry about a lot of facets. Before a deployment, the worst part of our preparation is always having to talk about, okay, 'What are your wishes? What do you want done?' Basically, you prepare yourself, you envision what the kids and I are going to do if the worst thing happens. Self defense teaches you that also—to run through all the scenarios in your head so you'll know how to react when the time comes. To a certain extent, after twenty years, it's something that you've reconciled. He might be killed. You've told yourself that a million times. The weird thing is, I wasn't really prepared for him to be injured. For some reason, I never really considered *that* scenario. I don't know why.

"When I got the call, the first thing that went through my mind was just, *Okay. He's not dead. We can get through this.* As time goes on you learn what you have to learn. You learn about the injuries. You learn about the drugs and the therapy. You learn about doctors and hospitals. You have to become your own best medical advocate. And you learn humility. When he was in the VA hospital in Richmond, they were calling him Mr. Maxwell for the first time in his life. It was such a loss of identity. It was humbling.

"Things are more different now than I would ever have envisioned," Shannon says. "But it's not worth crying about it or worrying about. You have to live for the moment. You make the best of it. Especially with kids, you have to do that, because they have enough concerns at their age. I grew up living in a very strong and determined family. You accomplish challenges. You attack them and you get through them, and grow because of them."

The Maxwells have lived in this house for four years; there is a bitter-sweet feeling to the birthday proceedings. Tim is leaving in a couple of days for Quantico. The family will follow soon. They have to pack up, buy a new house, sell this one, find new schools, new soccer and softball teams, new everything. Of course, the move is a sign that Maxwell is healing, moving forward, contributing. Perhaps he is not the same man he set out to be, but who knows: Had he not lost some of himself in Iraq, would he have ever contributed as much as he has?

"I use my story all the time in hospitals, when I'm visiting the wounded," Maxwell says. "I tell them about good luck and bad luck. I tell them about how I got blown up in an area that was supposedly secure. Come on? What's the odds of that?

"The thing is," he says, his thick hands set earnestly upon his khaki-clad thighs, his voice small and conspiratorial, "I never even fired my frickin' weapon at anybody when I was over there. Never. Not in twenty years. I'm not happy about that, but I'm okay with it. It is how it is."

He looks out across the yard. One neighbor is blowing grass cuttings off his driveway, another is trimming a hedge—the little two-stroke engines rev and whine in harmony. A bunch of kids are playing pirate in a trailered fishing boat; a couple of teenage goth-boys on ridiculously small bicycles pedal past, trailing attitude. "Some of these young marines, they have a lot of mixed feelings when they get back," Maxwell says. "Like Kinnee. He got injured after only three months of combat. He didn't have no firefights. He feels like a pussy. I tell 'em, 'Hey, look at me.' I've had six pumps, three of 'em in a combat zone. But I'm always in a platoon that never gets no action. When people call me a hero, how do you think I feel? Don't call me no hero. What did I do?"

He tilts back in the chair, the hind legs wrinkle and wobble owing to the cheap material, a little taste of danger he seems to enjoy. He sets his eyes to the horizon, to the place where the tall and lush green trees become the glinty gray sky, which is heavy with the portent of another summer shower. His ice-blue eyes reflect his determination. The awkward cast of his face, the slight lag on the right side, lends him an air of bewilderment. There are big changes in the offing. He has no idea what lies ahead. He has no idea if he is up to the challenge. In private moments, frankly, he is damned concerned.

But he's been trained to put one foot in front of the other. That is what he will do. He will move to Quantico. He will work for the new regiment. He will continue to help wounded marines. He will try to be of use.

# # #

At 0530 hours the first floor of Maxwell Hall is deserted, the only sound the hum of the fluorescent lighting. Lance Corporal Robert J. Wild is pulling watch at the fitness center. He sits in an office chair behind a typical front desk. Before him is an array of treadmills and ellipticals and other workout machines, TVs hanging from the ceilings, tuned to FOX News. His elbow rests on the Formica counter; his palm supports his chin. He stares out the window into the gathering dawn, the brick building across the way, the muddy waters of the New River shrouded in fog. Blond and boyishly handsome, he brings to mind a smaller, slighter version of the actor Brad Pitt—Brad's younger brother, perhaps, playing a skateboard dude from Moline, Illinois, who lived in a lot of foster homes before joining the marines at seventeen.

"I forgot you were coming," he says to me, flashing his endearing smile. His nickname is Wildman. The tone of his voice is flat and matter-of-fact. "I can't remember nothin'. That's why I have this Palm Pilot. To remind me of my fuckin' appointments. Only sometimes I forget to program them in."

His eyebrows rise; his face registers something between concern and puzzlement. "I was only there for four months. I got back November 1. I've been married since February—six months. It was a quickie thing. I went out to a club and met her; I've always had this attraction for older women. She's thirty-eight. It was weird at first 'cause she has four kids. Her son is twenty and her daughters are nineteen, seventeen, and fifteen, and the nineteen-year-old is pregnant. She just got married to a marine also.

The seventeen-year-old is pregnant too. Her man just joined the army. My wife's son used to be a pro skateboarder, but now he does vinyl siding. My wife is a doctor. She works at Greenville Memorial hospital. She's a respiratory therapist. I didn't even know that until we'd been dating for a while. Before that I—"

The words come bubbling out of him. You get the impression that what he is saying is unfiltered truth, inside stuff gurgling to the surface like sweet water from a small natural spring. I ask him the proper spelling of his names. I ask him his birth date. It turns out to be today, July 13. He is 22 years old.

"Friday the thirteenth," he notes, as if it is evidence of something, as if it happens every year the same way.

I ask the date of his injury.

"There's this religious belief that the Hajis have, it's called Ramadan," he says, pulling the little stylus off of his Palm Pilot to keep his hands busy. "It's forty days and forty nights where they don't eat or drink anything during the daytime. They fast because they believe that if they do this, when they go to heaven, they'll be granted forty virgins, something like that. And they have this one day at the end of Ramadan, I forget what it's called, but it's a special day, a day when they show their faith to their God or their leader or whoever by attacking us. If they die on that day, they'll get that stuff in heaven, the virgins and stuff. That was the day I got whacked: October 19th of 06. Me and my buddy Dam Semrau were in a four-by-four post on top of a building. We got hit by a rocket-propelled grenade. I got thrown head-first into a wall. I injured my C spine and tore all the ligaments in my neck. I was in a neck brace for, like, four months.

"Now I can't think too well," he continues, replacing the stylus, picking up his phone, opening it to check for messages. "Like before, I was really active and I wanted to do everything. Now I don't do the things I used to do The main problem is my frontal lobe. It's not functioning. Frontal lobes. There are two. When you look at them on these tests, there's no activity. It's where you get your personality and your emotions and all kinds of stuff. Short term things I can't remember. I can remember old stuff. Or if I repeat something enough to make it long term then I can remember it. Like people's names, I can't remember. I had trouble remembering my wife's name for a long time. It's hard because it makes you feel like you're stupid. People don't understand what your problem is. You seem perfectly normal. They look at you funny. They don't understand that you've been blown up. So all they do is judge you.

"Before, I was really fun. I'm not much of anything anymore. Like, I used to like to do hobbies. I used to like to play sports. I used to love to weight lift. I loved to draw and build things. I actually went to school for two years to be a carpenter. In school I did woodworking. I built an entertainment center, a couple of shelves, stuff like that. It was fun, because I know that I made this, and now somebody wants to buy it from me. It makes you feel good. The funnest thing was building houses. I once built a 2,000 square foot house for a foster family. I was a foster kid for a long time because my mom couldn't keep me. Later we got back together. Before I went in the marines, I got to live with her again. My mom works at Ryan's Steakhouse as a baker. My stepdad's name is Reggie Baker. Well, he's not really my step dad because they're not married, but he's the closest thing I ever had to a dad. My real father was in the marines, too. He got kicked out for selling cocaine and dealing drugs and doing other stuff. My family's pretty, like, low on the totem pole. Like, we have no rich relatives, no wealthy relatives, we're all pretty, you know, standard living. And everybody thought because I was a little problem child that I was going to turn out to be like my father, and that's the last thing I wanted. I wanted to join the marines to prove to myself and to my family that I'm not, you know, that I'm gonna be better than him. And I already did more in six months on this deployment than my whole family has ever done in their whole lives. Like, I was the best driver in the battalion. My nickname was Ricky Bobby from that comedy movie. That name came directly from the CO. I was the driver of the lead truck. I never, ever got my crew blown up, not even one time."

Wildman reaches over and grabs a remote control. He aims it at the nearest television, begins flipping the channels. He settles on ESPN. All the rest of the monitors stay on FOX News.

"Now I'm depressed," he says. "It's affecting my marriage. It's affected my, you know, my friends because I just have real bad anger problems. I guess I'm a little frustrated, a little mad. Like, the other day, in the rec room, I got bitched out for not vacuuming or something and I just flipped out. I mean, I don't even live in the barracks, I live with my wife. But whenever I'm here I usually take the initiative and clean up, so that way we can get dismissed early. And usually everybody else just sits around. This time I had a fuckin' killer headache and I just didn't feel like cleaning up. And this guy's all up my ass about why didn't I vacuum. And I just flipped out, I was like, 'What? Are you talking to me? DO I HAVE BITCH WRIT-TEN ACROSS MY FOREHEAD!?!'

"I guess I'm just tired of the Marine Corps. It's nobody's fault. It was good for me before—until I got messed up. Right now I couldn't even go to college and learn anything, because my brain isn't functioning enough to where I could remember what you taught me yesterday."

He pulls a Newport cigarette out of the package, gestures toward the door. We walk outside, take a seat on the concrete steps.

He lights up, drags deeply. "It kinda makes you feel like a failure," he says.

"Why?" I ask.

"Because you signed a contract but you couldn't do your four years. You couldn't do your job."

"But you got blown up. It's not like you went AWOL or something."

"It's not what you picture when you sign up."

"I guess if you did, you wouldn't sign up in the first place."

"Young, dumb, full of cum."

"That's what they say."

"I can't remember half the time what I ate yesterday, or what I had a conversation about ten minutes ago. I'm always, like, trying real hard to think."

"Don't you feel like there's been any improvement at all?"

"No."

"Not any?"

"I think it's getting worse."

I look at this kid. It's his birthday. I don't know what to say. Dawn is breaking, but it's too cloudy to see the sun rising over the river. The air is damp and cool, that time of day people always say makes them feel hopeful, full of possibility. I put my hand on his shoulder and squeeze, and then I pat his back a few times—hard, manly pats, like you'd do with a big friendly dog.

Wildman takes another deep drag of his Newport. He looks at me with his Brad Pitt eyes. "It's cool, bro, don't worry about it. It's a normal thing for me."

2
Generation H

F IVE MINUTES," lisps the sidewalk diva, a caramel-colored Puerto Rican boy wearing eyeliner and a hooded sweatshirt on a deep-downtown corner of Second Avenue.

"Wait over there." He vogues his loose wrist toward a grimy brick wall riotous with graffiti, his long, varnished fingernail glinting beneath the streetlight, indicating a line of customers waiting to be served, a dozen white kids in their twenties—nose rings and goatees, a couple of rep ties.

"A fuckin' line?" Mark asks, incredulous, annoyed, surveying the group that is queued up earnestly like ticket holders outside a midnight showing of a foreign film. Mark's eyes are big and blue. His pupils are pinholes. There is a hard kind of beauty to his face, a slight concavity like a model's or a rocker's. He sniffles, blots his nose with a knuckle. He's not sick yet but he feels a little clammy, a little bit ill at ease—the way he always feels when it's getting to be that time. "Gimme a break," Mark implores. He's been copping Hammer brand heroin on this corner for longer than he cares to remember. "I ain't waitin' in no line."

"Then get the fok outta here!" the boy trills, launching into his best imitation of Rosie Perez, his neck unhinged, his head bobbing from side to side, his tapered finger waggling back and forth, scolding. "And don' lemme see you back here for at least two days!"

For one brief moment, Mark sees himself pummeling the little queer—a quick right cross, a smashed nose, blood all over that pretty teenage face. He may have grown up in the suburbs, he may have been cut from a fresh loaf of white bread, but he's twenty-eight now, he's lived in New York City for six hard years. He's been robbed, evicted, disappointed, shortchanged, jailed. He's walked in on his girlfriend going down on another woman. He's pounded the sodden chest of his best friend, trying to bring him back to life. He snorts ten bags of heroin a day. He doesn't need this shit.

Mark reels away on his heavy boots, his need to cop overwhelming his need for vengeance. He heads up Second Avenue. *What's the world coming to?* he wonders, and then he frowns, thinking what a prosaic thought he's just had, what a cliché. *Christ, I sound like my father.* Mark loves his father; don't get him wrong. It's just that his father is like everyone else. They talk in clichés. They never achieve their great dreams. *Is there nothing new to say?*

Mark has been in this frame of mind lately. It probably began four months ago, when his friend OD'd, taking their band's recording contract to the grave with him. Since then, everything has felt futile and boring: his friends, the clubs, his whole life. Nothing is fulfilling. No one he knows is happy. Everyone seems to have a kind of psychic slash mark bifurcating their lives. Waitress slash sculptor. Bartender slash musician. It's like the whole world is on hold, phone cradled to ear, Muzak playing.

His girlfriend isn't helping any either. She's a secretary slash actress. She has turned into Oprah. She calls him an abuser, a co-dependent, a victim of low self-esteem. She wants him to join some group or to begin seeing someone. Mark tries to explain: He can't be classified. *I am not everyone else. I am me.* What does Oprah know? What does his girlfriend know? She became his girlfriend only because they both needed a place to live; the piece of paper that holds them together is a joint lease. They've been together for two years, about the duration of his habit.

Mark pulls the collar of his jacket closer to his neck. It's getting cold. If he was properly high, he wouldn't even feel the cold, he wouldn't care. He considers his options. *Think.* Seventh Street is out—the most obvious spot in town, too many East Village poseurs. Ludlow is out—home of the regulars, the near-fatally hip from Max Fish, the Pink Pony, and the Hat. Clinton and Delancey—a major thoroughfare for the bridge-and-tunnel crowd. Second and Avenue A—young execs at the southeast border of their courage.

Passing a bodega, Mark hears two men in a doorway speaking urgently in Spanish. He brightens, remembering a trip to Spanish Harlem he once made. He went with an older guy, a little field trip, a little dope-fiend anthropology. Uptown, the spots have been the same for forty years. The dope is purer; the people are nicer. There are no lines, not a white face for miles, certainly no earnest young ones with carefully sculpted facial hair. *That's it! Spanish Harlem. I can cop in Spanish Harlem!*

He steps off the curb, raises his hand to hail a taxi. Abruptly, he lowers it. *What am I thinking?* East 117th Street is a $20 cab ride away. You can get two bags for that price, if you can find them. Mark has spent almost $15,000 in the past few months, an inheritance from his grandma. Most of it wasn't on cabs.

What time is it? Only eight? How about Bowery and Third? Mark hangs a left on Second Street. The wind blows, an arctic gust. Trash skitters. Tenements and factory lofts lean in over his head. His pace quickens. He thinks about the book *Junky*. His friends call it the Bible of Dope. Mark has read it four times. In the preface, William S. Burroughs lays down something he calls the junk equation: "Junk is not, like alcohol or weed, a means to increased enjoyment of life. Junk is not a kick. It is a way of life." For a while, Mark had the quote taped to the fridge. His girlfriend ripped it down.

Mark had planned not to be in this position tonight, pockets empty, on a wild-goose chase. He was going to wake up early and see a guy at a record company, then go score some dope. But he ended up sleeping until his girlfriend came home from work and started bitching, and by then it was Miller Time on a Friday afternoon—in glitzy office towers all across the city, the work whistles had blown, and all the poseurs and dabblers and weekend warriors were hailing cabs to the kingdom of Somnus.

Every Friday lately, it's the same. Demand outstrips supply; the count is down, the quality is down. Wait five minutes, they tell you. You wait a half hour, standing amid mountains of green plastic garbage bags, each of them with chewed wounds in the side, the entry and exit holes of foraging rats.

It's a bitch when things get cool, Mark thinks. You find something on your own, you think you're pioneering, living in some rare space. And then you pick your head up one day and it feels like you're in one of those chic clubs, in a bathroom full of mirrors—hundreds of fractured images of yourself, glaring at you from every corner, fading into tiny horizons. Mark started doing heroin six years ago. Now, to his great inconvenience, dope is de rigueur: the fuel behind the music, the route to the sunken cheeks of the waifish model, the chemical prop in films and clubs, the self-administered antidote to diminished expectations and sensory overload in an era of ennui—180 channels and nothing on, nothing new anyway, and nothing to look forward to.

What a time to be young: war, famine, pestilence, plague, all of it in your living room—some of it, quite possibly, in your bed. So much input, so much reference and noise, so much news and film and product. Images and ideas from every era, past and present, rerunning at the same time. No wonder everything seems like one big cliché. This simulcast of greatest hits has rendered history irrelevant. There is no vantage point from which to see the long view. There is no time to understand evolution, the way new things build upon old. It just appears that everything's been done before, that anything you do or say or think is prosaic. Prosaic. Contrivance. Derivative. Cliché. The words of choice among Mark and his friends, these children of the nineties, call them Generation H.

Mark sometimes feels that his whole culture, his entire milieu, is beginning to seem like that beer commercial where they bang on the TV and reality gets shuffled. Hip TriBeCa clubs like Don Hill's mix seventies clothes with fifties music, Beat antiauthoritarianism with punk nihilism, grrrls taking back the night by running their own amateur striptease show, standing off in the shadows in their kitschy lingerie, tongue-kissing boys in full drag. Punch the remote. Change the channel. This is what you see: *Dazed and Confused.* Attention deficit disorder. Been there, done that. Why bother. Ho Hum. Fuck it. Kurt Cobain blowing his head off. River Phoenix convulsing on a sidewalk. Kristen Pfaff nodding out in a tub of lukewarm water.

Mark stops at the corner of Bowery and Second Street, rests his hands on his hips, catching his breath. He squints across the intersection, sees some hooded sweatshirts. *Is that them?* He bolts across four lanes of traffic, feinting around a passing car, his stride reminiscent of the high school flanker he was ten years ago. Back then, he surfed and skateboarded and played three varsity sports. He was an alcohol or weed man; drugs were a means to an increased enjoyment of life. But now he has found dope, or it has found him, cozied up and moved in gradually over the course of four casual years, until he woke up one morning two winters ago with the fever chills and diarrhea of a serious habit. Now he understands what Burroughs meant. Junk is not a lark. This is not fun. He's down on himself. Extremely down. He's begun to reevaluate. He's thinking about quitting. Thinking about getting ready to think about quitting. Turning over the possibility. It would be his second try.

Twenty feet from the northwest corner, Mark pulls up, downshifts to a cool saunter, eyeballs the action. Some people hanging around, but no dealers. Nothing happening. *Fuck!*

He squints northeast, across the intersection toward the corner of Third Street. *Is that them?*

He takes off at a run.

#

"Hey, Brian, Brian," Mark repeats into the telephone. "Pick up. Pick up . . . ."

Mark rolls his eyes. *He's probably shooting,* he thinks. Mark used a syringe for a while. You consume less dope that way. And you get an orgasmic rush. But you also develop abscesses in your arms. They fester and smell. It was all too sordid. Snorting is cleaner, easier, faster. It hurts your nose, makes it burn and weep, but there's less chance of dying. It's easy to regulate your dosage, one little snort at a time.

"All right," he says glumly into the voice mail. "Gimme a call."

He tosses the phone onto the bed. Over the headboard hangs an ornate, empty frame he found in the garbage. He calls it his self-portrait. It is Saturday, eleven or so in the evening. Mark's girlfriend is out of town; he has five dime bags stashed in the cavity of his right glove, which is stashed inside of his coat pocket. The night is ripe with potential.

If only he could think of something to do.

He picks up a pen and a pad of paper. "Bored bored bored," he writes, the beginning of a poem, or maybe a song. "Bored beyond belief/Belief beyond bored/Beyond belief/Beyond believing."

Mark works two nights a week, 4:00 p.m. to 4:00 a.m., tending bar in a trendy club. He makes $400 a night. Enough to cover the rent and the expenses. Not enough to keep him busy. Up until his friend died, it looked like their band might make it big. The group had formed during college: two English majors, an art major, and Mark, econ–poli sci. They weren't great musicians, but they each felt a need to make art, to express things buried inside. They considered themselves artists whose medium was music. For one glorious year, Mark didn't work any job other than music; his band toured the United States and Europe. It was a shoestring kind of deal in small clubs, but hey, it was a tour. Mark felt like a winner that year. Someone who'd defied the odds.

Mark opens his Casio digital phone book, begins scrolling down through the entries. When he got the Casio, he actually sat down and read the directions. You can rig it so it automatically gives the time zone for a specific city. He set it to Santa Fe, where his mom lives. His parents divorced when he was thirteen. She sent him the robe that is being used just now as a window shade. He hasn't seen her in a while. He picks up the phone.

"Scott. You home? Gimme a call when you get this message."

"Hey, Donovan, Don. *Hey!* You there? I'm watching Oil Can Boyd on the tube. Gimme a call."

He sighs and rises from the bed, shuffles out into the living room. It is a third-floor walk-up near Delancey Street, within sight of the Williamsburg Bridge. Over the past hundred years, his building, his neighborhood, has been occupied in successive waves by European immigrants, gangsters and performers, Beats, hippies, punks, denizens of the rock scene and the art scene, Puerto Ricans, Dominicans. These days, the Lower East Side is a frontier of sorts, a patchwork of renewal and decay, trendiness and squalor. The newest wave is the people like Mark, artsy 20-year-olds, piled together in railroad flats with bunks in the bedrooms and bathtubs in the kitchens.

Mark looks over at his bass guitar, leaning against the wall. He walks over, picks it up, puts it down. He was supposed to have a practice tonight, new people for a new band, but nobody showed. He stands motionless for a few seconds, preoccupied. He starts toward the sofa, then stops, then starts again. He picks up his coat, reaches into the pocket for the glove with his stash.

It's gone!

He wheels around, scans every surface in the room.

Tiny beads of sweat appear at his hairline. He skates on stocking-clad feet across the ruined parquet floor toward the kitchen, looks on the table, the counter, the floor. He opens the refrigerator. He unlocks the front door and peers down the hall.

He rests his head against the cool metal door frame. *Think. Think.*

At last, he finds the glove on the bed, next to the phone, where he left it. He plops down, exhausted and relieved. He removes the rectangular bags and counts them, *Onetwothreefourfive.* He puts four of the bags back into the cavity of the glove, lays the glove back on the bed. He opens one bag: Rips the heat-sealed plastic with his teeth, spits it onto the floor, unfolds the wax-paper packet, places it on the nightstand. Reaches into his pocket, pulls out a short length of drinking straw, retrieves the open bag. There is a line of white powder along the bottom, about an inch and a half long, a tenth of an inch thick. Dips the straw and snorts. Once in the left nostril, once in the right.

A burn in the nose, a medicinal scent, like a gelatin-cap vitamin from a natural-food store. His heart, his head, his limbs fill with a magnanimous swell of well-being. His body lightens, buoyed by a sudden absence of aches and pains. An odd, tranquil alertness sets in, a sense of being cut loose from the program, of floating in a dreamy place all his own.

Fuck it, fuck it, fuck it, Mark thinks. *Fuck it.* He lights a Camel, lies back on the bed, closes his eyes. His lungs feel wide-open. He draws deep; the ember flares. His left arm rises, as if free of gravity, levitating absently in the air above the bed.

Dope is cool, removed, placid, faintly erotic. It is warm and fuzzy, itchy, a little distracted, a few steps off the pace of real time. It acts on the central nervous system, blocking receptors called opioids, which register feelings of pain. By a curious quirk of nature, the shape of the heroin molecule resembles that of the body's own natural painkillers, the endorphins. When pain is registered—when you burn your finger, or break your leg—the brain releases endorphins to ease the hurt, to brighten your humor. Opiates work just like endorphins, though drug use delivers them in greater supply, to greater effect. Over time, however, you get used to the bigger kick. Endorphins alone don't really do it for you anymore. Life becomes even more depressing than before.

It takes your body time to get used to dope. The molecular fit isn't perfect, so it's not very pleasant at first. When a novice first does heroin, you initially feel energized and buzzed. Then you get itchy, and then you don't feel very good, and then all of a sudden your head breaks out in a sweat and you vomit copiously, the entire contents of your stomach, usually in projectile fashion. Following that, you remain queasy into the next day. It takes at least twenty-four hours for the drug to clear the system.

Soon you don't vomit anymore. Your body learns how to process the opiates. Food tastes better. Music sounds better. Your thoughts seem to be more interesting. That nagging stiff neck is gone. For six to eight hours, until you need your next fix, everything looks and feels *amazing*. If you are lonely or heartbroken, if your momma didn't love you, if your daddy took liberties, it doesn't seem to matter so much anymore. And sex becomes irrelevant. On dope you can't really get it up, though it feels good to be touched. If you can manage an erection, you get what they call a dope stick: hard for hours with no ability to climax.

Overall, high on dope, you have a euphoric feeling of being washed clean, of having intermittent sets of pleasant waves rolling through your arms and legs and dick and head and then washing away, away, washing away sensation, hurt, memories, leaving just a warm, hollow shell of the semi-present remains of your consciousness, lubricated on every surface with sweet numb.

Most of the heroin on the streets of New York is China White, grown in vast fields controlled by private armies in Myanmar, Thailand, and Laos, an area called the Golden Triangle. China White is brought to America by Chinese middlemen—some independent, some members of gangster triads—and in increasing amounts by Nigerians. The high level of purity has rendered needles unnecessary; it can be snorted or smoked. Seeing new opportunities, Colombian coke cartels began to diversify, planting poppies on the hillsides at home and in Peru and Bolivia. The Afghans, Pakistanis, and Mexicans are also harvesting record quantities. Annual retail sales in the United States are estimated at $10 billion.

Now, in his apartment on this boring Saturday night, a bag of dope melting inside his nasal passages, Mark opens his eyes, spies his notebook computer on the desk. He has been writing a lot lately. A stream-of-consciousness novel has emerged. He is calling it *Only the Stones Remain*. He breaks out another bag, fires up the Mac.

"The tracks run through a cut in a hill. It's very muddy down here, and now I can see the train. If I stay right where I'm standing now, I will be a bug on a windshield. Once I went to a pharmacy to refill a Valium prescription. I wanted to do a mellow bye-bye. The shit was out of date by two days. If you really want to die, there are too many very effective ways to do it. I guess I wasn't professional or at least serious enough about my career as a non-human.

"You know, it's funny. I talk about suicide and there's a shotgun in my closet. Prozac Nation my epididymis— This is the real nation. The ones who feel, think, know too much and don't want to live in the transition to perfection. I don't feel sorry for myself. I'm just bored to death and Dewar's with what's been left of me. How bad you WANT something is not important. Do you want to be a STAR or do you HAVE to make music, paint, write, act, or whatever? There is a difference. The only way you will ever find success is to know this.

"I hate advice.

"I really hate good advice."

# # #

On Monday night, Max Fish is filled with regulars, *Cheers* meets *The Twilight Zone*. There's a girl with a platinum crew cut and a tongue stud; a guy with an Elvis ducktail haircut, white leather jacket, and matching white belt; a hippie with muttonchops, a flag sewn over the crotch of his jeans; a Japanese couple wearing huge, multicolored afro wigs.

A guy with a ponytail top knot, the rest of his skull shaved clean, approaches Mark with a buddy in tow, a suit-type in a button-down collar. The ponytail guy screams over the loud music: "How you been? Haven't seen *you* in a while."

Though Ludlow Street is only a few blocks from his place, Mark hasn't been to Max Fish in some time. He's been so scarce lately, in fact, that there have been rumors floating around that he died. One idiot even called Mark's father with condolences.

Mark shakes hands with the ponytail guy. The preppy friend turns to the bar, orders beers for all, plus a shot of Cuervo for Mark. Mark kind of knows the ponytail guy, but he has no idea of his name. The three talk music for a while. The two friends were in a band together for a short time during college in Boston. It seems like everyone Mark meets was in a band once. Either that or they're looking to join one. In the verbal style of the day, slumming upper crust, the conversation is peppered with the word *actually*. Actually, the preppy is contemplating a move to New York. Actually, he and the ponytail guy are interested in getting a band going with Mark.

Actually, fuck you, Mark thinks. He feels like wringing their geeky poseur necks. He's only here in the bar because he's looking for someone, this friend of his, a connection. Waiting: another vital component of the junk equation. The talk turns to independent record labels; who's on the bill at CBGB; the latest album reviews in the new issue of *PrettyDecorating*, an alternative lit-crit tabloid.

There's a lull in the conversation, that inevitable point when you need to excuse yourself and go get another drink. Mark's eyes dance around the room. The other guys follow his lead, look around, too. Then the ponytail guy cuts his eyes to his friend and gets a certain expression on his face, a kind of resolve. He puffs himself up, leans close to Mark. "Hey, uh, listen," he says. "My friend wants to try some dope. You think you can help us cop? We'll buy you a bag or whatever."

Mark looks at the ponytail guy. In the back of the bar, playing pool, are several Dominicans. Everyone in the place knows they are drug dealers. Everyone except these two assholes. Outside the bar, in the shadows up and down the street, are more dealers. Around the corner is a bodega, one of dozens in the vicinity. On the shelves are a few dusty cans of food, some sundries—neither milk nor eggs. Its main business is drugs: Beetlejuice-brand heroin, no-name crack, powdered coke, you name it.

"I'm cleaning out my system right now." Mark says. "I'm going skiing tomorrow—meeting my father and my sister up in Vermont."

"That's cool, man," says the ponytail guy, he laughs awkwardly. "Gotta clean out once in a while. That's what I do."

Mark checks his watch, looks around one more time for his connection. "I gotta go, OK? Try talking to that guy over there. His name is Justin."

Mark finishes the beer in one gulp. Justin owes him twenty bucks. Let *him* deal with these poseur assholes.

#

The truth is, Mark is going skiing with his dad and sister. That's why he went to Max Fish tonight—to try to find some methadone. He's known about the trip for a month. For one month, he kept telling himself he was going to kick, that he was going to get around to kicking. And then, the next thing he knew, the month was over. He didn't even realize it. He only found out by accident. He was cleaning up the apartment for his girl-friend's return, removing all evidence of his weekend debauchery, when he chanced to flip the pages of his calendar to the right month, the right date. *Holy Fuck! The trip is tomorrow.* It was time for plan B: methadone.

A few days away from the city, some methadone to help him main-tain . . . . Maybe he can get clean. It seems like a good opportunity. It's really his only choice. He doesn't have enough money right now for a four days' supply of dope. If he tries to kick cold turkey, he'll be too sick to ski. Methadone will ease the symptoms.

One place to cop methadone is the clinic on Second Street and Avenue A. You can go early in the morning, find a junkie and buy "spit back," liquid methadone they stand in line for but don't swallow. To Mark, the image of collecting enough spit back for four days is disgusting. Luckily, in the great city of New York, there is always another way. Mark knows a guy who gets methadone pills from a guy who gets them from a doctor in East Texas. The problem now is finding him.

Mark walks north on Ludlow, crosses Houston Street, thinking to try the Ace Bar. To be honest, Mark has never *really* wanted to quit before. Yes, he has attempted to quit, but he couldn't imagine *never* doing dope again. Now, he says, he's admitted to himself that he wants to quit. He's ready to admit he has a problem if he can't quit.

"In the big picture, I have kind of allotted myself this time to be fucked up. It's taken me six years to get this fucked up. But only lately have I begun to get pissed at myself. I'm at a point where my best friend is dead, I'm out of money, I'm at a crossroads. I am twenty-eight years old. I still have options.

"I hate to admit it, but dope is the best thing in the world. I swear to God, it's like cheating death. I'm a thrill seeker, I guess. I don't want to brag, but I've done a lot of dangerous things. I've surfed big waves in Hawaii. I like to drive fast; I like to run from the cops. I've gotten into a lot of fights in my time with people bigger than me. There must be a subconscious thing about being threatened and having my back up against the wall. Doing dope is like backing yourself up against death. It's the ultimate.

"But then there's the other side. Like when I was still shooting, I went down face-first one time in the bathroom. My girlfriend had to walk me around the living room for two hours. It was so embarrassing. She'll never, ever, have any respect for me ever again. In one way, I feel like the closest thing you can have with a person is to reduce yourself to your most vulnerable in front of them. Then they completely know you. But then, on the other hand, it kind of puts you at a disadvantage. They lord it over you. Whatever you say is flawed to them. They can trump you with your weakness.

"For the longest time, doing dope has been a great novelty, but now it's real. I've gone through the money I've allowed myself. I've gone through the time and the people, I've burned the bridges I've allowed myself. Now it's getting serious. I can't afford to be a junkie anymore. This time I'm gonna quit."

# # #

Home from his ski trip, Mark starts the old Volvo he's borrowed, pulls out into the heavy traffic.

It took Mark four hours and five bars to find his methadone connection. The guy had only eleven pills left. Mark was forced to collect spit back the next morning. Like most black-market products, the methadone came with no directions.

On the drive to Vermont, he did all the dope he had, five bags. The next morning, he started the methadone. He got sick anyway. He snuck out of the condo his dad had rented, found a pay phone, called a friend who'd been in a program. The friend explained that it might take a couple of days for the methadone to kick in.

Mark did the best he could. The first two days, he was feverish and had bad diarrhea. He made a valiant effort, skiing with his dad and sis, pretending the runny nose was from the cold, having to dispose of his underwear at one point. (He'd wisely brought along an extra pair to the slopes). By the third day, Mark was so sick he couldn't ski. His dad made some comments. "What's wrong with Mark?" he asked. "Does he have the flu or is he not getting his *medicine*?" The way he said *medicine*, Mark felt like a piece of shit. The third day is when most junkies flee back to the streets for a bag. Mark lay in bed, drenched with sweat, chills rippling through his body. His stomach was cramped, his back was knotted. He smashed a fist into the pillow.

Then he remembered the Valium.

He rose, staggered to his suitcase, dug around. He found two ten-milligram Diazepam (hecho en Mexico) and swallowed them without water. He lay back down. Gratefully, he slept, long and deep.

They say that the fourth day is a little easier. Then the fifth day slams you almost as bad as the third. By the sixth, you get hungry. They call it the chucks. You want to eat everything in sight. By the seventh or eighth, you're home. That's it. Physically, the symptoms subside. From there it's a battle with your mind. Keeping yourself from buying.

On the morning of the fourth day, Mark woke early and packed his bag. He drove home and went directly to the divas.

Now it is the evening of the fifth day. Settling into a lane in the borrowed Volvo, he takes one hand off the wheel, reaches into his shirt pocket, produces a little rectangular package. He tears the plastic with his teeth, spits it out, unfolds the bag carefully, artfully—like a cardsharp working a poker chip between his fingers.

At a stoplight, he pulls out the straw, looks around, ducks his head, sniffs.

His face ignites—a large toothy smile, the teeth yellow and stained. And then the smile slowly melts. His face becomes a mask of apology, of deprecation, of failure. This was his second attempt at quitting. Strike two.

He makes a right turn, a left, another right. He reaches into his shirt pocket. "I'm gonna do another bag," he says. "I'm just gonna suck 'em down without any remorse or guilt right now. I gave my best effort for the last couple of days. I really tried to quit. I got pretty close. Now I deserve a little reward." He snorts again, once on each side. He throws the baggie out the window.

"Part of the whole problem is that you can just rationalize yourself into a corner. Now that I know I can do methadone, that I can get a prescription and I can eventually get off that way, it's giving me another excuse to put off quitting. I don't know—I guess, deep down, I've always been afraid of finding a cure. I don't want to be without it. Heroin is who I am."

He comes to a stoplight and brakes. First Avenue. A light rain is falling. He flips on the wipers, taps his fingers absently to a beat only he can hear.

And then a notion strikes. A large smile crosses his grill. "How about a field trip to Spanish Harlem?"

He turns left, uptown, into the night.

#

At precisely 11:20, same as every morning, Al the Chemist turns the corner at Rivington and heads north on Essex, muttering distractedly to himself. He is a big man, six feet, 240 pounds, in an aged corduroy jacket and dirty high-top tennis shoes. Fifty years old, he has the look of a professor—long gray flyaway hair, thick glasses, a pocket protector full of stuff.

Al stops at an artist's storefront. He rings the buzzer. The door opens. "How you doin'?" he asks.

He crosses the room, settles behind a desk, fishes a white plastic box out of his pants pocket. He puts the box on the desk and opens it, revealing a built-in digital clock and several bags of dope. From his pocket protector, he withdraws a pair of surgical scissors and a Bic pen without the ink cartridge inside. He picks up one bag, turns it to vertical, snips the packet. He unfolds, checks the count in the bag, flicks it with his middle finger, notes the time. "This will hit me in exactly twelve minutes," he says. He takes a hit, one in each nostril.

Al sits a while with his eyes closed, his hands in his lap, one folded gently atop the other. Then his eyes pop open. "Heroin restores normal physiological function for me," he says. "Without heroin, I have no sex drive, I have no desire for food, I have no energy. But when I take a snort of heroin, if you had me wired up and were monitoring all vital signs, you would find that twelve minutes after administration of the drug, all functions return to normal. When I'm under the influence of heroin, I immediately feel twenty years younger. For example, when I turned the corner from Rivington onto Essex, I felt about 70 years old. Ten minutes from now, I will feel about 30. Another bag, and I'll feel about 25."

He takes a deep breath and blows it out, as if he is exhaling the smoke from a cigarette. "I used to inject, but now I just snort. I stopped injecting heroin on December 18 of last year," he says. "That was the day my brother died of an OD.

"See, I came in the kitchen at 3:15 in the morning, and his head was on the table. I thought he was asleep, and I tried to wake him. I managed to get his eyes open, and they flickered a little bit. Then he died in my arms.

"I have no friends and no family. When my brother died, my life essentially came to an end. Technically, my heart was beating and I seemed to be breathing, but I died on December 18, a Sunday in 1994, at 3:15 a.m. I loved my brother very much. He wasn't just my brother, my step-brother; he was my best friend.

"You have to understand, my brother's death is the pivotal event in my life at this time. You would think that seeing my brother Robert die in my arms would stop me from using drugs. But I love drugs. I've been doing drugs for thirty years. Hard drugs: cocaine, methamphetamines, heroin. I've made my living studying and processing and synthesizing drugs. And doing drugs. I have a Ph.D. in chemistry, you know. And the thing is, since my brother died, I'm desperately lonely. See, he wasn't just my brother; he was my contact with the human race. He was my everything. It's like I've gone through surgery and had my right arm and my leg cut off and the right side of my head. That's how I feel, like half of me is missing.

"Now, I have a plan. I'm going to purchase some prescription drugs, a few amphetamines, a few barbiturates, some Ritalin and some Dilaudid. And I'm going to purchase two kilos of heroin. I can get the money. There's a way I know. And I'm going to take my drugs and go into my cave and clamp the door shut. And I will advise the city, state, and federal government that I'm deceased. See, a kilo would last a normal junkie fifty-four years, but my usage would be somewhat heavier. Plus, I'd like to be able to give some away. Or maybe sell some, if I needed money for food or clothes—

"Hey, let me ask you a small favor if I may. See, I'm very lonely. My friends are all dead. You know, everyone I've ever lived with is dead. If you happen to bump into anyone you think I could be friends with, I have a very broad range of interests: I'm not just a druggie, I'm interested in all phases of American society.

"Maybe some of the dope fiends you're interviewing for this article. Maybe you could introduce me. I mean, I know a couple people in the neighborhood, but I don't really have any friends. I'm sure we'd have stuff in common. I'd appreciate it."

3
Big

At TWILIGHT A FULL MOON has just risen over the terminal in El Monte,
bringing in the tide of commuters. The buses squeal and hiss and disgorge
their loads, and the platforms fill, and the people spill down the concrete
steps toward the kiss-and-ride, looking for their connections, the final
leg home.

Out on the avenue, a left-turn arrow clicks green. A small white Toyota
crosses the intersection, listing ponderously to port as it goes. It enters the
terminal parking lot, heads toward the area designated for compact cars.
The sky is a darkening azure, unusually clear for the San Gabriel Valley this
time of year, the autumnal haze of particulates and fumes having been
cleansed temporarily by a rare easterly wind, the storied Santa Ana.

The Toyota plies the rows, seeking a space. It is a Corolla three-door
hatchback, eighties vintage, bumper hanging, a hand-me-down from the
mother-in-law. With the motor home out of commission, hunkered in
the driveway beside the dead Lincoln and the semi-squashed VW Bug, the
Van Dykes have been forced to tag-team the Toyota. She's going to be late;
he's having dinner with a journalist, following at the moment a little distance behind in his own vehicle. He must park the Toyota somewhere in
this vast lot where she can find it.

A speed bump is sighted; the Toyota's breaks squeak, the car comes to a complete stop. Then, ever so slowly, the front tires creep over the little asphalt berm. At bottom, the chassis sags, the springs complain—a deep, mushy bounce that scrapes the belly of the car, setting up a series of jiggling aftershocks.

Back wheels clear, another bounce; the car turns left, then right. Charlie Van Dyke has a particular space in mind. After twelve years of marriage, you designate such things, you come to agreements on routines and conventions. It may be a vast city parking lot, the terminal where thousands of people from this particular patch of Southern California sprawl come each day to ride buses between lives and livelihoods, but that one parking space, over time, has become theirs—the property of their marriage, something known and understood. She will be looking to that spot. She will be frazzled, no doubt, after a long day, a long commute. Commuting. *Sheesh.* Charlie doesn't understand how people do it. He doesn't know how *she* can do it. He feels for her, but at least it's steady income and health insurance for them both. It occurs to him that for untold centuries, the fields have been located too far away from the village. If people really put their minds to it, couldn't they figure out a way to abolish the need for commuting? They could come up with a better way to live and work, something more spiritually and spatially conjoined, and people would be a lot happier, and the world—particularly California—would be a better place, the urge to hate a little less strong in everyone. Such is the nature of Charlie's running inner monologue. He is a thinker, a dreamer, a scholar, a believer, a lover, a high-tech renaissance man, able to figure out and teach himself—and usually improve upon—each new wrinkle of technology that comes available on the market.

Now, however, he must focus on smaller things, something he doesn't always do as well, things in the here and now that need attending to, like finding the Van Dyke parking space, willing it open, thinking perfectly open thoughts.

It's important for Charlie to come through for Kathie. He has always been her rock, her mountain. She relies on him, takes her cues from him, even talks like he does, very slowly, forming each word precisely, explaining everything completely. Her voice-mail message at the office is a three-act play.

They met over drama, in fact, in eleventh grade, when they were both seventeen, the subjects of an English teacher's matchmaking—seating chart manipulation on a fieldtrip to see the movie *Camelot*. It was an inspired pairing of misfits.

Charlie was on the AV squad, the leader of the nerd clique. Some types of people have always looked up to him, have always come to him for guidance and information. Others have always reviled him—scornful or mean or rude for no reason other than his appearance.

Kathie was tiny—five feet tall and ninety pounds. In first grade, she'd contracted rheumatic fever; she didn't return to school until she was twelve. The youngest child of two overprotective schoolteachers, she tended to see herself the way her parents saw her, as fragile and impaired, with scar tissue around the heart. When she finally returned to the classroom, the other kids considered her stuck-up and brainy; in reality, she was incredibly withdrawn, completely befuddled by people's reactions to her. What she learned from her experience is this: When you're insecure or different, when you don't participate, people will assume you're stuck up. They will think you are ignoring *them*. They will interpret this as hostility on your part, and anything bad that they are thinking about themselves they will project upon you. It's all about insecurity, she says, how it's so pervasive in our society. It took her years to come to this conclusion. Charlie was the one who helped explain.

In Kathie, Charlie found someone of intelligence and sensitivity, someone who understood what he was talking about, who liked puzzles with thousands of pieces, who could read almost as fast as he. She laughed at his humor, which was always on the warped side. She liked the things he liked: sendups and puns; the TV show *Deep Space Nine*; the Doctor Demento songs "Junk Food Junky" and "Happy Happy Joy Joy." In truth, she was his greatest fan—her giggly, snorting Horshack laugh always at the ready, her eyes sparkling behind her glasses, which are squarish and thick with oversized frames, just like his.

Late though it is, 7:30 or so, the parking lot is active. Wives, husbands, whole families await their loved ones on the asphalt shores of the home front. They sit inside cars, perch on trunks or on hoods, lean down to talk through an open window, to fit a pacifier into a bubbly little mouth. The sounds from car radios of salsa, classic rock, and rap mix with hypnotic Arabic strings and drums, all of it merging and swirling beneath the amber mercury vapor lamps.

The Toyota turns left again, down a row of parked cars, then right, down another.

And what do you know: There it is.

The Van Dyke space.

And it is *open*.

Hail the Goddess.

The Toyota pulls in and stops. There is the ratcheting sound of the parking brake. The car goes dark and silent; the engine ticks off heat. After a moment, the door squeaks open, the tinny cry of a tired hinge.

A sneaker appears, bright white, size 15 quadruple-E—thirteen and three-quarter inches long, six and five-eighths inches wide.

It is followed by a pink expanse of skin reminiscent of a small Christmas ham, Charlie's ankle—hairless, mottled, flaky, maybe eighteen inches around.

The sneaker plants itself on the asphalt, followed soon thereafter by its twin, and then a knee appears, pulling behind it a lumpy, forty-two inch thigh. The denim material strains at its double stitching—the Classic 5-Pocket Jean, model No. 2115 from a mail-order company called King Size. He wears size 72, the largest in the catalogue.

Charlie pushes down on the door frame with his large right hand, meanwhile knuckling his left thigh for leverage. Emitting a slight groan, followed by a sharp exhalation of air, like a weightlifter, he achieves a standing position, straightens his back.

Around the parking lot, everyone stares.

A skinny kid with freckles, standing by the rear of a mini-van, slaps his fat brother in his jiggly stomach and points. A young Asian guy lets his mouth drop. "Dios mio!" exclaims a gray-haired woman, poking her head out the window of her Chevy for a better view.

Charlie closes the door of the Toyota with a surprisingly gentle click—it is, after all, the last surviving vehicle in the Van Dyke fleet—and aims himself toward my full-size Chevy Caprice, waiting nearby. He's a little nervous. He's never been in this type of car before; he's hoping he fits. At Charlie's suggestion, I had requested to rent a Cadillac, a Sedan deVille. The deVille, besides being plush, easily accommodates his size. Also, the deVille was big enough that we could plan an outing with some of his friends, something he never gets to do, drive somewhere in the same car with his other fat friends, a pleasure he wanted to experience. By contrast, a Lincoln Mark IV, while large and comfortable by anyone's standards, does not fit Charlie. It has to do with the cut of the door, the relationship between the seat and the dashboard—we're talking here strictly about passenger seats. Driving either vehicle is out of the question—one reason the Lincoln has been left to rust in his driveway. Oddly, Charlie's Toyota fits him better than the Lincoln. Even so, with the seat set back as far as it will go, the steering wheel still rubs his stomach. In order to reach the wheel, he has to fully extend his arms. He grips the wheel with his fingertips, works in furious tiny strokes to make a turn.

It is the nature of Charlie's life that he must accommodate and jigger, plan ahead; the world just doesn't fit. His Timex Indiglo has the largest band available, ten inches, but it's impossible for him to use the watch's light: The push button is covered by a fold of flesh where the band bites. Even with the watch off, it's a struggle: His fingertip is too large to effectively press the little button.

Charlie is required by law to buy two seats on an plane. When he eats in a restaurant, he needs a chair without arms—a fairly sturdy one. For the record, he has bent a folding chair or two in his lifetime, but he has never broken a chair and fallen to the ground like in all those stupid comedy bits people find to be so amusing. Usually, at a restaurant, he is kept waiting for some time—it is clear they have an attitude about his fatness. Invariably, he is seated in the back of the house with the crying babies. Wherever he is seated, the tables must be far enough apart for him to walk between. Anything but a handicapped toilet stall is out. And though he can't sit in a booth or pass through some types of turnstiles, the chairs in movie theaters are usually no problem—"Fat flows," Charlie explains.

Sometimes, Charlie doesn't fit himself, either. Because of the sheer size of his body, his overall dimensions and proportions, the length of his arms relative to his girth, and so on, he cannot reach certain parts of himself. In the shower, he must use long brushes to wash himself. For the toilet, he has a jerry-rigged an assortment of pump spray bottles—a sort of home-made personal bidet. He cannot put on his own socks, so he doesn't bother. An itch between his shoulder blades is impossible to scratch. As for sex—suffice it to say that where there's a will there's a way.

It helps, he says, if your wife is five feet tall and is limber from practicing aikido. As they say in fat quarters, Kathie is a committed "cellulite surfer."

Charlie's stride is short, effortful, stiff-jointed, a bit breathless and—it must be said, with only the utmost respect—penguin-like: his dense forearms pump from the elbows, palms flat and facing backward, propelling him along. People gawk and point and laugh. He doesn't notice. Or so he says.

In medical terms, Charlie is *morbidly obese*, which means that he is more than 100 percent over his ideal weight. Charlie likes to say that if he would just lose enough to be 99 percent over his ideal, doctors would reclassify him as *grossly obese*. "Now that's a worthy objective," he deadpans.

To be considered merely *obese*, he'd have to lose 50 percent of his total body weight.

#

CHARLIE VAN DYKE is a fat man in a low-fat world. Once upon a time, fat meant jolly, godly, prosperous—think Buddha, Venus, a Roman senator, a Medieval friar, Rubens's women. Today, in our health-obsessed culture, fat is a symbol of shame—a sign of weakness and sloth and lack of discipline, an antisocial act.

According to surveys, about 40 percent of women and 25 percent of men are trying to lose weight. An additional one-third of both sexes are struggling to *maintain* their weight. They spend $40 billion a year on everything from fat-free Fig Newtons to surgical stomach stapling. In a poll, fat people who've had their stomachs reduced—a major procedure requiring an incision from sternum to groin—said they'd prefer to have a leg amputated or to go blind than to be fat.

Scientists say that two-thirds of people who lose weight regain it within the first year. Ninety-five percent will rebound within five years.

The last time Charlie weighed himself was fifteen years ago, at Weight Watchers. He weighed 550. At six feet three, he had a target weight, he was told, of 190. That was what he weighed in fifth grade, when he was five feet tall.

The first week on his Weight Watchers diet, Charlie lost twenty pounds. The second week, ten. After a year, he was down 104 pounds.

One year later, he'd gained back what he'd lost.

Plus, he'd put on an additional fifty pounds.

Charlie has been overweight his whole life. He was a twelve-pound newborn, a fat kid, a super-fat teenager. Today he wears shirt size 8XL: eighty-four inch chest, twenty-nine-inch neck, thirty-six inch sleeve, three full feet between the shoulders. Charlie is an expert in the areas of fat and dieting. He has lost hundreds of pounds. And each time he's lost weight—each and every time he's gone on a diet—he's eventually gained back that amount, plus an average of 50 percent more.

Yes, once in a great while, Charlie will eat four of the smaller Cadbury chocolate eggs at one sitting. He likes macaroni and cheese, potato soup, buffalo wings with gobs of blue cheese, lots of bread. He will leave his morsel of lobster soaking in the cup of butter for a full minute before eating it. And, yes, he drinks prodigiously—one Big Gulp-sized coffee (ten Equals, five creamers) and at least four peach Snapples a day. At mealtime he cleans his plate so utterly, so completely, that when he's finished, there is no evidence of what he's eaten, not a sesame seed or a drop of sauce left behind.

But, no, he doesn't gorge between meals. He doesn't eat a gallon of ice cream at a sitting, though he will order a large yogurt. He eats regular-sized portions. His table manners are good. He does manage to soil his shirts fairly regularly, the distance between the average tabletop and his mouth being what it is. He does not eat red meat, likes health food, has a well-developed palate, due to extra nerves in his nose and mouth, he says. Annually he is tapped as a judge for a local micro-beer brewing contest. The owners of the café around the corner have enlisted him to help with their new menu. He can eat 3,000 to 4,000 calories a day and not gain an ounce.

Believe it or not, fat has a purpose. If the body can be seen as a complex factory on a twenty-four-hour production schedule, then fat is the energy supply it constantly draws upon to run the machine. People cannot eat twenty-four hours a day, so the body converts raw fuel to fat and then runs off that.

Under a microscope, fat, or adipose tissue, looks like a bubble bath. At a slightly higher magnification, it resembles tapioca, packed globule to globule in a stringy intercellular glue, streaked with narrow filaments of connective tissue, blood vessels and nerves. Gram for gram, there is almost twice as much nourishment in fat as there is in carbohydrates or protein.

In other words, faced with the challenge of how to power its creatures—needing a biochemical Eveready Energizer to store the most energy in the least amount of space—God or nature (what have you) chose fat.

The problem shared by the millions of Americans who are overweight is that God or nature did not take into account the possible advent of refrigerators or fast food or even agriculture. We humans were constructed to be hunters and gatherers. We were set up for a life in which our primitive ancestors ate whenever they were lucky enough to find or kill something. When food is introduced, our bodies, by design, store energy for times when there isn't any food around. When there's plenty, our bodies make extra fat cells. Once you make a fat cell, you can never lose it. You can shrink it, but it will complain, sending out a chemical warning: *Help! The tank is nearing "E."* During times of privation, our bodies are designed to slow down and conserve fat. The heart and other vital muscles and organs will start breaking down before all the fat tissue is drained. When there is food again, the body *replenishes* fat cells at an even *higher* rate.

How much does Charlie weigh?

If you need a specific number, picture Konishiki, the American-born sumo wrestler Charlie so admires. Konishiki weighs 600 pounds. That's about right—600, 625, maybe 650, maybe a bit more. Like he says, he hasn't been on a scale in fifteen years. During that time, Charlie's weight has been stable. He's been wearing the same custom-made pinstripe suit for special occasions for nine years now, and it still fits perfectly. How many 44-year-old men can say that?

His secret?

He gave up dieting.

# # #

IN A THREE-ROOM OFFICE-WAREHOUSE, in a nondescript industrial park fifteen minutes from his house, Charlie and his friend Elaine are hard at work.

Elaine is five feet ten, 250 pounds. She is stuffing colorful pieces of tiny technology into green plastic circuit boards, the kind found inside a computer. She works from a prototype, which is clamped into an upright position beneath a spotlight on her desk. It looks like a three-dimensional model of a futuristic downtown, a functional little work of art that Charlie designed, part of a revolutionary new computerized locking system for tractor trailers, to keep merchandise safe from theft while in transport. They are on deadline with an order, working furiously, even though the company still owes Charlie money for the last batch. The sooner he gets these boards done, the sooner he'll get paid . . . he hopes.

Charlie sits at a custom-made drafting table, soldering the circuit boards Elaine finishes. He straddles a pneumatic task chair, his legs comfortably akimbo, his stomach dipped down between, as if he has a medicine ball adjoining his thighs. His zipper is twenty-one and a half inches long. Though he has lost his lap to his stomach, he has gained a kind of permanent desk. He'll sort mail atop his stomach, rest things there a moment—an arm, a book, the remote control for his boom box. Charlie searched high and low for a box with a remote—one less reason to move around. He tires easily. His back is bad. Though he can bend and pick up something from the floor, he prefers using a pair of grabbers. He has two different kinds, one for paper, one for cans.

In anthropological terms, Charlie's body has a barrel-chested pouter-pigeon shape. His forearms and legs are solid as rocks. When you think about it, Charlie probably lifts more weight daily than Mr. Universe. Each time he rises from his chair, he is squatting 650-odd pounds. Scratching his head is like lifting a fifty-pound barbell. It is mainly his mid-section that is so obviously constructed of fatty tissue. It sloshes and jiggles with every pot hole in a road. Charlie's stomach is a cousin of the common beer belly, known as a Falstaffian paunch. Men tend to collect their weight in the front—truncal fat. Women collect it in back and on the sides and down below. More often than you would think, a kid will walk up to Charlie, poke him in his belly, and say "You're fat!" Usually, Charlie will ignore him. Once—fed up, having a bad day—Charlie turned to the kid and replied, "Yeah? Well, you're ugly!"

People often tell Charlie that he has a handsome face buried beneath all that fat. "Thanks for the compliment," he muses. Strangers lean over and look into his shopping cart. Or they come up to him in the street and try to sell him diet products. "The problem you have—" they will begin, and Charlie will cut them off. "Excuse me," he will say. "The problem I have is *you*." Sometimes, when he is home with Kathie and feeling dramatic, he will mime one of his favorite scenes from the movie *Elephant Man*. He contorts his face, exhorts the heavens, cries out in pain (in an English accent), "I am not an animal. I am a human being!"

Behind Charlie's glasses, above his rosy Santa Claus cheeks, are sparkling brown eyes that Kathie thinks are very sexy. He has a cute little pug nose, always stuffy, making him tend to breathe audibly through his mouth, past teeth that are slightly bucked. You can imagine him as a little kid with luminous skin and freckles, the son of LaVerne and Shirley Van Dyke of Moline, Illinois.

Yes, LaVerne and Shirley.

LaVerne Van Dyke was known as Chub. He ran a gas station. He carted around enough spare parts in the back of the family station wagon to build another car. Chub's expertise as a mechanic may have something to do with Charlie's aversion to fixing cars, the reason there is a fleet of dead vehicles marooned in his driveway. Chub lives in California now too, not far from Kathie and Charlie. Recently, he's been having episodes of sleep apnea. Charlie visits when he can. Chub is very busy in his retirement. Two or three nights a week, he and his second wife go to church. Two other nights, they go to Overeaters Anonymous. Chub is the only man in the group. The stories the women tell? "Better than a soap opera," he says. "X-rated sometimes, too." They have a chant at OA: Three/Zero/One! It stands for three meals a day, zero snacks in between, one day at a time. At his last weigh-in, LaVerne was 324. In his prime, he was well over 400.

Shirley Van Dyke was raised in an orphanage. She went about 250. It is Charlie's burden to have smashed his mother's kidneys during gestation—or so goes the family lore. He remembers her having a tantrum one time when he was young, stomping around, telling him that it was all his fault. It is a painful memory. Charlie tries to remind himself that he didn't ask to be born, that he wasn't fat on purpose. She died a few years ago, at 54.

Charlie's salt-and-pepper beard covers his face, neck, and jaw, tangles down to the second button on his shirt, giving him the look of a prophet or holy man. From shoulder to shoulder, the material of his shirt rises and then falls, following the contours of his back, the characteristic fatty pad behind and just below his neck. In the past, there wasn't much choice about what clothes he wore. He'd find a store that carried his size and take whatever fit. Now he orders everything from King Size, a big-and-tall-men's catalogue targeted at America's 18.7 million obese men. Not only does King Size offer more variety; it also saves him from having to go out in public to shop. In most big-and-tall-men's stores, the largest size is 60. Charlie is a 72. Even the salespeople gawk.

As a freelance electronic engineer, Charlie specializes in microcontroller design. At the moment, he and Elaine are working on a PC board that runs a computerized, magnetic truck-door lock, invented by a partner and himself. With any luck, it will be patented and will revolutionize the truck-lock business. With any luck, Charlie will realize some of the profit—he's invented a few things before and has been screwed—and he will finally be able to upgrade his life a little bit: to buy a nice new vehicle, to stop screening his phone calls for bill collectors, to repair the earthquake-and-fire damage still evident inside his house. Kathie has declared their personal disaster area off limits to even the most intimate public. Since the fire, they've been holed up in the living room. There's a couch, a TV, a king-size water bed, all their clothes in boxes, the six cats. The dachshund, who started the fire by tearing up some paper over the furnace grate, has been living in the back yard ever since.

A CD of Indian music, Gandharva-Veda, is playing while Charlie and Elaine work. (He'd brought the Jefferson Airplane CD, but somehow this disk was in the jewel case instead.) The three rooms of his office—at the back there is an industrial garage door—are chockablock with stuff. If you can say anything about Charlie, it's that his life is very cluttered. Nothing is put away. It must be the energy level thing. He can't really walk that far without resting. There are files, a microwave, a coffeemaker, a refrigerator, boxes of stuff from the house fire. The front door is locked; the windows are shaded with mini-blinds. There is a meditative quality of busy stillness in the conditioned air, the two working together wordlessly to the sounds of sitar and tabla drum. After a while, Charlie puts up his soldering iron. "Sometimes," he says, apropos of nothing. "I feel like a black person walking into a bar in southern Georgia."

"Oh, yeah," says Elaine, picking right up on his meaning. She is bending a resistor to stuff into a board. "You can't tell a black joke or a Polish joke, but you can sure tell a *fat* joke."

"And every other commercial on TV has a fat guy as a punch line."

"Remember that real nice karaoke bar we went to?" Elaine asks. "Me and Dale and Rachel and Jeff? We walked in and everyone turned around and stared. I couldn't believe it. I just turned around and *left*. People actually came outside to watch us get into our cars."

"You just gotta get used to it," Charlie says. "The Lifestyle Police. It gets to a point, sometimes, that you just want to hide. But most of the time I don't pay attention. What it basically comes down to is that they're the ones with the problem, not me. *They're* the ones who have a problem with me being who I am."

"It's good you can get to that," Elaine says.

"It's a long process," Charlie says.

A lifelong process for a kid who was born fat. When he was in the nursery at the hospital, someone asked what a three-month-old was doing with the newborns.

Growing up, the only child of fat parents (who themselves had fat parents), Charlie was tormented by his father. "You wanna grow tits like a woman?" This from a guy nicknamed Chub. Charlie's mother always had him on a diet. Shirley Van Dyke spent much of her life wondering about her origins, trying to find her two sisters, from whom she'd been separated at an early age. She was a very dark and negative person who tried to lose her problems in baking. She was always making pecan pralines, divinity fudge, and peanut-butter cookies, dozens at a time, never only one variety.

Throughout his youth, it was made clear to Charlie that the world didn't fit him very well. He remembers the time he was riding along on his bike and decided to jump down a curb. He'd seen other kids do it a million times. When he came down in the street, the bike just fell apart—the handle bars came off, the front tire gave way. For a few feet, it felt like he was riding a unicycle. Then he crashed to earth.

As you would imagine, he was a reclusive kid, a homebody. He read a lot and built models; the events of his childhood kind of blur together. He does remember a lot of social problems at school: being a target, kids throwing rocks at him. When he was five or six years old, a couple of teenagers chased him down and started beating him. He remembers the pummeling of fists, trying to fight back, crying, snot rolling down his face. A ring of adults and kids gathered around to watch—Why did nobody intercede? Another time, someone threw a brick at his head. He required stitches.

Over the years, using his superior mind to do research, Charlie figured out how to take advantage of his bulk and strength. If he could get hold of his adversary, he realized, he could just sit on him and start pummeling. After a few fights, kids started leaving him alone. But now he had a new problem—the teachers thought he had behavior issues. In eighth grade, the gym teacher really hated him. He made Charlie run extra laps up a huge hill. He got a kick out of putting Charlie on the "skins" team so that he'd have to take off his shirt. As you would expect, the locker room was fraught. Even if you have a normal-sized penis, it's going to look small compared to your large stomach. Unlike other extremities, the penis does not gain weight.

When the Van Dykes moved to California—his mother having located her eldest sister at last—things began to change. Eligible in the more permissive state to opt out of phys. ed., Charlie joined the AV squad and discovered electronics. He found a niche among the nerds and misfits, a tiny little girlfriend named Kathie. It was weird, maybe attributable to the era of free love, but girls were always coming on to Charlie. "Some women just love the fat guys," he explains, though he hesitates to use the word *fetish*. Once, he was in the nurse's office and a girl on a cot across the room exposed a breast to him. Another girl, a hall monitor, would lift her skirt and show her panties as he went by, late to class. Another girl snuck him into the AV room and made a pass. It may have been some form of prank, but hell, Charlie didn't mind.

As a teenager, Charlie always had a job. He flipped burgers at Jack in the Box, scooped ice cream, delivered papers, made snow cones at the county fair. After a few years of community college, pursuing a major in electrical engineering, Charlie went to work as an electrical draftsman. For the past two decades, he has bounced from job to job, gaining experience as he went, moving up the ladder, becoming a supervisor, an engineer without a sheepskin. Sometimes, during dry spells, he has had to take other work. He's been a census-taker, a carpenter, a door-to-door vacuum-cleaner salesman—an interesting range of jobs for a guy with an IQ of around 140.

Though Charlie is an excellent employee, a monumental anxiety has always accompanied what he calls "the interview thing." He knows he's going in on the defensive, having to convince the prospective employers that "Hey, folks, I'm just an ordinary guy like the rest of you." But to some people, he says, "I'm a freak, something that shouldn't exist, an aberration of nature. It's like I'm their worst nightmare—that they'll wake up someday and be me." One prospective employer turned him down because the company's drafting tables were lined up too close together—he wouldn't have fit, they said. Another company that gave health-club memberships to employees told him he wouldn't mesh well with the other workers. A firm that did hire him instructed him not to sit on the new sofa in the waiting room. A petroleum company said he'd have to shave his beard. When he agreed to do that, they remembered that all employees were required to have a Nomex fireproof suit, in case of a disaster. As it turned out, they didn't have a fireproof suit large enough to fit him.

Charlie's reaction to all of this has been to go freelance. He is happy to be in his own space, eligible for the customary self-employment deductions—of course, he does his taxes himself—away from dress codes, gawkers, fat jokes, and health food pushers. Like he always says, "Don't let the assholes get you down; you gotta find your own solutions." Bobbing his head to the tabla drum, he picks up his soldering iron again and goes back to work.

"I'll tell you one thing," he says, holding the iron poised above the circuit board, both of which look Lilliputian in his hands. "Being fat teaches empathy. Blacks have had this same problem. Same as the Jews, the Arabs, the handicapped, people who have disfigurements or burns. If you think about it, almost everybody's a cripple. They just manifest it in different ways."

#

Late afternoon, a living room in Whittier, California. Charlie sits on a chair wearing a sweat suit. His eyes are closed, his hands rest upon his thighs, palms up; he looks like Santa Claus playing Buddha. Sitar music wends through the air. At his feet sit three very fat people and his very tiny wife—some of the members of their informal club, the Every Other Sunday Yoga and Potluck Supper Bunch.

To his friends, most of whom he met through the National Association to Advance Fat Acceptance (NAAFA), Charlie is known variously as the Guru, the Dean of Fat Men, and the Answer Man. This is one group that admires and respects him, looks to him as a role model, seeks his guidance and advice. He is, after all, a sagacious man, a man of many interests. He plows though a book on a different topic almost every night. Ask him anything; he knows some tidbit of information. He's like a search engine on the World Wide Web.

This afternoon, Charlie is demonstrating a new discipline he's been toying with, something he's calling "Chair Yoga." It is designed, naturally, for people like himself who have no facility to pretzel. Charlie believes, as the Buddhists believe, that it is important to recognize the way things really are. Having done that, you are able to work better within with your constraints, to flow around obstacles instead of trying to break them down. It's all about working *with* yourself instead of fighting *against* yourself—a kinder, gentler, more understanding form of self-control.

The living room belongs to Dale, a corporate headhunter who weighs nearly 400 pounds. Dale is dating Elaine, Charlie's circuit board stuffer. They've been together for six months. The third in attendance is Rachel. Her occupation, practiced on a contract basis, is executive relocation. Once people get their transfers, she helps arrange all the details of the move. Her boyfriend lives in San Francisco. They switch off driving the eight hours. It's better than flying. ("Flying? On an airplane? In those little seats? Don't even start!") Her age, she says, is twenty-nine. Her weight, she says, is 129. Then she laughs—table-shaking, water-glass-sloshing, a little too jolly. You'd probably classify her as supersized.

Rachel's mom was tall, thin, and blonde—a princess in the Rose Bowl Parade in Pasadena. Her dad was an interior lineman with a football scholarship to Georgia Tech. They had three children. The two sons looked exactly like the Mom—long and willowy and graceful. Rachel was built like her dad.

She started her first diet at age five. For lunch, her mom would give her a tomato and a pear. Or a lettuce-and-tomato sandwich, no bread. Her brothers would get PBJ and potato chips and a Ding Dong for desert. She was allowed no sweets. Her mom kept the Ding Dongs and the other junk food for the rest of the family in a locked box on the kitchen counter. Rachel learned to pick the lock with a bobby pin. Mom bought a combination lock. Rachel figured out that if you listened very hard and moved the tumblers very slowly, you could crack the combination.

At age seven, Rachel was put on the Mayo Clinic diet. The first day, she remembers, she was allowed a hard-boiled egg and a grapefruit. Since then she's been on hundreds of different diets: the banana-and-skim-milk diet; the protein-powder-and-water diet; Dr. Ding's Diet—900 calories and lots of pills, including amphetamines. During Dr. Ding's Diet, Rachel's room was the cleanest it had ever been. Sometimes, she stayed up all night long cleaning. When she started hallucinating, they took her off. Next came Dr. Ding's Revised Diet. Five hundred calories a day, more pills, and a weekly injection of urine from a pregnant woman.

Weight Watchers, Pritikin, Jenny Craig, NutriSystem, Slim-Fast (aka Shit-Fast)—she's tried them all. She has lost literally hundreds of pounds. During all those diets, even as she was shedding pound after pound, year after year, all she could think about was food. All she could think about was everything she was going to eat when she reached her target weight. She dreamt of food. She'd cut pictures of food out of magazines and put them in a folder along with the recipes she was going to make. Cream sauces, cream soups, creamed *everything*. The day she'd hit her target weight, she'd go immediately to 7-Eleven and celebrate with a box of Ding Dongs. And so the cycle would begin again. Lose fifty. Gain seventy-five.

The book that changed her life was called *Compulsive Eater No More*. There was a story in it about a young fat girl who loved M&M's. Nothing could stop her from sneaking them. Finally, her parents took her to a new doctor. He told the mother to give the girl an entire pillowcase full of M&M's to carry around with her—to let her eat as many M&Ms as she wanted.

The first month, the girl gained eleven pounds.

The second month, she gained two pounds.

The third month, she started losing weight.

And so it was that Rachel, a grown woman with a teenage son, got herself a pillowcase and loaded it up with Ding Dongs. She carried the Ding Dongs around for three months—in her car, to the office, even to the gym, and what she discovered at last was that all the Ding Dongs in the world weren't going to fill the emptiness she felt inside. She wasn't really hungry for Ding Dongs. "I had to realize. I hated myself."

What she needed, she says, was "Permission. Permission to eat all the Ding Dongs I wanted. Permission to weigh how much I weighed. Permission to be what I am: fat. When things are prohibited, you want them even more. It turns into a sickness. If you can just sample something, if it is normalized, you can control things better. Take a sample. Try some. Maybe you have too much in the beginning, but then you get over it. The mystery dissolves. You're able to better self-regulate."

This is precisely the kind of lesson that Charlie has learned in his intellectual searching. He has been meditating for twenty years, practicing yoga for about ten. He is a "citizen Siddha," he says, a teacher without portfolio. He's read Baba Ram Dass, Deepak Chopra, Carlos Castaneda, the Hindu Vedas, the Buddhists' texts, much more. Without his spiritual interests, he believes, he would probably be a very angry man. As it is, he seems enlightened, one of those rare people who appear to be at home in their own skin. Sitting there on his chair at the front of the room, Charlie's voice assumes a calm, hypnotic, quality.

"The postures I will be teaching are called *asanas*," he tells the assembled. "If you can't do a posture all the way, that's okay. Just picture it in your mind. If you only move an inch, that posture has been completed for you. As Professor Mohan said, 'We must always choose the hat to fit the head; we must not choose the hat and make the head fit it.'"

Wear the hat that fits.

Simple enough.

But what to do when the hat that fits is bigger than the biggest one available at any store in the mall?

# # #

SCIENTIFIC EVIDENCE now seems to indicate that some people are simply born to be fat. And if you are born to be fat, the world being the way it is, there is probably going to be a lot of attendant dysfunction, and you are probably going to end up being *really* fat. If such is the case, Charlie and Rachel and the rest agree, you must accept one thing: There is nothing much you can do about it. You are always going to be fat.

Some years ago now, scientists at Rockefeller University, in New York, pinpointed and cloned a gene that appeared to be involved in a signaling system that regulates body weight. The gene, called "ob," tells fat cells to secrete a protein to signal that the body has stored up enough fat to run the factory. The brain and other organs respond to the signal by altering the body's metabolism, telling it to stop storing fat. Some people are programmed to store more fat than others.

Given these findings—and studies of identical twins, which show weight as a function of genetics at least 90 percent of the time—science seems to be telling us now that fat is more the result of nature than nurture. Yes, our society exhibits a lot of pathology associated with eating, but that's another subject.

The fact is, it is not Charlie's fault that he's fat. He was born that way to Chub and Shirley.

More recently, medical researchers also confirmed something that Charlie has believed all along: *dieting may actually cause obesity.* Some other interesting findings:

- Nondieters who overeat occasionally tend to gain very little weight.
- People regain pounds very easily after a weight loss, and the regained weight is mostly fat.
- Obese people gain weight much more easily than nonobese people.
- Health risks and mortality rates currently associated with obesity may actually be the result of yo-yo dieting—the stress on the body of gaining and losing so much weight.
- There is evidence that each person has an individual set weight. One oft-cited expert suggests that the best weight for most people is simply the lowest one they've been able to maintain for a year as an adult without struggling.

Just some things to think about.

# # #

CHARLIE VAN DYKE was leery about doing this story, about opening up his life and offering himself up "like a suckling pig on a platter with a big apple in my mouth." But with the risk of humiliation comes a chance to speak his mind. This is what he wants you to know:

"I was born fat," he says. "I've *always* been fat. I don't even know what it's *like* to be thin. It's like being born blind—you have no idea what sight is. It's like being black. You can't do anything about it.

"After a while, it becomes a quality-of-life question. Do I want to spend my life dieting and struggling and yo-yoing up and down? Do I want to end up gaining even *more* weight than I just lost? I've known people who've had their jaws wired, who've had their stomachs stapled. I know people who've had part of their intestines removed. They end up not being able to absorb certain minerals. They're on supplements for the rest of their lives. Not to mention the tremendous problems with gas. There's a sizeable mortality rate on the various surgeries. Why don't they just line us up and shoot us?

"Nobody chooses to be fat; nobody really wants to be outside of society. If there was a way that I could safely be the proper size for my body, a little smaller, probably right around 250 or 300, something like that, I'd be tickled pink. But hey, you know what? They haven't found a way. They have *not* found a way. And I haven't found a way, either. I have to live my life now, as I am. I have to make the best of it. I have to wear the hat that fits."

In his case, size XXXXXL.

GQ, 1995

4

A Boy and
His Dog in Hell

THE KID IN THE ALLEY calls himself Zeke. He's waiting for Beo, his older brother. It's early yet, 8:00 in the evening in spring. Dogs bark behind a back-yard fence, rain drums on the hood of a car, rap rumbles from a boom box in an open window. Zeke cups his hand beside his mouth and lifts his chin toward the roof line. "Yoooooooooo!" he howls—a lone, shrill note that pierces the rot smell and the amber light and echoes across the ruins of North Philadelphia. Once upon a time, this area was populated by Irish and Italian immigrants; they worked in the factories along American Street, turning out ball bearings and steel rollers and conveyor belts, little parts of bigger parts that made the machine age run. Today the neighborhood is called Little Puerto Rico. The factories have moved to the suburbs, the Sunbelt, offshore. American Street is wide and empty.

"Yooooooooooo!" Zeke howls again. He tilts his ear and listens.

From a distance comes a faint response. "Yooooooooooo!"

Beo is coming. He's got the dog.

Zeke crosses a vacant lot, crunching over the tin cans and car parts and bedsprings and pieces of foam and Pampers that cover the ground like mulch. He jumps atop an old washing machine and lights a joint. The rain is harder now. He tugs the collar of his jacket to his neck. It is a 76ers jacket, red and shiny and much too large for a seventy-five-pound kid. The waistband hits him mid-thigh. The sleeves keep falling over his hands. He took it from somewhere, he can't remember; it was a while ago, before his last stretch at St. Michael's School for Boys. A name is stitched on the left chest in white letters: SAUL.

Zeke has been home from St. Michael's for two weeks. He likes being home, being free, doing anything he wants—like all day today, like tonight, a night sharp with the promise of dogs and drugs, blood and adventure. St. Michael's was far away from the neighborhood, in Tunkhannock, Pennsylvania, in the woods near the mountains. They locked him in there, and he went to school, took baths, watched TV. They tried to make him eat, but the food was nasty, nothing tasted like nothing. Zeke didn't know nobody but one boy. One night the boy tried to pinch Zeke's ass. Zeke punched his lights out. Or so he says.

To hear him tell it, Zeke should never have gone to jail in the first place. It was his lawyer's fault—his lawyer wouldn't let him talk to the judge. Had he been able to talk, Zeke says, he would have got himself off. Like he told that lawyer, he didn't fight no pit bull dogs to the death. He didn't hang no dogs from no roof with no telephone wire after they lost a fight. And he didn't know nothing about no ten dog bodies. He didn't do nothing.

The lawyer told him to shut up. Zeke was appearing before the same judge who'd sent him away the last time. This time, his sixth at St. Michael's, Zeke got five months. By his own rough count, that makes a total of three years that he has spent locked up in one place or another. He is thirteen years old. When he totals his time, he smiles and shows his dimples. He is a pretty boy, with high cheekbones and dark hair cropped close to his head. His eyes sparkle like the broken glass in the gutter.

Beo rounds the corner, issues a quiet "Yo." He's got the dog by a choke chain. It pulls him through the alley, weaving here and there to sniff and piss, wheezing a bit from the pressure of the chain around its neck. A young male pit bull, about one year old, it is fourteen inches tall at the shoulder, maybe twenty-five pounds. Its brown and tan coloring is called *brindle* by breeders and aficionados; on the street it's *tiger stripe*.

He's a good-looking animal, handsome in the same way a man can be—chiseled jaw and high cheekbones. His body looks like something by Nautilus, with a muscular chest and slightly bowed front legs, as if he'd done a lot of pushups and biceps curls. The waist is tapered, the ass small, the gait wide-legged and sturdy.

Zeke neither waves nor says hello. His expression says he doesn't give a shit whether Beo showed up or not. He doesn't even look at the dog. In Zeke's world, he says, "If you want something, you don't get it." Zeke don't want nothing from nobody. If he did, he'd take it himself.

Beo is fourteen, the oldest boy in his mother's brood of seven children by three fathers. Beo is four-foot-eleven, one inch taller than Zeke, five pounds heavier. He's wearing a leather jacket with the hood pulled up over his head. As he comes closer, his soft face and big brown eyes put you in mind of the time Tom Sawyer wore a bonnet to fool the old lady. Like Tom, Beo is a legend, at least around here.

"We tried to catch this kid for two years," says Sam McClain, a Philadelphia police officer. One morning at 6:00, McClain came to Beo's house with warrants for theft, receiving stolen property, dog fighting, cruelty to animals, and killing or maiming a domestic animal. The fire department set up ladders on either end of the block. Fifteen police officers covered the rooftops and the street.

"Somehow the kid got away," McClain says, only half-grudgingly.

Around the neighborhood, the stories about Beo have reached mythic proportions. One time, it is said, he was running through an alley, trying to elude the cops, and a pit bull flew out of nowhere and locked onto Beo's back. He flipped the dog over his shoulder and crushed its skull with a brick, never even breaking stride. In the next block, a stray German shepherd clamped onto Beo's leg. He beat it to death with a board. In the end, the cops found the two dead dogs but could not catch Beo. Or so it is said.

According to McClain, Beo is now wanted in connection with a murder. In March a kid answering Beo's description rode his BMX bike past an old woman at high speed and snatched her purse, knocking her down in the process. She died later from her injuries.

Beo says that he owns four pit bulls at the moment, scattered at three different houses in the neighborhood to protect them from confiscation by the SPCA. They are named Voltron, Hitler, Murder, and Atlas. By his own account, over the past three years, Beo has had, for varying lengths of time, literally hundreds of pits. He has fought them all, many to the death. They are never around for very long. In one recent five-day period, Beo and Zeke had eight different pits in their possession.

Most of the dogs are stolen; sometimes the boys will trade, either dog for dog or dog for dog plus considerations, like maybe a little cocaine. Both of the boys earn money selling powder cocaine on a street corner—they both have regular shifts. Like dedicated managers, Beo and Zeke put their dogs in training. They fatten them on twenty-five-cent-a-can dog food and leftover beans and rice, run them around the block behind their bicycles, feed them chicken blood to make them game, take them on safaris around the neighborhood hunting for cats and strays, shoot them up with black-market penicillin and vitamin B12 to help heal their wounds, rub them with motor oil to make their fur grow back over scarred areas.

Unlike his big-shot brother, Zeke has no dogs at the moment, though he had one last night—a white bitch he'd stolen to celebrate his return from St. Michael's. He named her Canna, short for Canna Be Stopped. She was a good fighter. But she wasn't as good as Beo's dog, Murder. The fight lasted only five minutes.

After the fight, Beo and Zeke threw Canna's carcass on a trash heap, then went hunting for a new dog. A couple of miles away, in a back yard, they found a black pit. They stole it and named it Blade. They knew the guy who sold Blade to the man in the house, so they passed the word through the streets: If Blade's original owner wanted him back, he could come see Beo and Zeke. He did. A trade was arranged. That's where Beo has been this evening. Now he's back now with the goods.

Beo lets go of the choke chain and the tiger-stripe pit makes a bee line for his little brother. Zeke jumps off the washer and kneels on the ground. The dog is all over him in an instant—licking and wagging and strutting.

Zeke swats the dog on its side, pulls its ears, ruffles its fur and makes him growl. He kisses him on the snout. "What his name?" he asks his older brother.

"Shit, I don't know, man." Beo's voice is husky, his dialect a mixture of Puerto Rican Spanglish and black Ebonics. "He crazy, though. He went after two cats on the way here."

"He *fat*," Zeke says. "He look *good!*"

"I gonna train him up. He gonna be a champ!"

"What his name?" Zeke asks again.

Beo bites on a hangnail, studies his brother for a moment. "What? You want him or somethin'?"

Scuffing his toe on the ground.

"You want him or not?"

"No, man," Zeke says. "*You* keep him."

Beo grabs the dog by the scruff of its neck, lifts him to eye level and growls. Then he looks over at his brother. They share a room together. Since they were little, they have always been together, side by side, best friends and worst enemies. The only thing that has ever kept them apart is St. Michaels. "If I give him to you, you gonna take good care of him?" Beo asks.

No answer.

"You won't let him get skinny?"

No answer. With Beo, you never know the right thing to say. Usually, it's best to say nothing.

Beo flings the dog at Zeke. It knocks him over; the two tumble as one across the wet cobblestones.

Zeke sits up, delighted. The dog licks his face. "We'll call you Diablito," he tells his new pit, Little Devil.

"We'll make him a champ!" Beo proclaims. He kicks Diablito in the hindquarters, sends him sprawling.

And then he laughs, "*Ah ha HA!*", the way he always does when he's around the pits: head back, eyes wide, left hand squeezing his balls.

# # #

ACCORDING TO THE *New York Times*, North Philadelphia is "the 'dog fight' capital of the East Coast." But this story could just as easily be set in New York or Miami or Detroit or Los Angeles. Wherever there are men and boys who need something to be proud of and known for, there are people fighting pit bulls.

On the hard streets of the city (and in the mall parking lots of the suburbs), you are what you own: your moped, your boom box, your sneakers, your bling, your pit. Having a pit is not like having any other kind of dog. Pits do more than eat and shit and walk on a leash. They fight. They are perfect for places like Little Puerto Rico—small enough to keep, tough enough to survive.

"The attraction is basic. Kids need an outlet," Officer McClain says. "You go home every day, you live somewhere shitty, your mother and father are fighting, you got your ass kicked last night. You need a pit to impress your peers, to make you feel good about yourself. With your pit on the street, you're somebody. You've got an enforcer at your side."

Pit-bull fighting has traditionally been the domain of skilled professionals—a mostly rural cult of outlaw aficionados who fight the dogs in regulation pits according to rules. They train and care for the animals as they would prizefighters. (More recently, the illegal sport has made headlines in stories involving rappers and athletes, most notably former Atlanta Falcons quarterback Michael Vick.) "Pit bulls have become the new macho dog of choice in the urban centers of the country," according to Randall Lockwood, the director of higher education for the Humane Society of the United States. More and more pits are being seen on the streets and in the neighborhoods of the nation's cities and towns. As their numbers grow, so does the litany of horror tales.

Law-enforcement officials have reported the increasing use of pit bulls as weapons in crimes ranging from street robbery to rape. "And I know of some cases," McClain says, "where police will hesitate to raid drug-selling sites because they are guarded by an army of pit bulls."

"Nowadays," McClain says, "you walk your pit down the street and people clear the way. It's about power. It's a fad. Every era has its fads. This era has pit bulls. This era is pretty twisted."

# # #

PIT BULLS TRACE their ancestry to the English bulldog, to a sport called bullbaiting. During the early nineteenth century, peasants would gather for an afternoon, tether a bull to a long lead, cover its horns with pitch, and poke it with sticks. Then they would let two or three bulldogs attack it.

With the passage of the English Humane Act of 1835, which outlawed bullbaiting, dog versus dog became a popular sport, especially in the coal-mining areas of Staffordshire. When the bulldog was brought to America, it was bred, successively, with the terrier, the bullmastiff, the Rottweiler, and the Rhodesian ridgeback. The result of all this selective breeding is known, variously, as the American pit bull terrier or as the American Staffordshire terrier. It is a dog that has been genetically engineered for fighting.

Most wild and domestic dogs, according to research by the Humane Society of the United States, fight to drive away rivals for food, mates, status, or territory. First, the dogs will square off and bluff—growling, barking, baring teeth. Fighting is usually a last resort; the engagements are brief. A fight ends when one of the dogs withdraws or surrenders by exposing its neck and belly.

Pit bulls, however, rarely bark or growl. They will attack without provocation. The gamest of them will fight for hours, until complete exhaustion or death. They wrestle with muscular front legs, lock on an opponent with sharp teeth and powerful jaws. They crush bones, puncture flesh, tear it free from the skeleton. If a dog shows his belly to a game pit, the pit will disembowel it.

A 55-pound pit bites with a force of 1,800 pounds per square inch. The average German shepherd or Doberman bites with half that force. And the pit's jaws have become specialized over the generations, so it can lock on an object with its front incisors and chew with its back molars at the same time.

According to researchers, pits have been genetically equipped with a higher tolerance for pain than most animals. Pit bulls can climb trees or hang from a tire by their teeth for hours. In Holland, a forty-pound pit recently pulled a two-ton trailer 100 meters along a straightaway.

Defenders of the breed speak of a highly misunderstood dog. Like gun enthusiasts, they fault the human element—the pit-bull owners who misuse their dogs. They extol the virtues of the pit bull—innate intelligence, loyalty, and fine character. In an eloquent paean to the pit bull that appeared in *Harper's Magazine*, Vickie Hearne, a writing instructor at Yale University, rhapsodized over "the seriousness of mind of this breed," its purity of heart, its "awareness of all the shifting gestalts of the spiritual and emotional life around" it. The article—entitled, "Lo, Hear the Gentle Pit Bull!"—portrays the pit as a complex, highly refined dog that is capable of acting with "moral clarity," the result of "qualities that have to do with real love, love with teeth."

Only in the latter part of the twentieth century did the pit bull become maligned. In the early 1900s, the pit was portrayed as the canine embodiment of American virtues—a dog of independence, ingenuity, tenacity, cooperation, and good humor. Petey from *The Little Rascals* was a pit bull. A famous 1914 painting by Wallace Robinson depicts an English bulldog, a Russian wolfhound, a German dachshund, and an American pit bull terrier. Each dog wears the military uniform of its country. The

American pit bull is at the center of the lineup, the hero of the piece, which is entitled *I'm Neutral but Not Afraid of Any of Them.*

# # #

Nine in the evening. Beo and Zeke are in the living room of their family's row house. Beo is pounding a screwdriver repetitively into a piece of cardboard. *Bang, bang, bang.* Zeke is smoking a Newport cigarette. Diablito is asleep at his feet.

"Hey, Zeke."

"What?"

"Who ax you?" Beo laughs his maniacal laugh, "*Ah ha HA!*"

"Fuck you!"

"Shut *up.*"

"*You* shut up!"

"I'm gonna bust yo ass," Beo says, and then he smiles, huge and toothy. They both crack up.

"Hey, pussy," Zeke challenges, "who put the soda in their Cheerios with milk?"

"*Ah ha HA!* I only did that so you wouldn't want none."

And so it goes, another night of non sequiturs. Beo and Zeke don't go to school. They've never been to a movie. They don't know what a magazine is; they've never heard of *Rolling Stone*—or the Rolling Stones, either. When they have money, they go to the "Indian store," the only business in a several block radius, a liquor store and general market owned by a Pakistani. They have never seen an answering machine, have never used a computer or played a video tape. Their television gets only three channels. The only time they've ever been out of this part of the city was when they had to go to court or to jail or to St. Michaels. Most of what they know comes from rap songs, TV, and life on the streets. Neither one of the boys reads very well, but between them they know every hiding place, every abandoned house, every path through every alley in the neighborhood. When they are engaged in illegal activities, they set up lookouts like a team of well-trained guerrillas, covering all lines of approach. If someone says scatter, they're gone like smoke in the wind.

The origins of the Puerto Rican community in Philadelphia go back to 1943, when a number of workers—who had come to the mainland on labor contracts with the Campbell Soup Company in Camden, New Jersey—took up residence in Philadelphia. By the late 1940s, as economic conditions on their home island worsened, many others followed, hoping to find high-paying jobs in the area's factories. By the early 1950s, there were direct air flights from San Juan to Philadelphia, making it an attractive alternative to New York City, which already had a thriving Puerto Rican community of its own.

Unfortunately, the influx of the Puerto Ricans coincided with the end of the great days of manufacturing in Philadelphia. As was the case in the rest of the industrialized Northeast, factories were shutting down or moving out. During the 1970s, the number of manufacturing jobs in Philadelphia declined by 40 percent. The population of the city declined by 13 percent. The number of Puerto Ricans increased by 76 percent.

During the 1980s and early 1990s, Puerto Ricans had the lowest levels of education and income and the highest rates of teen pregnancy, infant mortality, and criminal arrests in the city. According to a report by Temple University's Institute for Public Policy Studies, there was little hope for relief. "Puerto Ricans have a hard time in Philadelphia. . . . As serious as [their] needs may be, they are only one group among many poor people living in a city with limited means to help them."

Despite their disadvantages, when you spend time with Beo and Zeke, it doesn't seem that they mind being semiliterate and truly needy. They wear name brands like Adidas and Lees. They have fancy BMX bikes. They have regular employment in the shadow economy—their shifts on the corner selling cocaine. And now they have a new pit bull, Diablito. It doesn't seem to matter that they have no future. This is life as they know it. It's the only one they have.

The living room is dark and warm. Heating is included in the rent, which is good, considering that their last house burned down after one of the little cousins got too close to a space heater and caught her dress on fire. There is a water-stained hole in the ceiling, beneath some bathtub pipes, and you can hear the leak—*drip, drip, drip*—mixing with sounds of laughter and shouting and the heavy bass of rap songs that filter through the shaded front windows. As the evening wears on, the rest of the Garcia brood lands in the living room with Beo and Zeke. Mami and Popi remain upstairs. You hear them occasionally, like Charlie Brown's parents in *Peanuts*, but they rarely make an appearance.

Sister Angelina is sixteen. Her baby is thirteen months old, named Nikki after a character on a daytime soap. Nikki's eyes are bandaged because Angelina accidentally used the lice shampoo instead of the baby shampoo.

Renata is fifteen. She's just come back from the store with a bottle of soda called Malta. She says that if you're pregnant, you can drink a Malta and take two of these pills called Cortal and you won't be pregnant anymore. Her boyfriend is named Angel. Beo and Zeke refer to him as their brother-in-law. He brings presents all the time; he is allowed to sleep in Renata's room. He deals coke for the Blue Tape Gang up the street. In Little Puerto Rico, gangs are identified by the color of the tape that is used to seal the little glassine envelopes of cocaine—blue, red, black. The gangs control their own corners. White people drive into the neighborhood, catch a runner on a corner to score. The coke is mostly powder, with a few small rocks, a bad burn. Both Beo and Zeke work for Angel. On the corner where they stand, there are a few scraggly trees with white crosses spray-painted on the trunks, places where kids Beo's age and older have been shot to death in the gang wars.

Ten year old Maria is busying herself at the coffee table in the living room, using a butcher knife to cut apart an imitation pearl necklace she found somewhere in the neighborhood. Seven year old Elena is playing roughly with a little kitten, throwing it up and down like a ball. Elena says the kitten has already used up three of its lives. One time Popi threw it out of the third-floor window. It didn't land on its feet, it didn't move. But then, after a while, it got itself back up and climbed the front steps into the house. Another time, the baby sat on it. It seemed dead, so Angel soccer-kicked it into a wall. But two hours later it came back to life and walked shakily to its bowl and took a drink of water. Elena can't remember the third time but she knows it happened. The kitten is cross-eyed. It has no name.

Beo watches idly as Elena plays with the kitten. All of a sudden, he snatches the kitten by the scruff of its neck and starts teasing Diablito with it. He bounces the terrified, cross-eyed kitten on the dog's nose, throws it at him, picks it up before the dog can pounce. The kitten shrieks. Elena shrieks at Beo. Zeke shrieks at Elena. Maria shrieks at Beo. Angelina shrieks at Maria.

Then Renata hollers that she's gonna punch somebody out if they don't shut up. She sounds serious. A scuffle ensues, the volume maxed, everyone shrieking and screaming and laughing and scowling and swatting, literally bouncing off the walls . . .

And then a bellow from above—Popi!

The stairs shake. *Boom, boom, BOOM!*

Juan Garcia is the father of the four youngest children, including Beo and Zeke. He came here from Puerto Rico in the late 1950s. He says he works for a Jew, landscaping rich people's houses on the Main Line—when there is work. Popi hates the dogs. Last week he called the SPCA. They came and took away three pits.

By the time his feet hit the living room floor, Beo and Zeke have vanished.

# # #

"TELL 'EM, ZEKE, tell about Tough Boy," prompts Beo.

"Tough Boy—he *tough*," Zeke says proudly.

"Tell about that time with the *bike*."

It's nearly midnight. Beo and Zeke and Diablito have fled to their basement hangout down the street. There are seven boys in attendance, ranging in age from thirteen to sixteen: Sam, Emilio, Macho, Louie, and Li'l Man. All of them have pit bulls. The basement is downstairs from where Louie lives. The kids crash here all the time. It's decorated with old mattresses and sofas, posters of professional wrestlers, a boom box that Zeke stole out of a car the other night. As the hours pass, boys come and go from the basement. Each time there's a knock at the door, everyone freezes. Every boy in the room has done something illegal today—stolen something, received stolen property, bought or sold drugs, fought their stolen pit bulls, gotten into a fight, snatched a purse. As Beo likes to say, "You ain't broke no laws 'til you get caught."

"Check it out," Zeke says, happy for once to have center stage. "I was riding my bike in the alley, and Beo had Tough Boy. And Beo say, 'Sic him!' you know, so Tough Boy runs me down and grabs my back tire, flips me right off the bike. Then he just held the bike straight up in the air, you know, by the rim."

"*Ah ha HA!*" Beo laughs. "He *strong*. Zeke was teasing me, you know. He was tellin' me how Tough Boy was a mutt and shit. But really he was *jealous* of him."

"I was not jealous of him!"

"Yes, you *was*. You used to talk a lot of shit."

"I hated that motherfucker!" Zeke says. "I *hated* him."

"Only 'cause he kilt that pit of yours. Tell 'em how Tough Boy kilt that pit of yours."

"Terminator?"

"*That* motherfucker."

"Check it out," says Zeke, "I had this pit, right? He a champ. Name Terminator. He eat up one of Beo's dogs, a tiger stripe named Buzzsaw. After the fight, Beo had to carry his shit home. His ears was hanging off and shit."

"Das right," says Beo, taking up the story himself. "So after that, I went and I traded this boy dog I had—he was all white, name Cocaine. I went to this guy I know and say, gimme a real killer. So I gave him Cocaine—plus I gave him a gram of Blue Tape—Cocaine plus *cocaine*! And that's how I got Tough Boy. I come back with him and tell Zeke that Tough Boy gonna kill *his* dog. And Zeke say, 'No, man. No *way*.'

"We went to the third floor of this old house and they rumbled. Tough Boy and Terminator. Tough Boy shook him all up. He hit him on the neck. He crunched him on the leg. He bit his fuckin' ear off. Terminator be hollering and screaming, bleeding and pissing and shitting, trying to run away. *Ah ha HA!*" Beo laughed. "That lousy ass motherfuckin' mutt almost jumped out the window!"

"He *did* jump out the window!"

"'Cause he a little pussy like you, motherfucker!" Beo says.

"I got a champ now," Zeke says. He raises his chin. "Diablito gonna tear your ass up! He gonna tear your shit right up."

"Yeah?"

"Yeah, mothafucka."

"Let's bang 'em!" calls Macho.

"Let's rumble!" says Sam.

"Let's shake 'em up!" yells Louie.

"*Ah ha HA!*" laughs Beo—head back, eyes wide, left hand squeezing his balls.

#

THE BOYS WALK through the alley in a hard rain, across a vacant lot toward a fenced-in schoolyard. Beo has Diablito, Li'l Man has Voltron, Louie has Death Man, and Macho has Darth Vader. The dogs pull the boys through the alley, wheezing from the pressure of the choke chains around their necks. Zeke tries to take Diablito's leash out of Beo's hand. "Give him *here*," he implores. "He's *my* dog."

"Who give him to you?" Beo sneers.

By the time they reach the schoolyard, the rain has begun to let up. They find a dark spot near a fence. The boys form a ring. In the center, it's Diablito versus Death Man, Beo versus Louie.

The boys stand five feet apart, face to face. They keep the dogs between their knees, squeezing to hold them in place, meanwhile riling the dogs, pinching and scratching at the fur behind their ribs, hissing into their ears, "*Ssssssssssic, sssssssssssic.*" Shortly, the dogs catch on and nature takes its course. They growl and bare teeth, strain forward. The boys let go. The dogs charge. Beo laughs and squeezes his balls, "*Ah ha HA!*"

Bang! They collide. You feel the ground shake.

Death Man gets a deep neck lock.

Diablito cries and disengages. He turns tail and runs.

Zeke's face falls. He doesn't say a word.

Beo corrals Diablito, sets him up again between his knees, facing Death Man.

Again, a neck lock. Diablito utters a squeal so horrible and wrenching that it turns your stomach. He shakes free and runs again.

"Pussy!" everyone taunts.

Zeke looks like he's about to cry.

Darth Vader is next, a black pit with distended teats, a new litter. She's fast. She locks Diablito just behind the head. There is much growling and squealing. There is blood.

Next is Voltron. He is Beo's dog, midnight black. "*Ah ha HA!*"

It is over quickly.

Diablito is lying on his side on the fissured concrete of the basketball court. His breathing is shallow. His blood mixes with a puddle of rain water. His brown eyes, fearful and confused, search the faces of the boys and dogs that surround him.

Beo calls Zeke a pussy.

Louie calls Zeke a pussy.

Macho calls Zeke a pussy.

Li'l Man calls Zeke a pussy.

Zeke kicks Diablito. He calls the dog a pussy.

Then the boys head back to the basement.

# # #

Late afternoon the next day, Zeke's living room.

It's raining again. It's quiet. There is no one around. Beo is working his usual shift on the corner, selling cocaine. Zeke has taken the cushions off of the sofa and placed them on the floor against a heating vent.

"When your dog lose," he says, "you probably get a little mad, 'cause everybody sayin' your dog lost and your dog a pussy and you a pussy. You get a little mad, but you don't get embarrassed. *No way.* 'Cause everybody be laughin', right? But *you* know you're gonna come back with revenge. Big-time revenge. You gonna tear their shit up. You gonna shake up their dog. You gonna kill their shit. And that's when *you* start bragging, too. That's when *you* be havin' a big smile on your face.

"Diablito was a mutt. Motherfucker wouldn't fight. Kept turnin' his back. Shit. He was a pussy. He don't deserve to live noways."

Zeke closes his eyes and takes a hit off a joint. Diablito is certainly dead by now. Someone has probably called the SPCA; they will come and collect the body from the school yard. Zeke had Diablito for less than one day. Like he says, "You can't care too much about shit, 'cause sooner or later, it be gone."

Spending time with him out in the streets, you almost forget Zeke's age. He seems as street smart and savvy as any grown man, drinking and snorting and smoking, fighting dogs in a schoolyard, selling drugs for money to buy dog food, committing all kinds of crimes, petty and other-wise. But here, in the warm darkness of his family's tenement living room, it is easy to see Zeke as he really is—thirteen years old, seventy-five pounds, curled up in the corner in a stolen 76ers jacket that is way too big for him.

"When I get older," Zeke says, his voice soft and dreamy, "I ain't gonna hustle or nothin'. I'm gonna buy me a car, a little Mazda with one of those racing engines. I'm gonna buy me a house, some furniture. I'm gonna put the house in the city, but far, far away from my family. I don't want those motherfuckers coming to my house.

"I'm gonna have slaves in my house. I'll sleep late, and I'll have lady slaves fanning me, rubbing my back. I'll wake up, they'll wash me up, wash my hair, hook me up. Then I'll be ready for them to carry me to the kitchen so I can eat my breakfast. And I'll be fuckin' all the lady slaves, too. Some badass bitches. All of them Puerto Rican. And some black ones. And some white ones. Different ones all the time.

"I ain't gonna have no company. Nobody can visit. It the king's house. Nobody visits the king. Like, if you come over, they open the door, my slaves do, and they say, 'What you want?' And you'll say, 'This is Mike, King Zeke know me, I'm baldheaded. I brought some drugs to give to Zeke.' And they'll say, 'All right, but you gonna have to wait.'

"If I decide to let you in, I'll tell 'em all right. Then my slave will come back down. He'll open the iron door, *bang*. He'll open the wood door, *bang*. He'll open the screen door. Come right on in. See the king. Me. I'm over here. You kneel."

Zeke giggles, then he closes his eyes. The pot is low quality; it makes your lids heavy. Cradled in the lullaby of the dripping rain, he nods for a while, a beautiful, mocha-skinned boy with long, thick eyelashes.

Outside the window, someone walks past with a boom box. The boy stirs from his nap, stretches, and yawns.

Zeke picks up the beat from the passing song, makes it into his own. He taps on the wall with his knuckles, blows a bass beat through his lips, beatboxing. Then he begins to recite. This is Zeke's Rap.

My name is Zeke
I'm at the mike
I'll tell you 'bout
My whole damn life
I fight the pits
I'm number one
Look a me havin'
So much fun
To the beat ya'll
To the beat ya'll
To the beat ya'll

Rolling Stone, 1987

5
The Smartest Man
in America

B Y SOME ACCOUNTS, Christopher Michael Langan is the smartest man in America.

He is certainly the smartest nightclub bouncer in America, endowed with an IQ that has been measured at 195, a score that puts him on par with the likes of Leonardo da Vinci, Ludwig Wittgenstein, and René Descartes, three of the brightest minds in human history. Chris is six feet tall and weighs 275 pounds, a great Minotaur of a man with a basso profundo voice. A former cowboy, construction worker, and Park Service firefighter, he has a fifty-two-inch chest, twenty-two-inch biceps, a cranial circumference of twenty-five and a half inches—a colossal head, more than three standard deviations above the norm. Known in his younger days to play a mean lead guitar, he has light blue eyes, a dry-look Elvis pompadour, and a large chip on his shoulder, something you come to understand once you hear his story.

"It ain't easy being green," he says in typical fatuous style, quoting Kermit the Frog, resigned yet undiscouraged—the cocky, perverse, some-what defensive assuredness of a person who has always been the smartest in any group, perhaps the loneliest, too. The distribution of IQs through the population forms a bell curve, with the very smartest on one side, the severely disabled on the other. The IQ of the average human is about 100.

The IQ of the average college graduate is about 120. IQs like Chris's exist among us at a rate of roughly one in one hundred million. In a world designed for average, folks like Chris don't always fit very well. Forty-two years old, he pulls down $6,000 a year. He lives in a tiny, cluttered one-room cabin overlooking a field of heavy machinery in Eastport, Long Island—a short drive from the tony Hamptons—which he shares with his cat, Ramona, and his 1985 shovelhead Harley-Davidson, parked at the moment near the sink in the kitchen.

Thanks to the magic of the World Wide Web, over the past fifteen years, more than a dozen affinity groups for people with superhigh IQs have been formed. More exclusive than Mensa—which accepts those with a minimum IQ of 132, one of every fifty people—clubs like the Triple 9 Society, the Prometheus Society, and the Mega Society (with IQ requirements of 148, 164, and 176, respectively) provide electronic fellowship to an eccentric, far-flung population known as HiQ Society. Though the clubs, like all subcultures, have become petri dishes for ego squabbles and political infighting, they nevertheless supply the comfort of fraternity in a world that doesn't think fast enough, doesn't get the reference, doesn't grasp the point.

Chris's mom was a spirited young woman, the black-sheep daughter of a wealthy shipping executive. She frequented San Francisco's City Lights Bookstore, rubbed shoulders with the Beats. Chris's dad, the story goes, died of a heart attack before Chris was born. To this day, he's not sure if his mother was telling him truth. She's dead now, so that information has gone to the grave. A kernel of truth: There is stuff even the smartest man in America can't know.

Chris began talking at six months of age, reading at three years. He skipped kindergarten through second grade, started his schooling in third. Though his IQ was never tested when he was a child, he says, "It was simply recognized that I was some kind of kid genius. My schoolmates saw me as the teacher's pet, this little freak." When he was still an infant, his mother married a struggling Hollywood actor. They had two sons and then divorced. When he was five, she married "a mean, hard-drinking tyrant," Chris says. "He figured the best way to raise three boys would be to set up his own military platoon. Living with him was like ten years of boot camp, only at boot camp you don't get the shit beaten out of you every day with a garrison belt, and in boot camp you're not living in abject poverty."

At 6:00 each morning, his stepfather would sound reveille on an authentic bugle. His three little soldiers lined up at attention, heels touching, feet cocked at forty-five degrees, thumbs along trouser seams. He'd stand before each of the boys and feign a punch, usually a right jab that he'd stop an inch or two shy of their noses. If one of the kids flinched, he would sock him for real. Chris's body was always covered with welts. The fresh ones were pink and red, the older ones black and blue, the oldest green and yellow. "I looked like a Jackson Pollock painting," Chris remembers.

By the time he was twelve, Chris got into lifting weights. "When you're the littlest and the smartest, and you're wearing rags, and you come to school with a fat lip and all these marks on you, you're treated like scum by the rest of the kids. I just decided enough was enough. I developed my strength, worked on my hand speed. I learned how to beat up kids who were twice my size. I got a reputation for being a tough guy. By that time, I was mostly doing independent study—they didn't know what to teach me anymore, but nobody was going to take me out and put me in college on the fast track, so I just did what they told me. I went to study hall and worked on my own, taught myself advanced math, physics, philosophy, Latin and Greek, all that. Meanwhile, all the parents were taking their kids out of study hall because they didn't want them anywhere near me. They thought I was going to beat them up."

One morning when he was fourteen, Chris awoke to a flash of white light, followed by intense pain across his eyes. Just home from an all-night drunk, his stepfather had wrapped his garrison belt around his fist and punched Chris while he slept. Since he was four years old, Chris had never once talked back. It was always, *No, sir, Yes, sir*; for all the abuse he'd taken, he'd never even said *boo*. Now something snapped. Chris went mental. He jumped out of bed half blinded and flew at his stepfather, knocked him across the room, against the wall, out the door. In the front yard, for all to see, Chris issued a merciless beating to the man who had beaten him so many times. Then he told him to leave and never return. He didn't.

Chris got into college on a scholarship. He lost the scholarship when his mother forgot to sign the financial forms. He took a year off, earned money fighting forest fires, enrolled at another college. Then his car broke down. It was the middle of winter. He had no money to fix it. He had to walk fifteen rural miles in the snow every day or face expulsion. School officials were unwilling to give him a break. "There I was, paying my own money, taking classes from people who were obviously my intellectual inferiors," he says. "I just figured, Hey, I need this like a moose needs a hat rack! I could literally teach these people more than they could teach me, and, on top of that, they had no understanding, they didn't want to help me out in the least. To this day, I have no respect for academics. I call them *acadummies*. That was the end of my formal education."

Over the years, Chris developed what he says is known in social-psychology textbooks as a double-life strategy. "On one side, you're a regular guy. You go to work, you do your job, you exchange pleasantries. On the other side, you come home and you begin doing equations in your head. You kind of retreat into your own world. You make it work for you the best you can."

When Chris isn't busy working as a bartender, or training summer luminaries like the writer Tom Wolfe at the local health club, or wrestling with drunken rich people at the door of the nightclub, or chatting up the young ladies (his big weakness, he admits), he is often found hunched over his homebuilt computer, drinking tepid tea from a spaghetti-sauce jar, working on something he calls the CTMU, his Cognition Theoretic Model of the Universe. The result of ten years of solitary labor, the CTMU—pronounced *cat-mew* for short—is a true Theory of Everything, Chris says, a cross between John Archibald Wheeler's Participatory Universe and Stephen Hawking's Imaginary Time theory of cosmology.

Simply put, the CTMU explains the meaning and substance of reality. It resolves—once and for all time, he says—"many of the most intractable paradoxes known to physical science while bestowing on human consciousness a level of meaning that was previously approached only by religion and mysticism." The culmination of "the modern logico-linguistic philosophical tradition," the CTMU "reunites the estranged couple consisting of rationalistic philosophy and empirical science." Though Chris has invited criticism of his theories from all quarters, he has yet to hear anything approaching a valid argument against any of his conclusions or computations. Neither has he found a publisher.

"Sometimes I wonder what it would have been like to be ordinary," Chris says. "Not that I'd trade. I just wonder sometimes."

# # #

STEVE SCHUESSLER HAS AN IQ of 185, which ranks him higher than Charles Darwin and Bobby Fischer, around one in 10 million.

A contract researcher for a nonprofit environmental think tank, Steve studied mime for several years with a disciple of Marcel Marceau. On his Web page, Steve notes that he's a Baha'i vegetarian windsurfer. His voice is thin and reedy, the words carefully enunciated. He has the sort of flighty aspect of the joyously effeminate, a tendency to flutter and float his hands to and fro, to cock his head coyly, to giggle and mug. In practice, he says, he is steadfastly heterosexual, with a penchant for supple young students of dance and yoga, two of his long-standing enthusiasms. It's been more than two years since his last sexual encounter. He hopes to break luck soon.

A recovering agoraphobic who once made a local name for himself playing blindfolded chess, Steve enjoys setting odd goals for himself; one time he set for himself the goal of going to a party and seeing whether he could be the last one there at the end of the night, dancing the craziest. In his spare time, he runs Web sites for two of the HiQ societies. He is looking forward to an upcoming appointment with a psychologist who wants to do a PET scan of his brain. Steve is anxious to find out if he has larger-than-normal inferior parietal lobes, as Einstein did. Either way, he plans to post the results on his Web site as soon as possible.

Though Steve responded quickly to a request for an interview, he refuses to divulge his age, explaining that he is rabidly opposed to ageism. When he was six, he explains further, tests found that he had the intellectual development of a twelve-year-old and the emotional development of a four-year-old. "People's expectations about one's development are pinned to age rather than to capacity," he says. "This is something I really feel bad about—people's expectations for life's little guideposts and progressions. It seems to me that HiQ people either get a doctorate at nineteen and then burn out at a young age—they become hermits and collect subway tokens or whatever—or they'll wait and investigate many, many different ideas and paths and maybe get an advanced degree at the age of fifty or sixty.

"There is a little lizard called the axolotl. It's one of my favorite Scrabble words. It's a strange little creature that looks like an immature salamander throughout its entire life. But if you treat it with drugs a certain way, it will turn into what appears to be an adult salamander. There are those who view a certain lack of emotional development as being childlike. Notice I didn't use the word *childish*. I said child*like*. There is a certain curiosity, a certain believing in the moment, that a lot of people lose by the time they're seven or nine years old. I feel like I probably never lost that. I still have a childlike sense of wonder and curiosity."

Other out-of-bounds topics include the names of Steve's parents, his place of birth, the universities he's attended and quit. When questioned directly, Steve refuses to share any specific details about his life, past or present, preferring to respond with streams of interesting factoids and well-informed opinions, giving the impression that he is not so much a complex human personality as he is a walking amalgam of disparate bits of information. He prefers to explain his life experience by way of elliptical anecdotes from his three favorite movies about young geniuses: *Little Man Tate, Searching For Bobby Fischer,* and *Good Will Hunting.* The scene in which the young genius is lonely and alone in a crowd. The scene in which the pre-med girlfriend becomes upset because her genius janitor boyfriend understands organic chemistry better than she does. Ask Steve a question he doesn't like, and he freezes for painfully long minutes, squinting his gray eyes intensely, staring into the unfocused middle distance, the muscles in his jaw clenching and relaxing. One detail he volunteers without prompting: He colors his wispy, elbow-length hair with Clairol's "Lightest Auburn." He carries a ponytail scrunchie in the right front pocket of his pants, a comb and a round brush in the right rear.

Steve lives illegally in med-student housing near the University of Houston—a two bedroom apartment. There are boxes and random pieces of furniture and computer parts all over the living room and dining room. Steve's bedroom is a dim study in timeless utilitarian order—the blinds drawn, the space dominated by a futon, some overweighted bookshelves, and a pair of networked computers that carry 26 gigabytes of memory—he calls it his TAN, his Tiny Area Network. Because he does not own a car, he relies on friends to get around the sprawling city. His most steady ride is named Bill, whom he met while working at Kinko's.

Steve has studied subjects as diverse as quantum physics, classical philosophy, Latin, Greek, electrical engineering, communications theory, and the history of exploration. Even so, he has never earned a college diploma. This makes him feel somewhat inadequate and defensive. "The blessing part of high intelligence is that it seems that you're equipped with a telescope and a microscope, and other people have binoculars and a magnifying glass. The curse part is probably when you have a feeling that there is so much that you could be doing but haven't lived up to the possibilities.

"It's easy, when you're interested in lots of things, to get sidetracked. You start studying one thing, and that leads to the next thing, which is also interesting. Before you know it, months have gone by and you're very far afield. I enjoy the sharp upward learning curve associated with new knowledge, but, frankly, I often become bored with the tedious plateau associated with expertise."

Unfortunately, Steve says, expertise is far more marketable. "You want to find work where you can utilize your talents," he says, "but how do you put on a resume that you're probably going to see things more clearly, have better ideas for strategies, have a better overall view than anybody else in the entire company? And do people really want somebody like that? Highly intelligent people are not seen as team players. They're seen as loners with their own ideas, as people who are difficult to deal with. Some people get more despondent and isolated as they age, and it's very, very difficult. Others take that as a challenge—how to interact with other people, how to talk with other people. I kind of took that route. I took a lot of drama courses, read a lot of things. If you become actively hostile against the environment around you, that's like a certain kind of hell."

Gina LoSasso is a short, garrulous woman with a heavy Brooklyn accent and purple eye shadow that matches the satin bra strap peeking out flirtatiously from the shoulder of her floral blouse-and-shorts ensemble. Though she is by no means the smartest woman in America—that title goes to Marilyn Mach vos Savant, the *Parade* magazine columnist—she is way up there, with an IQ around 168, higher than that of Mozart or Thomas Jefferson. Since men with extremely high IQs (and men with extremely low IQs) are fifty times more plentiful than women, Gina estimates, the incidence of females in the population with an IQ similar to hers is about one in 3.4 million.

Gina is forty-three years old, twice-divorced, the mother of two—a twenty-year-old daughter and an eight-year-old son. She recently received her Ph.D. in clinical neuropsychology from Wayne State University in Detroit, having completed her bachelor's, master's, and doctoral programs in just under five years. She earned a great number of her undergraduate credits through something called the College Level Examination Program. She'd pick a test that seemed doable—marketing, management, literature, computer science, biology—get one basic textbook on the subject, study it, take the exam. She averaged about two tests a month. She scored in the high 90s on all the exams except biology, which she still managed to pass.

In her first e-mail to me, Gina opined that highly intelligent women make the best lovers. She believes that her high libido and her high intelligence are both related to a higher than normal percentage of testosterone in her system. When she was young, in fact, she wanted to be a boy; she refused to answer to any name other than Billy. These days, she thoroughly enjoys being a girl, especially given the man-woman ratio in her circles. Gina is currently the only female on the list of the top fifty American players in the International Correspondence Chess Federation. A former member of the U.S. Chess Olympiad Team, Gina lived in Brussels for many years as a professional chess player, traveling the European circuit. Her second husband, an international master whom she married when she was thirty-two, was fourteen years her junior.

Before she found chess—through a correspondence league associated with Mensa—Gina managed a weight-loss clinic, flunked out of three colleges, attended computer-programming school, sold copiers, made sand-art terrariums, sold candy behind the counter at a movie theater. As soon as she played in her first chess tournament, she realized two things. Number one, this was what she wanted to do with her life. Number two, her marriage to her first husband—a construction worker from the old neighborhood in Brooklyn—was over. She felt the same way when she was accepted into her doctoral program; she informed her second husband that she wanted a divorce. Gina has never had a problem letting go, forging ahead, concentrating on her own needs, making tough decisions—like leaving her daughter behind with her father while she pursued her dreams of playing chess. She abhors hanging around.

Though she tested off the charts in standardized examinations as a child, she hated school, often refused to go, barely graduated. Because she liked to talk and goof around a lot, and because she was good looking—not to mention the thick Brooklyn accent—people always mistook her for an airhead. She liked it that way, because she was self-conscious about being too smart and didn't want to be thought of as a nerd. In fact, in her youth, she was somewhat of a hellion. As a young teenager, she frequently hitchhiked to Greenwich Village. She'd pick an apartment building, gain entry, listen at doors for the sounds of a party in progress. If one sounded interesting, she'd knock. She spent much of her fourteenth year in a residential drug-treatment program.

Gina's mom worked as a civilian employee of the police department. Her dad was an electrician and an alcoholic who left the family when she was sixteen. Often he'd build elaborate wooden and electronic puzzles that he'd take to work for the purpose of stumping his coworkers. When Gina solved the puzzles handily, he'd become angry. He'd storm out of the house and head for the local pub.

Puzzles and games have always been Gina's passion and forte. She loves playing Scrabble, breaking tough encryption codes. She often plays computer games like Jessball and Myst for upward of six hours at a time. One of her favorite activities is riding her exercise bike while staring at her lava lamp. It helps clear her mind, she says; it's also great for her thighs. She keeps the bike in her bedroom, beside a large four-poster bed with a gauzy black canopy and sexy silken sheets. She is skilled at calligraphy, macramé, and jewelry making. "When people like me want to do something, we just do it," she says, typically unabashed. "From learning a musical instrument to learning how to tile your bathroom. You just get an instruction book and figure it out. It's a real empowering feeling, knowing that you can do almost anything you try. The hard part, of course, is trying. When I know that I can do a presentation better, with little or no preparation, than the average person can with all kinds of preparation, it's hard for me to get motivated. I can be very industrious, but I have a lazy side. Or not lazy, really. It's just, like, I wanna do what I wanna do, you know?"

Gina believes that high intelligence works against you, because mundane things are very difficult, and the world is full of mundane things structured for the average person. Waiting in line, paying bills, filling out forms, taking required courses, driving her son to school, answering routine questions, following arbitrary rules—life to her can sometimes be excruciatingly dull. Another difficult obstacle, she says, is finding the patience to communicate properly with others. Though she is a people person of the highest order and has many good friends, she isn't always easy to get along with. She expects those around her to make leaps they sometimes fail to make. She easily becomes impatient: Why should she have to belabor a point to make herself understood? Sometimes she feels like snapping her fingers to speed people along. *Come on, come on, keep up!* And though she hates to say it, she can't stand watching her son play chess. He's already an accomplished player, having won his first trophy at four. She is proud of him, yes. But the kids' game is so slow it annoys her. They take all year to see a move. Sometimes she just wants to stand up in her seat in the audience and scream. *Knight takes queen, fer chrissakes!*

Like many of her HiQ fellows, Gina is admittedly obsessive-compulsive. Upon our first meeting, she proffers a three-ring binder complete with section tabs—a compendium of personal tidbits, FAQs, and background readings. She likes to be in charge. She likes to be the center of conversation and attention. She has a need for order and control. Often, when she buys a pair of shoes, she ends up returning them to the store because the right shoe is not identical in every way to the left. She loves to argue but has a difficult time agreeing to disagree. She believes that there is always an answer waiting to be found, and she will go to great lengths to dig it up, to prove herself right. *Maude is Edith's cousin! Muhammad Ali is more popular than Pele!* Currently, Gina is embroiled in a dispute with her new boyfriend, a ponytailed HiQ postal employee she met on the Web. The argument arose after he made an obscure joke about losing his Thomas Pynchon doll. Gina didn't get it. The boyfriend said she must be an idiot if she didn't get it. She held fast to her opinion that his joke didn't make sense. She went so far as to research her position, telling the joke to her doctoral colleagues—clearly not idiots—carefully noting their reactions. They didn't get it, either. She is very proud of her new credential: Ph.D. Those three letters appended to her name are very important to her, partially because it is a label that everyone can see. It says, with little need for interpretation, that she is *certifiably* smart. When you're special, you want people to accord you that extra bit of deference and respect. It's hard when they don't know you. Those three little letters go a long way. It helps explain how she was able to endure the tedious process of earning a doctorate in the first place.

Since her boyfriend lives in Virginia, they communicate mostly by e-mail and phone. Gina also has a torrid ongoing e-mail correspondence with America's smartest man Chris Langan, the bouncer/cosmologist, though they've never actually met. She has printed out both sides of their e-mail correspondence; she keeps the hard copies in a three-ring binder beneath her desk—an X-rated, HiQ version of *Love Letters*. She is moving soon to Connecticut to take up her postdoctoral studies at Norwalk Hospital, a ferry ride away from Long Island. The next three-ring binder has yet to be filled.

"I'd love to clone myself, I really would." She smiles at the preposterous sound of the idea, continuing deliciously. "I would know how to raise me to reach my full potential. I think sometimes that if I'd been raised by a normal family, with opportunities to go to the best schools and stuff like that, I might have been a neurosurgeon or something by now. But then again, there's a side of me that's very creative and undisciplined, and maybe it's better to embrace that. Look at all the fun I've had. I've partied a lot. I've dined with heads of state and heroin addicts. I've lived in Brooklyn and Brussels, traveled to Moscow and Dubai. I've had a very broad, incredible life. I'm very philosophical about my whole experience growing up in the inner city and struggling and being different, because I'm here now, and I'm at a really good point. I can say that everything has worked out."

RONALD K. HOEFLIN IS a mild man with graying hair who wears his watch on a string around his neck.

Fifty-five years old and legally blind, he lives in Manhattan, in a $106-a-month apartment in Hell's Kitchen. He has three cats—Big Boy, Princess, and Wild Thing—and a collection of faux Frankart lamps, curvaceous female forms holding colorful globes, that lend a bawdy air to his tiny, ultra-neat bachelor pad, all of the furniture in which was found abandoned on the streets. Framed on his wall are three mandalas, photocopied from a series of twenty-four drawn by a patient of Carl Jung. The colorful works are symbolic of the patient's creative struggle and development. Though Ron can't make out the detail without his magnifying glass, the mandalas give him comfort in his solitary labors, he says, as does the crystal statue on his desk—Atlas balancing the world on his shoulders.

Sweet-natured and eager to please, Ron volunteers the fact that he has no friends. He seems nervous and awkward in public; he often goes days without meaningful conversation. When he does speak, the words gush forth so rapidly that he sounds as if he's using a foreign tongue; understanding him takes a bit of practice. Once every two or three months—whether he needs it or not, he jokes—he goes on a date with a woman friend from Long Island. He's also begun corresponding with a woman in Florida. She has promised to come visit. "I'm looking for a bright woman who'd like to have bright children, if any such woman exists out there who can tolerate my low vision, modest income, and shyness," he says matter-of-factly.

Ron's father was an electrical engineer and ballroom dancer who worked his way through college playing violin in dance bands. His mother was an opera singer. Born and raised in St. Louis, Ron spent his youth "running around the neighborhood like a wild Indian." Due to his poor vision, he was never much of a reader; neither could he see the chalkboard in school. Nevertheless, when tested, he was found to be several grades ahead of his class, the fifth brightest student in his entire district. Though he remembers being upset that he wasn't the *brightest* in his entire district, all of the adults in his sphere were pleasantly surprised. No one, including Ron, could explain how he knew so much—where he'd learned all the big words and complex theorems. It was as if the knowledge had come to him *a priori*.

Though Ron dropped out of his first three colleges, he now has two bachelor's degrees, two master's degrees, and a Ph.D. in philosophy. He modestly claims an IQ of only 164, though he says that arriving at a final number is tricky. "I've gotten scores ranging from 125 to 175, depending upon what cognitive abilities they're tapping into," he says. "The fact is, nobody really knows exactly what you're supposed to be measuring when you're measuring IQ."

Ron is a self-taught expert in HiQ testing. He is credited with creating two of the world's most difficult IQ tests, the Mega and the Titan. Ron is fascinated with human potential, human limits. He is interested in world records of every kind: running times, weight-lifting records, home-run tallies, the number of digits of Pi a person can memorize. Since 1979, he has founded four HiQ societies, mostly because he was interested in the psychometric possibilities of forming such groups, given the numerical rarities involved. He makes his living by publishing monthly journals for two of the clubs and by scoring his tests for twenty-five dollars each. That he lives in one of the most expensive cities in the world with annual earnings of about $7,000 is perhaps the truest testament to his genius.

Seven days a week, at precisely three in the afternoon, Ron walks to a Wendy's restaurant fifteen blocks from his place. He orders a chef's salad and a large iced tea, then retires upstairs to the second-floor dining room, sits at his regular table by the window. After reading the *New York Times* and the *New York Post*, he reads exactly ten pages of philosophy—no more, no less—searching for examples to include in the book he's been writing for the past seven years, *Decoding Philosophy: Cybernetic Patterns in Philosophy and Related Disciplines—A Theory of Categories.* An expansion of ideas he first explored ten years ago in an essay for which he was awarded a prize by the American Philosophical Association, Ron's book offers a revolutionary new system for categorizing and analyzing all of the world's known philosophies. Handwritten on six-by-eight inch notepaper—printed neatly in black ink; corrected with white streaks of Liquid Paper; edited with scissors and tape—the book runs about one million words. He keeps it filed in manila folders on two shelves in his apartment. Though he is aware that the book is much too long to be published, he forges ahead. Within the next year, he hopes, he'll be finished.

Ron owns a computer but has never hooked it up, which adds to his sense of isolation. Though he has a reputation among fellow HiQs for being a technophobe, it's not the technology that daunts him so much as it is the idea of embarking on a whole new area of interest. Many years ago, he eschewed the notion of regular employment because he thought he would be squandering his time, that he wouldn't be improving himself in any way during all of those hours he had to work just for the sake of making money. While some HiQ types prefer to rip open a new gadget or enthusiasm, ditch the instructions, and wing it, Ron is the kind of person who wants to read every word in every manual before he'll start anything new. As it is, he is known as a prodigious letter writer. "I've been using the mail for fifty years," he says. "Why stop now?" He feels the same about his financial position. "I'm sort of used to it. It's a trade-off. Money on one hand, leisure and independence on the other. I'm not really enough of a people-person to become wealthy, so I figure, what the heck, you know? I'm used to my condition. I have food and shelter and clothing. You don't have to be a genius to know that those are the most important things of all."

Ron's outward life is a series of comfortable routines. By putting the mundane tasks on a sort of deeply entrenched autopilot, he says, his mind is free to ponder larger questions. He always takes the same routes to Wendy's, to the post office, to the grocery, to the bank. He always goes at the exact same times, says the exact same things to the people who serve him. Every night for dinner, he buys two pieces of fried chicken, a can of corn, a can of peaches. Food is food, you know? Fuel for the body and mind. Later in the evening, while watching one of the five premium cable movie channels that are his only extravagance, he enjoys a scoop of strawberry ice cream. He loves the quiet of the dark, stays up all night watching movies, listening to classical music, writing essays. He sleeps until one in the afternoon. "I'm not saying it's a good life or a bad life. It's my life. It serves its purpose," he says.

When Ron was in sixth grade, a girl in his class invited everyone to her birthday party. When he arrived, she looked surprised. "Ron," she exclaimed. "I didn't expect you to come!" He doesn't remember now whether he stayed at the party, but he does remember the feeling he had, the lesson he learned. "Even though people invite you, it doesn't mean they are sincere about it. The truth is that people with average intelligence are a bit resentful. Throughout their entire schooling, they've had to compete with these people who seem to find it easy to get straight As, and they're working hard just to get Bs and Cs. If you were normal size, and you had to spend every day of your life out on a football field being run over by a three-hundred-pound guy, you'd start to resent him, wouldn't you? It's the same as that.

"There's a theory about genius. It's sort of like the 'tragic-flaw theory' in tragedy. You see it in a lot of cases of highly intelligent, highly creative people. For example, Sir Isaac Newton's mother abandoned him at the age of three to remarry. Her new husband didn't want young Isaac around, so he went to live with his aunt. He never recovered from the abandonment, could never achieve friendships with anybody throughout his entire life. His creativity in mathematics was really his way of saying, 'I'm a worthwhile person.'

"That's what a genius-type person, typically, will try to say through his work. He or she is saying, 'Even though you may not realize it, and even though I sometimes hate myself, I'm going to try and prove to you that I have some reason for being alive, that I have something important to contribute.' It's like you're born out of sync with the world, and you have to try to adjust. Your way of compensating is taking your greatest talent and just pushing it to the limits."

Esquire, 1999

6

The Ice Age

ONE NIGHT WHILE HE SLEPT, special agents from the DEA entered Robert Li's bedroom and planted a tiny speaker in his brain. The device was top secret; it transmitted and received. It read his thoughts, broadcast voices, tracked him by satellite everywhere he went.

At work in the produce department of the local supermarket, he'd notice now and then that certain shoppers would stop their carts and spy on him. Men, women, teenagers, he could hear them talking. They'd be saying stuff like, "He's spraying the lettuce now."

At home he'd hear noises. He'd look out the window, but no one was there. Sometimes, if he looked quick enough, he could catch a glimpse of a shirt collar in the bushes, the bill of a baseball cap behind the fence. Once he saw a man with a walkie-talkie standing near his car. "I know what you're thinking," the man said into his handset. Li rushed outside. The man was gone.

After that, Li stayed in his room. The broadcasts got louder. He dug around in his ear with a paper clip, but he couldn't find anything. Neither could the ear, nose, and throat doctor who patched him up on three different occasions. "Then I started thinking maybe things were planted in my walls, planted in my radio," Li says. "I took apart everything in my room you could think of. I'd spend hours—ten, twelve, fifteen straight hours—just taking something apart, looking for a mike or something like that. Do you know how many parts a TV set has? I couldn't find anything. Then I had to put it back together."

At the moment, Li is sitting on his bed, propped on pillows against the wall, grinding his teeth. Twenty-eight years old, he is an attractive mixture of Chinese, Caucasian, and Hawaiian—dark and mop haired, with hooded eyes and a square, Dudley Do-Right chin. This is his parents' place, a modest wood-frame house on the windward side of the island of Oahu, in the state of Hawaii, nine or ten miles over the mountains from Waikiki. It's a small room, the scene of his boyhood: wood paneling, a shelf full of model cars, a collection along the window ledge of spent disposable lighters.

Li reaches into his shirt pocket and pulls out a clear glass tube with a hollow ball at one end, a fluted mouthpiece at the other. At the top of the ball is a small hole; at the bottom, a little clump of crystals. The crystals are shiny and translucent, like sea salt or rock candy. Li covers the hole with his finger, teases the glass ball with a tight blue flame. In a few seconds the crystals melt, then bubble, then vaporize. Smoke swirls inside the ball, wispy, clean, and white. He sucks it through the tube, inhales deeply. There is no smell. He says it tastes like vanilla. Others say it tastes like green apples, star fruit, the way plumeria smells. At last, he exhales. He opens his eyes and smiles.

The first time Li smoked ice was six years ago. Before that, he wasn't a druggie; he didn't even smoke *pakalolo*, Hawaiian pot. Since high school, weekends had been a case of beer, cruising the streets of Waikiki, gawking at tourists, stopping in at clubs like Masquerades or the Rock and Roll Clinic, maybe going in with some friends to buy the services of one of the hookers strolling downtown Waikiki. Occasionally, he did a little cocaine, maybe shared half a gram, not enough to get jangled, just something to take the woozy feeling off the beer.

Then one night, he was on his dinner break—he was working the p.m. shift at a grocery store. His buddy, Ron, asked if he wanted to try something. Each smoked about four hits. "It felt different," Li remembers. "I didn't know the high, so I didn't *know* I was high. But I noticed I kept talking more. I was more friendly towards people. Usually I'm kind of quiet. It made me feel happy, you know, and it made me want to work more— harder and faster, too. I was stocking shelves like a banshee. I was *really* stocking those shelves. Great rows. Perfect balance. I really concentrated. I hardly took any breaks."

Soon, Li bought his own pipe. You can get one at any number of head shops or Korean liquor stores on the island. At the Korean stores, you have to ask for a "liquid-incense burner." If you say "pipe," they pretend not to understand. For the next six months, Li smoked crystal before work at least four or five times a week. A week's worth cost him only about thirty dollars. It is an easy drug to do no matter where you are. You put it in the pipe, heat, smoke. When you're done, the liquid cools and recrystallizes, sticks to the bottom of the pipe. You can just stash it in your sock and go—being careful that it's cool first (many ice users suffer burns in this fashion). The pipe stays loaded and ready. Nobody at work could really tell that Li was high on drugs. He just seemed garrulous and happy. He got his work done. He was a model employee.

Unlike cocaine, which requires a re-administration every fifteen minutes, the feeling of high-energy well-being that Li got from smoking a few hits of ice lasted six to eight hours. Even so, as time passed, taking hits off the pipe became his main preoccupation.

Smoking is a sensual exercise: the flame, the bubbles, the swirl. It was something he just kept thinking about, something he wanted to do again and again. At work, he started taking more and more breaks. Between breaks he'd think about the next break. Outside of work, all he ever wanted to do was smoke or visit people who smoked. In the beginning, ice makes you want to share. In time, you become increasingly paranoid and isolated.

Li would stay up for three or four days and then crash. As he was coming down, his mind would race and his heart would pound, armies marching through his brain. Then, just as he'd start settling down, an odd electric jolt would run through his body, and he'd be up again, wide awake. Finally, he'd sleep, fifteen to twenty hours at a time.

Then he'd wake up and smoke some more, usually before he got out of bed.

A year passed. Li lost thirty pounds. His eyes looked sunken. His skin turned greenish yellow. He started calling in sick at work. He stayed in his room. "I'd start thinking about what's broken around the house, how to fix it," he says. "Sometimes I'd actually fix something. Most times I'd just think how to make things. Things just for the drugs. A better pipe. Or trying to make something to hold the pipe in my car, so that it only took one hand to operate the lighter and the pipe."

Sometime during his second year of daily use, Li became convinced that the DEA had planted a speaker in his brain. "It's like, whatever I'd be doing, the voices would tell me what I was doing," he explains. "Like, they'd be narrating what I would be doing. It would be my thoughts; I'd hear it in somebody else's voice. Or I'd think something, and then the voices would say, 'I heard what you just thought!' It's like they were playing with me. They were always teasing me. *They.* I always say *they.* Sometimes you think it's your friends. Sometimes you think it's undercovers. Then I thought at one point that maybe it was this special agency that helped you get off drugs. I thought maybe my parents paid these people to trip me out so bad that I'd stop using."

Li was fired from his job. For the next two and a half years, he stayed home and smoked ice. When he thinks about that period of time, it's kind of like a movie he saw once, grainy and hazy, a shadow of memories. His parents knew what he was doing behind his closed door. He told them he was smoking ice because he didn't want them to think he was smoking crack—he didn't want them to worry. Since he'd worked for many years and always lived at home, he had a lot of money saved. He spent all of it on ice. He also exhausted a $5,000 line of credit he'd opened to restore an old Mustang he'd bought. He sold the Mustang. He ran his credit cards to the limit with instant cash advances.

"I heard the voices every single damn day for two or three years," Li says. "It was really bugging the shit out of me. The part that bugged me the most was thinking that my thoughts were being read. I actually thought that my parents and my friends could hear what I was thinking. I'd have fights with my parents and I'd say, 'You guys know what I'm thinking!' And they would tell me, 'No, it's just the drugs, talking.' And I would refuse to believe it. I'd be like, 'You guys are playing this game with me. Just tell me how you're doing it, and I'll quit.' All my friends noticed I was weird. They said they liked me better when I was straight. I agreed with them. I knew it was true. But what could I say? I liked the drugs."

Six months ago, the voices got so bad that Li finally agreed to get help. He stopped smoking, got some medication from a clinic. The voices went away. He got a custodial job. He spent a lot of time thinking about the past six years. Six years he'd done ice. It was like he'd missed this huge chunk of his life. All that time and money flushed down the toilet.

"Then you start thinking of the good times you had with your friends. You wish you could go through it again. You want to reminisce. It doesn't seem like bad memories. You can think of the hard times, but mostly it's only the good times you think of."

He managed to stay straight for three months.

Li raises his pipe and heats the bowl. The smoke swirls; he takes another hit. "I only do it once in a while now," he says. "Like maybe a couple of days a week, but not *every* day. It feels great. It's like a new high. I get the voices, but it's not strong like it used to be. I guess I've learned a lot so I can cope with it better now."

#

ICE IS A SMOKABLE version of crystal methamphetamine, essentially the same drug as the pep pills and speed of yesteryear, the crank of motor-cycle gangs and heartland dopers, the meth of today. What's different is the form: whole crystals; the method of ingestion: smoking; and the purity: about 90 percent. Manufactured with easily purchased, over-the-counter ingredients, ice ranges in color from translucent to milky white to yellowish brown. Fifty dollars buys one-tenth of a gram on the street, in papers or glassine envelopes. Coke sells at fifty dollars for one-half gram, but meth's high lasts much longer. Shipments of ice have been intercepted coming into Hawaii from Taiwan, Hong Kong, Thailand, the Philippines, and Korea, which law-enforcement officials say is the world's major producer. Ice is the fusion of two Asian traditions—smoking drugs and using amphetamines. It is called *shabu* by the Japanese, *hiroppon* by the Koreans, *yaamaa* by the Thais, and *batu* by the Filipinos.

Ice is not a drug that actually gets you "high." It doesn't make you drunk like alcohol or stoned like pot. It doesn't give you a rush, take you on a trip, or even bend reality. It in the beginning, before the toxic effects build up, the thing that ice does is make you feel bright, awake, and happy. You feel good about yourself, no matter how bad things may be. You can work and produce on ice. You don't care anymore that your job is boring or that your boss is a schmuck. You see the goodness in others.

You see your place in the universe and the golden possibilities of things to come. Just a few hits of ice and all is well.

Housewives become superwomen, finding more time and energy to handle kids, job, marital duties, and still have time for themselves. Adolescents say that ice makes them feel secure, well adjusted, and better able to express their inner feelings. Truckers, accountants, store clerks, hotel and restaurant workers, data processors, mechanics—mainstream, middle-class Americans—say they do it to help overcome the malaise of daily life, because it helps them accept who they are.

In time, however, the long-term effects of meth begin to kick in. Rick, a maintenance man, heard Samoan war drums and was convinced someone was out to kill him. He turned himself over to the police to avoid assassination. Connie, a messenger, believed her body was covered with bugs. She went so far as to call the health department and have her whole house fumigated. Jack went outside several nights a week and rammed his truck into the trash cans in his driveway. Derek, a data programmer, also thought he had a DEA implant. He used *his* to contact famous men like former General Motors honcho Lee Iacocca for discussions about corporate management. Jasmine, the manager of a fast-food restaurant, spent hours cleaning her kitchen floor with a toothbrush. Tommie, a truck driver, heard voices from random speakers he would pass—the PA system at a used car lot would taunt him. The radio in his truck would be turned to the off position, but somehow it would still call his name. Auditory hallucinations, so chillingly real.

Ice affects people the way it does because of its similarity to a group of natural chemicals in the brain called sympathomimetic amines. These amines, which include norepinephrine, epinephrine, and dopamine, function as neurotransmitters, the chemical facilitators of human reactions and feelings.

Amphetamines cause the release of these chemicals into the brain and body. The physical effects depend upon the user, the environment, the dose, the purity, and the method of administration. With small doses, users experience increased blood pressure, slower heart rate and weaker heart contractions. With greater doses, heart rate and force of heart contractions accelerate. Other effects include dilated pupils, light sensitivity, blurred vision, and dry mouth, as well as increased breathing rate and muscle tension.

Users also feel fidgety and anxious. They enjoy repeating simple tasks over and over, like stringing beads, playing darts, cleaning bathroom tiles. In the beginning, before reaching a toxic state, ice users feel euphoric and alert. They feel powerful, confident, uninhibited, impulsive, and horny. Men experience easy and durable erections. Orgasms for both sexes are delayed and intense. Often, users think their performance on the job has improved, and sometimes their ability to carry out simple manual tasks may actually be greater. Usually, improvement is delusional. You just *think* you're doing more. You're manic. You're *into* it.

After a time, the brain becomes flooded with dopamine. The resulting chemical imbalance is the same as noted in the brains of paranoid schizophrenics. In fact, researchers first began understanding schizophrenia when they applied the medical models developed through the study of "speed freaks" in the 1960s. Like schizophrenics, ice addicts can be treated with drugs such as Thorazine and Haldol; some patients continue to hear voices for as long as six months after quitting. As the acute symptoms of addiction set in, the intensity, efficiency, and euphoria vanish. Users need larger and larger doses just to feel well.

Smoking is the fastest method of drug delivery. Inhaled into the lungs, the amphetamine is absorbed immediately into the bloodstream through millions of tiny vessels. The blood then flows into the left side of the heart, where it is pumped into the brain. When injected, the drug travels from the vein through the body, to the right side of the heart, to the lungs, to the left side of the heart and then to the brain. This way, the drug takes longer to kick in, but users experience a more intense rush. When ice is smoked, there is little or no rush.

Ice may cause the arteries in the heart and brain to shrivel. Pulmonary edema, an excess of fluid in the lungs, has also been seen, as have strokes and cerebral hemorrhages. Early reports show that ice use by pregnant women causes decreased blood flow to the fetus, resulting in underdeveloped limbs, organs, and brain. The long-term effects of ice are not known.

#

Two years ago, before she tried ice, Carol Gomez was twenty-six, married, the mother of three kids. The Hawaiian-born daughter of a hard-working immigrant Filipino stevedore, she'd married at fifteen.

When her eldest child reached eleven, Carol was still young. She wanted to start a career. With the support of her husband, a hotel bellman, she got a job at a pizza restaurant. In a year she became assistant manager.

Carol loved her job, but the schedule was hectic. She was working late one night, trying to finish the books, worrying about what her husband was going to say, worrying about who was going to feed and bathe the kids. When her manager came in the office, she told him her predicament. "Try this," he said. "Just take one hit."

Carol remembers: "I was trying to be Superwoman: do the dishes, wash the clothes, raise the kids, go to work, come home, cook dinner, do the paperwork I brought home. So I started hitting the pipe. I felt really productive. I got things done. It was like an answer to everything."

Things went well for six months. Carol was promoted to manager with a salary of $40,000 a year. She worked harder, smoked more. "We were short-handed, so I started doing all the jobs myself," Carol says. "After a while, the drug started coming into the workplace. Everybody in management was doing it. I got really frustrated with everything. I kept thinking, 'I need that pipe, I need that pipe.' But really, it was making me more confused, more frustrated.

"One thing I noticed about this drug was that it brings out the feelings—the worst part of you. In the beginning, it brings out the best part. But when you have no sleep for four days, your mind and body get out of sync. You can't function. I always had my pipe in my sock. I'd go to the bathroom, take a hit, do more work. I started to get very unorganized. Before, I was very organized, a good delegator. But after a while, my assistant manager had to take hold of me. She'd say, 'Forget this, do that! No, do this! Don't forget that!'

"When you're a manager, you hear everybody's sad story. I started feeling for those sad stories. All my employees were on the stuff. They were having problems with their husbands or wives or boyfriends. I started to counsel them. I would tell them, 'This drug is bad, you should get off of it,' and then I'd go into the bathroom and do another couple hits."

Inevitably, Carol's husband started doing ice. Her brother and sister-in-law moved into her house—they were also using and selling. Everyone they knew was smoking. There was fighting, stealing, hoarding, power play, shifting alliances. Home was a nightmare. One night, Carol called the cops and had her husband arrested. "I got to a point where I wanted to die because nobody heard me," she says. "I wanted my husband to be my friend, to try and listen to me for once. I was crying out for help in the worst way, and at that point I couldn't even help myself. He couldn't help himself either, but I started blaming him. Blaming everybody but me.

"Then one time my oldest kid got me real mad, and I gave him one good uppercut—I hit him right in the jaw. I don't even remember the reason. I was so hyped up, you know? I never really listened to what was going on around me. I was just lost in my thoughts, always lost in my own thoughts. This one time my son just did something, and, I don't know, this rage just came out. I plugged him."

That night, filled with remorse, Carol gathered up all the pills in her house and swallowed them. She was ready to die.

"Somehow, by a miracle, I woke up the next morning. The radio was on. The first thing I heard was this, like, public service announcement. *If you have to wake up and hit that pipe, you're an addict.* I heard it and I got up. I looked at myself in the mirror. It was true, I was an addict. It never really occurred to me before. It just sneaks up on you."

Carol has been clean now for seventy-three days. She got help after another big argument with her husband—he'd threatened to go to court and have the kids taken away.

"A lot of people who do ice are in high-demanding jobs," Carol says. "In society today, so much is expected of you. Ice makes you feel more productive, helps you do things you want to accomplish. That's why people do ice. It makes you an achiever. It's the American way."

# # #

ICE, OR CRYSTAL METH, is one of a family of central-nervous-system stimulants called amphetamines. Some sources attribute the discovery of amphetamines to a German scientist in 1887; others to a Japanese in 1919. What is clear is that sometime around the turn of this century, pharmaceutical researchers figured out the chemical structure of the natural substance the brain manufactures to react to stress and synthesized it in the lab. Amphetamines are copies of the brain's natural stimulant.

It wasn't until 1932 that any practical use for amphetamines was discovered. That year, the drug company Smith, Kline and French marketed a Benzedrine inhaler for treatment of lung congestion, asthma, colds, and hay fever. As people discovered the euphoriant effects of Benzedrine, the first abuse of the drug began. By breaking open the inhaler and pouring a soft drink over the drug-impregnated filter paper inside, users could extract the basic amphetamine. The manufacturer soon changed to a different chemical that did not have a stimulant effect on the brain.

Over the next decade, despite isolated instances of abuse, amphetamines became known as a kind of universal tonic. The drug industry developed a list of thirty-nine generally accepted uses for amphetamines, including treatment of schizophrenia; morphine, codeine, and tobacco addiction; heart block; head injury; infantile cerebral palsy; radiation sickness; low blood pressure; sea-sickness; and persistent herpes.

The drug was promoted as nonaddictive. Amphetamine derivatives, such as methamphetamine, were developed in both oral and intravenous preparations. A warning was included with the drug, indicating that doses higher than recommended might cause restlessness and sleeplessness. Physicians at the time, according to the literature, were sure there were no significant side effects. In 1937, amphetamines were used in the treatment of hyperactive children, Parkinson's disease, depression, and narcolepsy. When narcolepsy patients reported a loss of appetite, it was discovered that amphetamines also worked as an anorexic, an appetite depressant for weight loss.

World War II saw heavy use of amphetamines. According to the National Institute on Drug Abuse, 200 million amphetamine tablets were distributed to U.S. troops during the war to "increase activity in battle and to stave off hunger and sleep," according to a government report. The drug was also distributed by the British and Germans, as well as the Japanese, who also made amphetamines available to industrial workers at home to enhance output. Left after the war with large stores of the drug, Japanese pharmaceutical companies mounted a publicity campaign aimed at the general public, suggesting that speed would help ease the sorrow and depression of the lost war. This led to the first documented reports of amphetamine abuse in Asia.

To avoid the need for a prescription in the post-WWII United States, millions of units of amphetamines were still sold by drug companies to shady entrepreneurs in care of post-office boxes. From there, amphetamines found their way into diners, taverns, and gas stations. Known as bennies or pep pills, they were used by college students, athletes, truckers, and housewives, in addition to the thousands of veterans who returned from the war with amphetamine habits. The earliest incidence of intravenous abuse of amphetamines was found among American GIs stationed in Korea and Japan in the early 1950s. The soldiers learned to mix the drug—then called splash—with heroin and inject the combination. This came to be known as a speedball. Over time, all amphetamines became known as speed.

In the early 1960s, doctors in San Francisco began prescribing amphetamine injections for treatment of heroin addiction. Widespread abuse followed as San Francisco pharmacies began selling injectable amphetamines without prescriptions, or with crudely forged prescriptions, or sometimes through bogus telephone orders from users posing as doctors. This era also saw the advent of "scrip-writers," crooked physicians who would write out a script for the right price.

Soon after, federal, state, and local law-enforcement agencies cracked down on speed. Drug companies withdrew their liquid, injectable products from general distribution, though the products remained available to hospitals. To capitalize on the lucrative market abandoned by legitimate producers, illegal meth labs cropped up all over the Bay Area.

The height of 1960s speed abuse began with the Summer of Love, in 1967, when thousands of teenagers left home and thumbed to Haight-Ashbury, looking to get in on a new age of sex, drugs, and rock 'n' roll. At first, pot and LSD were the drugs of choice for the masses of flower children; there was little speed and little violence. As kids arrived in increasing numbers, the original flower children—who saw drugs as a path to love, peace, and mind expansion—were overrun by the newcomers. These new kids were willing to try anything they could get their hands on. The speed labs met the need.

The popularity of speed was abetted, historians say, by the tenor of the anti-marijuana and anti-LSD campaigns that were being mounted at the time by the federal government. So bogusly *Reefer Madness* in tone, the public service announcements made outrageous claims—one ad claimed that using LSD would cause chromosome damage, resulting in mutant babies. A study of the Haight in 1967 by two psychiatrists concluded, "The horrible reactions to marijuana and LSD predicted by various authorities were virtually never seen. The runaways generally took this to mean that all the widely advertised dangers of drugs were establishment lies. This further alienated them from the social structure and made them more willing to experiment with all sorts of chemicals."

The hippie "establishment" launched its own campaign against speed, anchored by the memorable slogan "Speed Kills." Beat poet Allen Ginsberg told the *L.A. Free Press*, "Let's issue a general declaration to all the underground community, *contra speedamos ex cathedra*. Speed is antisocial, paranoid making, it's a drag, bad for your body, bad for your mind, generally speaking, in the long run uncreative, and it's a plague in the whole dope industry. All the nice gentle dope fiends are getting screwed up by the real horror monster Frankenstein speed freaks who are going around stealing and bad-mouthing everybody."

Despite the work of Ginsberg and anti-speed warnings from the likes of the Beatles, Timothy Leary, and Frank Zappa, the use of amphetamines continued to grow. According to a report by a Canadian commission, the slogan Speed Kills "may, paradoxically, have carried more attractive than deterrent power."

###

BUCK IS SEVENTEEN, a tenth-grader. His parents are of Hawaiian descent. Danny is sixteen, a ninth grader. His parents are second-generation Japanese. Well dressed and handsome, they are sitting at a picnic table under the shade of a banyan tree. Like most teenagers here, they speak with a singsong accent, littering their sentences with pidgin, the local dialect. They sound a little like Jamaicans, little more sing than song.

"Usually when I buy the ice, I buy 200 bucks' worth," Buck is saying. "I buy my whole paycheck, and what I do is break 'em down, make $50 papers. You sell some of the papers, make your profit. Then you get your stash for smoke, and you buy one more."

"Yeah, but some days you smoke the whole stash," Danny says.

"And the next day you're all broke," Buck says. "You're asking your grandparents for borrow money or something."

"You got to get that money," Danny says.

"What happens," Buck says, "is I'm high already, and I want more. I want to amp. I want to have a good one. Don't want to sleep for four, five days, a whole week. So you go to the other side of the island, *brah*. You rob houses. *Boom*. You pawn the stuff, you buy the drugs, you rent one hotel room, you smoke. Or, you know Levi jeans? A friend and I walk in the store, rip off five pairs, *brah*. You walk back in and return them. You don't even need the receipt.

"No *shiiit!*" Danny says.

"Especially around Christmas," Buck says.

"Really?"

"Then you get, like, one eight ball," Buck says, meaning 3.5 grams of ice. "If the three of us were smoking it, it would last one whole day and one night, and till the next day, *brah*, like until twelve o'clock, when you'd be needing more. You'd be scraping the pipe, using the Q-Tip, the piece of metal, anything you can think of to scrape out the pipe to get another hit."

"Drugs is *fucked*, man."

"You be doing it *every* day."

"Every *fucking* day."

"Me and my radio, my six-pack, my pipe," Buck says.

"Everything all set, then you enjoy," Danny says.

"You cruise."

"You call up one *chick*." Danny says. He grins large.

"Let's party," Buck says. He is grinning too.

"And then, when you're up for a couple of days, a week, you can't even move."

"You sit down and phase."

"You can't walk."

"You don't want to do shit," Buck says. "You just want to smoke some more and smoke some more and just stay awake. You want to sit there with a gun and watch the windows."

"You think, 'Fuck this drug, I can quit, I can stop,'" Danny says. "But then you jus' don't want to. You like it too much."

"Everything is drug-related. All you talk about is getting it, dropping it off, getting money, finding a safe place."

"You stop going to school. You neglect your family. It's like you have no morals."

"Just to get that high."

"It's your life, *brah*, and you don't even give a fuck."

7
Kobe Bryant Doesn't
Want Your Love

THE BALL TRACES a high arcing parabola through the air; Kobe Bryant bobs in place on the balls of his feet, holding his pose, frozen for a split second in his brand new, Nike-issue, red-white-and-blue Zoom Kobe II's, size 16, made especially for international competition, his impossibly long, Pilates-sculpted arm, bark brown and moist and smelling of complimentary hotel lotion, still extended overhead like a kid raising his hand in class. The names of his daughters Natalia Diamante and Gianna Maria-Onore—he pronounces them with the proper Italian inflections, the *t* in Natalia more of a hardened *th* sound; the *r* rolled in Maria—are tattooed on the meat of his right forearm, which is now facing the basket, his wrist still holding its perfect gooseneck follow-through, a gesture at once so strong and so delicate, like something from ballet, and so essential, adding as it does the ball's backward rotation, the shooter's touch, which acts as a damper around the rim, helping to ensure that the 9.5-inch-diameter ball will fall with greater frequency through the 18-inch-diameter hole.

A few years ago, Kobe fractured the fourth metacarpal bone in his right hand. He missed the first fifteen games of the season; he used the opportunity to learn to shoot jump shots with his left, which he has since been known to do in games. While it was healing, the finger just adjacent to the break, the ring finger, spent a lot of time taped to his pinkie. In the end, Kobe discovered, his four fingers were no longer evenly spaced; now they were separated, two and two. As a result, his touch on the ball was different, his shooting percentage was down. Studying film, he noticed that his shots were rotating slightly to the right.

To correct the flaw—or really, to learn to accommodate this tiny change in his anatomy that had upset the precision of his stroke, honed over countless hours over the course of his twenty-nine years, on countless courts and playgrounds from Italy to Philadelphia to Los Angeles— Kobe spent the summer in the gym, making one hundred thousand shots. That's one hundred thousand shots *made*, he explains: He doesn't practice *taking* shots—he practices *making* them. If you're clear on the difference between the two ideas, on the ramifications of the differing mindsets, you can start drawing a bead on Kobe Bryant, who may well be one of the most misunderstood figures in sports today. It is a tragic misunderstanding, for his sake and for ours. You can blame it on the press. You can blame it on the way the world revolves around fame and money. You can blame it on Kobe himself.

Unbelievably, the youngest-ever all-star in the NBA is about to begin his twelfth season. Lately, somewhat grudgingly, people are beginning to acknowledge him as the greatest all-around player still active in the game, mentioned as a peer of Wilt Chamberlain, Larry Bird, and Michael Jordan. This year, Kobe will make upwards of $45 million from salary, endorsements, and business ventures. He is constantly in the news, usually on the wrong side of public favor as he continues to play for a once glorious team, the Los Angeles Lakers, that is working its way back again into prominence. Spending five days with Kobe—a dozen hours, really, spread over five days—is to glimpse the life of a highly skilled craftsman. He sees his work as his art, his calling. Like Jason Bourne and James Bond, two of his cinematic heroes, Kobe sees himself as an uber-practitioner: a modern warrior able to solve any problem, able to train his way into dominance. He is the self-styled black mamba, the largest venomous snake in Africa, known for its speed, aggression, and striking ability. All those sweaty commercials for Sprite and Nike? Those were his idea. Film my workout, he suggested, that is the essence of me: the guy who guts it out on *every* rep. Kobe's logo, which you will hear more about in the coming years, is called the Sheath. It is drawn to resemble the sheath of a samurai's sword. The sword is the raw talent, Kobe explains, the sheath is the package it's kept in—everything you go through, your calluses and your baggage, what you learn.

"*Scito hoc super omnia . . . Tempus neminem non manet . . . Carpe diem,*" he proclaims in Latin (which he learned in elementary school in Italy, where he lived from age six to thirteen while his father played pro basketball) on the home page of his Web site, KB24.COM. "Know this above all else . . . Fully use every point, moment, and hour that you have. Time waits for no man . . . Seize the day."

He wakes up at 5:30 every morning to work out. He eats five times a day, a special diet, stressing not just the ingredients but the way they're cooked. He studies tape of past, present, and world players with the curiosity of a scientist in the lab. (As a kid, he used to study bubble-gum basketball cards in order to see which moves the players were showcasing and "which of their muscles were firing to make the moves happen.") He can look at a random still photo of himself making a particular shot from a game and tell you exactly when and where and what happened. He has spent hours at a time chasing tennis balls along the floor, running the same patterns again and again on an empty court to get his cuts right for the triangle offense, running steps, running suicides, running distance. After his first season as a pro, when he was the Laker's sixth man, his summer workouts stressed ways to keep himself mentally involved in the game so he could come off the bench ready to contribute. Before Phil Jackson was ever even mentioned as a possible coach, Kobe contacted Tex Winter, the godfather of the triangle offense, just because he was a student of the game and wanted to learn *everything*. In his first season without Shaq, he added fifteen pounds of muscle to handle the heavier workload he expected. The summer of 2007, he lost eighteen pounds, partially due to his need to watch his cholesterol (a family history of diabetes and heart disease) and partially to take some strain off his body in general and his knees in particular, which have been operated on several times, including once in Colorado—an ill-fated trip undertaken with life-altering results, more on which later.

According to his specifications, Kobe's shoes have been designed with a special alloy band inside the arch to cut, he believes, hundredths of a second off his reaction time. For the same reason, he's asked Nike to design a sock-and-shoe system for him, maybe something like pro soccer players have. That fraction of a second he loses when his foot slides inside the shoe is the time it takes him to blow by a defender, he says. When he ices his knees, he ices the backs as well as the fronts, something that is usually not done because it takes more time. He has also asked Nike to design a new kind of warm-up that will wick heat away from his knees and thus enhance recovery time; recovery time, he says with conviction, is the most important element of working out.

With one ball and one rebounder, shooting his usual 80 to 90 percent in practice (with no defender), Kobe can make five hundred shots in about sixty minutes. Last year, as a result of all that practice, all those hundreds of thousands of makes, Kobe scored at least fifty points in four consecutive games and led the league in scoring for the second time. Two years ago, he turned in an electrifying eighty-one-point performance at home against Toronto, the second highest total on record, after seven-footer Wilt Chamberlain's hundred-point game (unlike Kobe's, all of Chamberlain's shots came from within fifteen feet of the basket). The reaction to Kobe and his achievements has been puzzling, as it has been since the beginning of his career, when he was voted into the All-Star game as a second-year player (he was the sixth man on the Lakers at the time) and then criticized for inciting an electric duel with the reigning king, Michael Jordan. Perhaps no figure in NBA history has been at once more respected and more reviled than Kobe Bryant.

Now, in the gym, the ball falls perfectly through the center of the iron rim, ripples the bottom of the net with a distinctive, thrilling *swish*. Kobe nods his head once, almost imperceptibly, as if to say, *That's what I'm talkin' about*, an expression he uses with exuberance when he's in private, when something catches his fancy, when something he believes is borne out. A picture of Kobe seldom witnessed: his perfect white teeth bared in the large carefree smile of a young man who loves watermelon and those yummy ice cream Kahlua drinks he and his wife had the other night for dessert at the restaurant in Las Vegas before seeing the show *Ka*, and who is lately in love with the Harry Potter series, which he read at a breakneck pace, trying to beat out his wife, the first books he's read since twelfth grade, when he became obsessed with the sci-fi thriller *Ender's Game*, about a specially bred boy-warrior who suffers greatly from isolation and rivalry but triumphs in the end.

###

THE DOORBELL CHIMES musically. Kobe and his party have arrived, a contained but complex weather system of youthful energy and expensive perfume.

Leading the way is the bodyguard, Rico, a soft-spoken man of unremarkable size. A former LAPD SWAT-team member with a background in martial arts, it is said that Rico (his first name is Cameron; nobody thinks it fits) is trained to hold off a surging crowd long enough for Kobe to get to safety. In a few days, Kobe will be off on a Nike-sponsored tour of Asia, six cities in seven days, where his apparel sells through at almost twice the normal rate and where surging crowds are actually a threat. Worldwide, Kobe apparel outsells that of all other NBA players: The undisputed fact of his statistical dominance seems to outweigh the perceived negatives of his personal history—the aloofness and selfishness of his earlier career; the Colorado sexual-assault case that was dropped by prosecutors and the civil suit that was settled out of court; his pissing match with America's beloved clown-giant Shaquille O'Neal; his on-again, off-again insistence on being traded from the Lakers.

Jerry Sawyer is Kobe's marketing manager, six foot two with Malcolm X–style black-frame glasses and an enviable collection of vintage sneakers. His father managed boxers; one of them was Leon Spinks. Jerry carries two different communication devices in the pockets of his oversized shorts. He's one of the four pillars of Zambezi Ink, Kobe's mixed-media ad agency. Like record labels owned by rappers, Zambezi is Kobe's attempt to harness the means of production. Jerry also does a lot of other things for Kobe, from screening press contacts (like me) to dealing with charitable causes, like the After-School All-Stars, an enrichment program for needy kids in L.A., which we visited together one day with the predictable uproar (snapshot: a large cooking class of middle-school-aged black and Latina girls learning to make potato salad, wearing hairnets and plastic gloves and holding knives, screeching at the top of their lungs). Jerry was also charged with making sure that Kobe's black-and-white polka-dot polyester sport coat, custom-made for him by Gucci (as are many of his clothes; he sits at the dining-room table with his wife and chooses swatches), was pressed and delivered for this photo shoot, which is finally about to happen in this borrowed suite in the Wynn Tower on the

Strip in Las Vegas, where Kobe is playing in a summer tournament with the U.S. National Team, attempting to qualify for the Beijing Olympics. The Wynn is booked solid the entire month with basketball royalty—between the National Team and Michael Jordan's annual Dream Camp, anybody who is anybody is here, from Carmello Anthony to Spencer Haywood to the two Coach John Thompsons, senior and junior. The scene in the exclusive Tower lobby—stone Buddha, mirrored ceiling tiles, seven-foot men on blackberries, pampered women on overstuffed sofas surrounded by shopping bags—is something to behold.

Clutching tight to Kobe's hand is the former Vanessa Urbieta Cornejo Laine, twenty-five, she of the infamous $4 million purple makeup diamond. Kobe met Vanessa—and her mother, who was along as a chaperone—on the set of a video shoot for his rap album, an experiment in cross-marketing that came and went with little fanfare. (Note: Try Googling the lyrics of "K.O.B.E.," performed in duet with the model and TV personality Tyra Banks.) At the time, Vanessa was still a seventeen-year-old high school junior. Kobe himself was only twenty-one, a four-year veteran of the NBA. (You will recall, perhaps, that he took the pop singer Brandy to his own senior prom.) Criticized early in his career for holding himself separate from his teammates—while they were playing cards, going to clubs, and discussing child-support payments, Kobe was playing pay-per-view Nintendo and ordering room service—Vanessa seemed more his speed. A sheltered Catholic school girl from Orange County, she was as close to her family as he was to his; after residing with his own parents for two years, Kobe had only recently started living on his own. Vanessa had only recently begun booking jobs as a dancer and an extra on videos; she'd been discovered outside a hip-hop concert by a music producer, who'd been struck by her head-swiveling looks. Kobe tells me unabashedly that when he met her, it was love at first sight. They've been together every possible moment since. The first week, he flooded the administrative office at her high school with flowers for her; he'd pick her up after the bell in his black Mercedes, causing a stampede of lookie-loos.

Vanessa's dark beauty and silken, coal-black hair bring to mind the kind of idealized Mexicana frequently seen in tattoos sported by Latino gangbangers. She is known by some as Kobe's Yoko. I have seen her, purring and demure, at Kobe's side in her four-inch heels, her makeup and wardrobe obviously the work of someone with ample time and money on her hands, bringing to mind the image of a tower-kept princess before her mirror, primped to the last eyelash, the last curl, the last bangle. In public, she patiently endures the endless cell-phone pictures taken by all comers—who seem to be lying in wait around every corner, all the time—graciously thanking each person who tells her how beautiful she is: "You're so very kind," she will say, her smile royal and Splenda sweet. "Thank you so very much." And I have seen her go *off*—like a mother bear, like a cornered cat, like a streetwalker on D.C.'s notorious Fourteenth Street strip, zero to sixty in a snap of her manicured fingers, hurling a string of expletives outside the Lakers' dressing room at a fat guy who she perceived had been looking at her daughter in an inappropriate fashion. She might well own the record for the most *motherfuckers* in one sentence.

Kobe calls her *Mamacita*. He holds her hand everywhere they go. Sometimes he speaks to her in Spanish. Later this afternoon, when his fruit plate finally arrives, Kobe will ask her: "*Quieres un poquito de fruta, Mamacita?*" Kobe and Vanessa are teaching their kids Spanish and English. Sometimes, Kobe throws in some Italian, too. He'll say *mangia*, for instance, telling them to eat. Natalia, four, known as Nani, will look at him like he's crazy. "You're not saying the *Spanish* word, Daddy," she will chide. Nani, of course, is tall for her age. Kobe's older sister, with whom he is very close, is six two. Kobe's mother, Pam, as long as we're doing this, is five ten. His father is six nine. Joseph Washington "Jellybean" Bryant, a product of Philly and La Salle University, left college early for the NBA through the "hardship draft," after showing financial need. He was nick-named for his love of sweets. (He named his son after the pampered Japanese beef: Kobe Bean Bryant.) The rap on Joe is that Kobe didn't get his work ethic from Joe's side of the family. Joe was known as a show-boat. He played eight years in the NBA, four with his hometown Philadelphia 76ers, who stuck him under the basket in their old-school, East Coast-style offense. Jellybean thought of himself as more of a Magic Johnson-type playmaker who was being held back from achieving great-ness. In Italy, he finally became the player he dreamed of being, high scoring (he had two fifty-plus point games) and beloved; Kobe remembers the fans singing songs about his dad.

When Kobe was a toddler, he'd put on his little Sixers uniform and watch his dad on television. At home in the living room, Kobe would pre-tend to play in the game, mimicking his dad's moves, taking time-outs for

water when the team did. As Kobe got older, he would end up playing for
the same Italian club team as his dad, only in a younger division, wearing
the exact same game uniform for real. Frequently, Joe would bring Kobe to
his own practices. At age eleven, a team from Bologna tried to buy Kobe
from his parents. By thirteen, he was beating his dad's teammates in games
of one-on-one. Kobe's daughter is athletic, he can already tell. Nani is playing soccer, a game Kobe still loves. (He picked his U.S.A. team number, 10,
because it was the number of his favorite soccer players: Pele, Maradona,
Ronaldinho.) Usually, when he plays games with Nani—the younger, nick-
named Gigi, is only eighteen months—Kobe lets her win. Occasionally, he
goes ahead and beats her at something. He's noticed she plays a lot harder
the next time around. His daughters' all-time favorite game is something
called Tickle Man. As you might expect, it involves Daddy.

This weekend, with the Tickle Man in Vegas playing his own big boy
game and Mamacita here to keep him company, the girls are home in their
big house in guard-gated Ocean Ridge, near Newport, California, being
watched by Vanessa's mom, Sofia Laine. Vanessa's mom and her birth
father divorced when she was a baby, after which he returned home to his
native Baja, Mexico. Sofia and Vanessa moved into her sister's spare room;
she went to work as a shipping clerk at an electronics firm. Eventually, she
met and married Stephan Laine, eight years her junior, a middle-manager
at the firm. That began Vanessa's middle class upbringing in Orange
County. Not long after Vanessa learned she was pregnant with Kobe's first
child, Sofia Laine filed for divorce. Her estranged husband told the *LA
Times* that Kobe and Vanessa had lavished his wife with so many surprise
gifts—a house full of furniture, a Mercedes-Benz S-500; $120,000 in
cash; payment of phone, dental, and credit card bills; payoff of their
mortgage—that he began to fear his wife's respect for him was crumbling.
Robert Laine, Stephan's elderly father, told the *Times*, "All of a sudden, it
wasn't 'What does Steve want for dinner?' It was, 'What does Kobe want?'"

In Kobe's estimation, his mother-in-law "is the best. She's a huge
sports fan. We can sit down and watch basketball, boxing, football—she
loves all that stuff." Kobe and Vanessa have lived in the Newport house
since their marriage in 2001. It is not publicly known whether it is still
decorated, as was earlier reported, with his *Star Wars* memorabilia and her
Disneyana. Presumably, it is big, with a lot of kids' stuff everywhere. The
Bryants are proud to say they do not employ a nanny.

After much discussion with the hotel's management, the photographer, Nigel Parry—an affable Brit known for his stunning black-and-white pictures—managed to secure this suite for a photo session. Once the date was set with Kobe's people, Jerry e-mailed *Esquire's* photo editor, saying that Kobe needed to have his own stylist for the shoot and that Vanessa Bryant would fill that role. *Esquire* assented, offering Vanessa its standard $250 payment. Jerry countered with a request for "a more typical" rate, somewhat higher. After a bit more back-and-forth, a compromise was happily achieved.

Now, upon arriving in the suite and making everyone's acquaintance, Kobe and his crew set about their first order of business: ordering the aforementioned fruit platter. Vanessa, who has asked to be identified as Lady V in the photo credits, dives right in, voicing her concern with Nigel's choice of black and white for the photos. As it happens, she has picked out a wardrobe of black-and-white clothes—prints on prints, everything custom Gucci, even the lizard-skin shoes—all of it to be dramatically offset by the red paisley on a Neiman Marcus one-hundredth-anniversary tie. "The brown seamless has gotta go, too," she tells Nigel, referring to the backdrop that he and his three assistants have so painstakingly raised, the particular shade no doubt an important element of his art. She turns and addresses her husband. She is obviously livid. "Did you know this was going to be black and white?"

For one long moment, the room becomes very still. We all look toward the big man. At six six and 207, Kobe dwarfs most of us by nearly a foot. On the court, however, next to the rest of his U.S.A. teammates—huge specimens like Dwight Howard, six eleven and 265— he appears to be somewhat small and wiry, almost delicate.

Kobe regards his wife intently. "I didn't know that," he says, a neutral tone. "I did not know that."

"It *needs* to be color," she says with conviction. "Otherwise, we can't see the *red* in the tie."

"Can you shoot both?" Kobe asks Nigel. His voice is deep, up from subbasement. The accent is a blend of foreign vowels and put-on Ebonics (he was brought up speaking proper English and Italian in wealthy enclaves).

"We can shoot both," Nigel says.

Lady V is not convinced. "You do *have* color, right?"

"Ain't no big deal," Kobe says, sweet but preemptively, raising his chin, exposing the large escarpment of his Adam's apple just beneath. "It's all good," he sings.

And so it is. With help from Vanessa and Jerry, Kobe gets dressed and into a seated position in front of the brown seamless. Nigel and his assistants go to work, the flash pops, followed by the electric whine of the recharger. Lady V chooses a couch off to the side. I stand next to her, so as to be close. I don't think Nigel likes us being in Kobe's line of sight, and for that I apologize. My first duty is to my audio, the little tape recorder in my hand, sprockets turning.

"That looks really sexy," Lady V says. *Pop. Whine.*

"I only have two facial expressions," Kobe muses. "Smiling Kobe and Intense Kobe."

"Not much of a range, there, huh?"

"Look smack-dead on to me," Nigel says. "Bring your eyes down." *Pop. Whine.*

"Not so fierce," says Vanessa.

"Fierce is good," Nigel says. "I like fierce."

"He's fierce in every photo! A little softer."

"She don't want me to be intense all the time," Kobe explains.

"Yeah, it's the same picture in every magazine. And at Nike. I love when he smiles."

"We're changin' it up over at Nike this time around," Kobe tells her. Yesterday, he had a meeting with Nike designers, his player rep, and his agent, Rob Pelinka, who played college ball with the NCAA Division I–champion Michigan Wolverines, on the same team as the Fab Five. (He was open on the wing at the moment Chris Webber called the fateful illegal time-out, or so the story goes.) At the meeting, they previewed Kobe's new fall line of apparel. Per his suggestion, it had a retro, old-school theme, circa *Yo! MTV Raps.*

"You should see these shirts they made," He tells his wife. "One of 'em looks like it comes with a complimentary *bong!*"

"Yeah?" she says, a little unsure.

"It's got some pink-and-green checkerboard and shit." Big smile—he's actually telling the truth.

"That's it," says Nigel. "That's awesome." *Pop. Whine.* "You *do* have a great smile."

"This is the Kool-Aid smile," Kobe says, adjusting the jellybean-sized ruby he is wearing as a solitaire in his left ear.

"*Awwww,*" Vanessa coos. "That's like the pictures we have at home. I love it when he smiles." The look on her face says that she has been smitten all over again by her man.

"By the way," Kobe says, keeping the game going. "They made me a pink tracksuit."

"Oh no, they did *not,*" exclaims Vanessa, her tone straight out of O.C., her head swivel straight out of Compton.

A deep voice, musically: "Oh yes, they *did.*"

"What *shade* of pink?" she challenges.

"I don't know. Pink. Dusty pink."

"Like mauve? Or like bubble gum?"

"Bubble gum," he declares, enjoying himself. The Nike rep had sold it to him as a manly "dusty-gray-pink." He flashes a huge and untroubled smile.

"That's nice, excellent," Nigel says. "Now: No smile. Intense."

"Like when you're looking at Nani and Gigi," Vanessa says.

"But I can't help smiling when I look at them."

"Like when you're fixing one of their boo-boos."

"That's right," says Nigel. *Pop. Whine.*

"I forgot to tell you," Vanessa says. "Nani spilled some Kool-Aid on the couch today. She told me when I called. She said, 'Mami, I have to tell you something. Grandma gave me Kool-Aid and I spilt it on your couch.'"

Annoyed: "The white couch?"

"My mom says she got it out 'cause she was quick. My mom was like, 'I *told* her not to.' You know, she's not allowed to take any juice in there. But give her credit. Nani told me herself what she did, thank God. I'm like, 'I appreciate your honesty, Nani. Don't do it again.'"

"Man, I wish they were here," Kobe says wistfully. "They'd be running around this whole place. Nani is such a poser," he tells Nigel proudly.

"Yeah?" Nigel asks, a bit distracted. It's easier to take portraits when people aren't talking so much.

"She'll do a million different poses for you," Kobe says.

"That's nice," Nigel says. *Pop. Whine.* "Would you mind taking your jacket off?"

"Nope," Kobe says without hesitation.

"Nope," Lady V reiterates.

"Huh?" Nigel asks, taken aback. He looks from Kobe to Lady V and back again.

"No go," confirms Kobe, a command tone. He cuts his eyes to his wife, who nods her head once, almost imperceptibly, as if to say, *That's what I'm talkin' about.*

And then the doorbell chimes musically. The fruit plate has finally arrived.

#

TWO DAYS LATER in Kobe's suite, the thirtieth floor. Mamacita is gone, whether out shopping or gambling or back home with the girls, it is not for me to know. Kobe drags a barstool over to the living room, where there are two plush and fabulous sofas and a coffee table, so as not to have to bend his knees so acutely when he sits down. When you're six foot six and chronically suffering pain, low grade or otherwise, the world can be a very cruel place. "Ain't gettin' any younger," he explains.

Yesterday, a Sunday with no scheduled Team U.S.A. practice, Kobe went to the gym and made five hundred shots. With two balls and two rebounders, he managed to do it in one hour, stopping only long enough to chat with Indiana's legendary coach Bobby Knight. They'd never met before; Kobe was overjoyed. By all accounts, he looked like a kid meeting Kobe for the first time. Then last night, in another Tower suite, he spent two hours signing nine hundred autographs for the Upper Deck company—a feat made all the more difficult by the heavy "camera pen" that documents the execution of each numbered signature. (Among the items offered: a limited edition of 124 Kobe-inscribed, laser-engraved basketballs for $699.99 each.) This morning, he was supposed to be up early working out and doing Pilates, but he canceled.

"You get to the point where you learn to listen to your body and make adjustments from there," he explains. He speaks of his physical self in terms of a finely tuned machine, which of course it is.

I sit on the sofa. He is on the barstool. It is awkward; I feel like I'm sitting at the foot of the Lincoln Memorial. I drag another barstool over to the living room. Now I feel like I'm doing a talk show, with Rico the bodyguard as our audience, sitting quietly in a corner. Kobe is warm and chatty. I've been around awhile; he has become accustomed to me—though I was still not allowed to ride in a car with him or to be with him alone or to spend any unstructured time with him at all. But at least now he's *feelin'* me, as they say in the L. The other day, at the photo shoot, by way of jocular greeting, Kobe's big open palm suddenly whipped down from on high and slapped me pretty hard in the solar plexus. "What up, Mikey?" he said playfully. Luckily, I flexed in time to avoid getting the wind knocked out of me.

For the next ninety minutes, we talk. About how he loves sharks and would like to go down in a shark cage, and how he would like to skydive, both after he retires. How, as an adolescent, he grew so fast that he had horrible Osgood-Schlatter disease—it was so bad that it hurt when someone even so much as breathed on his knees. How he just bought an Akita to go with his two Pomeranians. How having untrained dogs should be a crime, a form of abuse. How Michael Jordan has become a confidante and how his advice "is like getting advice from that Buddha that sits on top of the mountain, who has everything figured out and passes on some of his knowledge to the next guy who's trying to climb that mountain." How awed he felt one time in Taiwan in this big arena with five thousand screaming kids who had come just to see him run a little clinic. He remembers standing there thinking, *This is weird. This is just insane. I'm goofy. I'm silly. I play basketball.*

We talk about the philosophy of his logo, the Sheath. We talk a bit about baggage, how it's the place you store your energy. We also talk about his image in the league, how he got off to a bad start and never recovered. "When I first came into the NBA," he says, "I was one of the first to come out of high school. I was seventeen years old. At the time the NBA was much more grown-up. It wasn't like now. I was naïve. I thought that when you come into the NBA, you just play basketball all day. The thing I was most excited about was not having to worry anymore about writing papers or doing homework. It was basketball all day, this is awesome.

"The aloofness thing, honestly, I didn't really hear about it until later. A lot of it was just my youth again, because I didn't read the papers. I didn't watch, like, the news. I had no clue what was going on, what people were saying about me. It sounds silly to say, but it's true. And I think because of that, a lot of people looked at it like 'Woah, he must be arrogant.' But I didn't know what the hell was going on. I had a reporter one day come up to me and ask me about it, you know, 'People think you're arrogant, what's up with that?' And it absolutely just seemed to come out of left field. I was just like, 'What are you talking about?' And he was like, 'Haven't you read the papers?' From that day forward, I started reading the papers."

I ask him about Colorado, about the young woman there, the alleged rape. He starts to say something and then he stops himself, like maybe he wants to talk but knows he shouldn't. I push him a little bit. He laughs and shakes his head. "I'm not sure I can dive into that one without really *diving* into that one."

"Can you dive into some of it?" I ask.

There is a long silence.

"I . . . uh . . . hum," he says. "I don't know how to touch on that without really sayin'—you know what I'm sayin'?"

What about the whole thing with Shaq, about the whole thing with wanting to be traded from the Lakers?

"If I had to do it all over again, I just never would have said *anything* in the press," he says. "Some things need to remain behind closed doors. Do the fans really need to know everything? Do you need to know everything 'bout what goes on in your neighbor's house? Do you even want to?

"I just want to continue to push. To just become as good as I possibly can be, to see what other aspect of the game I can get better at. 'Cuz you know, it's fun. I just enjoy doing it. When you enjoy doing it, you wanna find out new ways to do it. Like the eighty-one game? I had worked extremely hard the summer before that. That game was a culmination of days and days of hard work. But the most important thing about that game—and I know it's going in the history books and all that—the best thing about that game is it feels good because we won. It was a tough one. We had lost, like, two or three games in a row; it was just a rough patch. And it was my grandfather's birthday, who had passed away not too long ago, and my grandma was at the game, and my wife and daughter were at the game, so it was special, yes. But to me, winning is everything. That's the challenge, the ultimate challenge—how do you get to that elite level as a *group*? Right now, I don't care about points or any of that stuff. It's how do you get to that elite level and remain at that elite level as a unit. What are the things you need to do?

"You have to be open-minded and not be rigid. If you're rigid, that's weakness. All you can do is forget about the bad stuff and then move on. You just kind of roll with it, you just kind of learn. I will not make the same mistakes in the future that I have made in the past. I will make new mistakes, I am sure. And I will learn from them, too. You have to be fluid. Your body changes. As that happens, your moves need to change, your training program needs to change. You have to be able to adapt.

"I am going to work extremely hard. I'm not going to cheat the game. I am going to take all the steps and do all the work necessary. It's like, God blessed me with the ability to do this. I'm not going to shortchange that blessing. I'm going to go out there and do the best that I can every single time."

Kobe excuses himself to leave for Vegas's Thomas & Mack arena, a tune-up game for the impending twelve-day international tournament. Over the coming two weeks, Kobe and his U.S.A. team will outclass all comers, winning by an average of more than thirty points, clinching a berth in the Olympics, earning the once-proud U.S.A basketball team its first gold medal in international competition in seven years. And while Kobe will go off for twenty-seven points in the grudge match against Argentina, which won the gold in the last Olympics, throughout the rest of the series, he will distinguish himself with his leadership, his tenacious defense, his artful passing. In every game, he will ask to be assigned to play defense against the opponent's best scorer. He will hold Brazil's NBA standout, Leandro Barbosa, the tournament's leading scorer, to just four points. Kobe will also be among the leaders in minutes and assists. He will be the heart of Team U.S.A.

That's what I'm talkin' about.

Esquire, 2007

## 8

Thailand's Home for Wayward Vets

THE MOUTH AT THE BAR is John Murdock—chopper pilot, sandwich maker, tennis pro with one student, a resident alien of Thailand with corkscrews of chest hair and a gift for the grandiose. He's poking a hole in the air with his finger, and his quarter-pound Rolex is flashing, and his blue eyes are flaring, and if you didn't know he was in a bar in Patpong, in Bangkok, bathed in neon and reeking of beer, you'd be sure he was back in Vietnam in '68, Lieutenant Murdock, *Lieutenant Cocksure*, driving his U.S. Army Cobra down hard on a tree line, firing bursts of obscenities at some gooks.

"C'mon puss wad. I'll spot you thirty-love, two-to-one odds, and I'll still wipe your ass all over the court."

What he's doing is challenging Paul Jones, a British deep-sea diver, to a simple game of tennis. 'Nam comes up later, of course, after a few more Singha beers. Right now, the rap is all about green ones and red ones and purple ones, preferably purple ones, 500-*baht* notes, worth about twenty-five dollars each. Scam as art, art as life, life as "survival of the fittest, or it's on skid row for the kid," as Murdock likes to say in his too tight smile in his eighth month without a proper job.

But not without a plan. So what if no one's hiring chopper pilots at the moment. When you decide, as Murdock has, that there's a place to live that's better than America, you hustle to make sure it doesn't blow back in your face. Sure, he can always go home to the farm in Pomfret, Connecticut. But when you're thirty-eight years old and you've been in the States for only two weeks in the past ten years— when you've been telling everyone you ever knew that life in Thailand is a piece of cake for a vet, nothing like back in the States—you don't just show up at the airport one day with your trunk. No way. *You make plans, see. You use your head, you understand? You make it work.* You sell sandwiches here at the Grand Prix bar on Saturdays. You talk about finding investors, expanding into weekdays and burgers. You hear that a hotel chain is looking for tennis pros. *Shazam!* You become a tennis pro, so utterly convinced of your own prowess that you're ready to play anyone who'll put his *baht* where your mouth is. *Hey, I'm thinking of the future. I'm trying to make some money here. You can make a million bucks if you got the right angle. I can do anything. Anything, you understand? You just gotta line up the suckers and let it roll.*

"C'mon," he taunts, poking the finger again toward Jones, his tight, nasal, Connecticut Yankee honk rising an octave with the challenge. "You said you've been takin' lessons, right? One thousand *baht.* Two purple ones. *C'mon,* ya lousy limey, ya queen-mother lover."

Jones is watching the video screen sunk into the wall above them, the Grand Prix's 9:00 p.m. showing of *Dirty Harry.* He has a steady job, makes beaucoup bucks. He turns his head, fixes Murdock with a look, turns back to the video, takes a slug of his beer. *Fuckin' Murdock. Somebody needs to shut him down before he crash lands.*

Behind the bar, the owner of the Grand Prix shakes his head, an expression of mock pity. Rick Menard is a stocky ex-army aircraft mechanic with a patch over one eye, cataract surgery. He looks contentedly bored, polishing a glass, watching three of his Thai go-go girls dancing on the stage, meanwhile daydreaming about the kind of kitchen cabinets he's going to order for his new, two million-*baht* condo. Sex sells in Bangkok, the most aptly named city in the world; Menard is one of the ones making trips to the bank. The girls range from cream to mocha, with ebony hair and a certain perplexed innocence in their eyes, spangled bikinis on their boyish little bodies. They dance to Michael Jackson, humping in the back-beat with half a heart.

Next to Jones is another Viet vet; he says his name is Hamber Moody. He's on leave from his electronics job in Saudi Arabia. Black and lanky with a goatee, he goes on about "sand niggers," his exorbitant overtime pay, his growing savings account, his myriad "bitches." Next to him is a retired air force pilot, laying over in Bangkok on his way home to Tulsa. He also works in Saudi. One of the bar girls has her rump dug meaningfully into his crotch. The button pinned on her left bikini cup identifies her as Number 12.

The group sits together along the rail, not too far from the shithouse. Once upon a time, a man could get a blow job while taking a dump in any bar in Bangkok, or so they say. You can probably get one in the Grand Prix, but you'd have to arrange it yourself—there are no girls on permanent station in the loo. Then again, if that's what you really wanted, you'd probably have no trouble finding it within a short distance. This, after all, is Patpong—three square blocks of skin and sin, joints like the Pink Pig, the African Queen, the Sexy Bar. The night streets are nuts to butts with *farangs*—the derogatory Thai term for white folk—strutting and gaping, hunting for beer and pussy, man's most essential needs. There are girls on high chairs outside the doors of musky bars; wooden racks of American cigarettes; food vendors in bamboo hats with carts full of bubbling pots of mystery food; ragamuffins begging for one *baht*, selling flowers, asking for bonbons; little old Thai men hustling, imploring, handing out show bills for featured performances of the Pussy Smoke Cigarette Show, the Pussy Write Letter Show, the Pussy Drink Beer Show. Tinsel streamers on the lampposts, hot chili peppers, thumping disco and nonchalant lust in the air, a lawless tide of scooters and minicars and motor rickshaws on the narrow streets—a place where any man, no matter how old or fat or pockmarked, can be Hugh Hefner for an evening, as long as he has a couple of purple ones in his pocket. There may be loneliness in Bangkok, but no one is ever alone.

This is the nightly haunt of John Murdock and the Patpong Commandos, as the local *Soldier of Fortune* magazine correspondent likes to call the regulars. The U.S. Defense Department says there are 1,100 Vietnam-era veterans residing in Thailand. Patpong is their headquarters. Here is where you drink until your face goes numb. Here is where you find your love object of the evening. Here is your frat house, your locker room, your Elks club—Bangkok's home for wayward vets.

Here are the regulars—Murdock, Menard, and Al Dawson, news editor for the *Bangkok Post*, an army vet who stayed on with UPI news service after his hitch. Jack Shirley is part-owner of the Tavvern, another bar around the corner. Shirley says he worked, before retiring, as a "special adviser" to the governments of Thailand, Laos, and Vietnam, "attached to the U.S. Defense Department." Shirley's friend, Tony Poe, comes down occasionally from his tapioca farm. A former CIA man, Poe is said to have walked every mile of Laos on foot, to have killed uncounted numbers with his bare hands, the right of which is missing two fingers, lost in some unspeakable way. A guy called Book says he's a former navy SEAL. A huge man, with legs as wide as an average man's waist, he once bit off a guy's ear in a bar fight. "Then he spit it out on the floor and walked back to his stool like nothing had happened," Murdock says. Lurch is ex–Special Forces. One night, the record on the jukebox started to skip. "He pulled out a .38 and drilled the fucker six times," recalls Menard, who didn't bother handing him a bill for repairs.

L.T. "Cowboy" Edwards, retired air force sergeant, also hangs now and then, though mostly you'll find him in the New Loretta Café, his own bar across town on Sukhumvit Road, downing his daily ration of two six-packs of beer and two fifths of Johnnie Walker Black. Not too far from the Loretta is Soi Cowboy, a street named in Edwards' honor. Edwards likes to point out that only two other Westerners have ever been so distinguished: Red Cross founder Henri Dunant and country singer Bobby Dee. On Soi Cowboy you can find another regular, retired air force sergeant Josh Gaines, proprietor of J's Soul Food, purveyor of the finest fried chicken and salt pork and chitlins this side of North Carolina.

Farther upcountry, in the lush flatlands to the north, retired air force intelligence sergeant Doug Martin lives in a tiny and isolated village, a rice farmer with ten acres of paddy, two water buffalo, a Thai wife, and three kids. Father John Tabor, a former navy Seabee, remained in South Vietnam after his hitch to study for the Catholic priesthood. He fled the country in 1978, after being imprisoned by the communists for six months, and came to Thailand to work in refugee camps along the border. In Udonthani, 300 miles north of Bangkok, VFW Post 10249 boasts eighty members, a group of whom shows up every day to burp and fart and drink one another under the table before the sun goes down.

"Why do we stay?" repeats John Murdock, incredulous, super-animated as always, swilling another Singha beer. "It's the night life. It's the food, the climate, the lovely, lovely ladies. You gotta understand. 'Nam was a big fuckin' high. You remember what it was like. You don't want to live without that charge. You want to have something of that left. In some ways, living here, I still got it. I've stayed in the same line of work—flying choppers. I stayed in the same part of the world. 'Nam sucked, sure. But what a lot of people don't talk about is how much fun it was, too. There was a lot of good times with the bad, like when we were laying back in the hooch, drinking like hell, going downtown, sneaking out of the compound—'cause we had a little house of ill repute around the corner. Here we are. We're still in Southeast Asia—"

"We're just not in the army no more," Menard adds.

"We're not restricted within certain confines of what they call respectable behavior at home," Murdock says with a wink.

So what if Murdock sometimes hungers for a Big Mac or if Dawson would love a thick, juicy cut of prime rib. Or if Doug Martin, the rice farmer, can't plow his fields himself because his water buffalo doesn't like his smell, or if, after eleven years of marriage, he still can't get his Thai wife to sit down to dinner with him. And so what if *Monday Night Football* doesn't get to the Bangkok VFW post until three weeks later on a Thursday, or if the willing and seemingly demure Thai women have a scary reputation for taking razors to penises in fits of jealous rage—it is a fact that Bangkok boasts the world's most advanced penis reattachment clinic. So what if Menard felt like an idiot on his last visit to the States. Is it his fault a kid had to explain to him that the faucets in the bathroom at JFK airport turned off automatically? So what if Harry Reid, commander of the VFW post in Udonthani, where he plans to live until he dies, doesn't really like the Thai people he has to be around every single day, including his own wife.

So life isn't exactly perfect. So what? What life is? You think the guy on Long Island likes commuting into New York? You think the tractor doesn't break down in Bucksnort, Tennessee? Everybody's got his load to bear. At least it's cheaper here. At least there's opportunity. Where else but Thailand, asks Menard, could a high-school dropout aircraft mechanic purchase himself a two million–*baht* condo? Where else but Thailand, asks Josh Gaines, could the son of a mechanic and a maid have the one-and-only soul-food emporium in the entire country? Even Cowboy, a man with a healthy ego, has to admit that the chance of having a street in the States named after him would probably be slim. (He readily admits that only in Thailand could he divorce nine wives without paying a cent of alimony.) Where else but Thailand could Murdock have afforded a full-time servant on a sandwich maker's salary? Or purchase potent Thai stick at the equivalent of $100 a kilo? Where else would Harry Reid have risen to the rank of commander of his VFW post? Back in Columbus, Ohio, he settled for the number-three spot on his bowling team.

"For various reasons," Dawson says, "a lot of people here are doing much better than they could have ever dreamed in the States. Some of them aren't smart enough, some wouldn't have had enough money, or a combination of both. Some are not as frightened to try something bold in a country like Thailand. There's a bit of racism involved, maybe, a natural feeling of superiority between themselves and the little brown people running around . . . . Sure, there are some hard-luck stories. There's probably a good bit of escapism, too. But basically, it's a bunch of guys over here who think they just might have found a better way."

Welcome to Thailand—last frontier of the American Dream.

It was late 1966 when Doug Martin returned to the States from his first stint in Vietnam. Boy, was he ever glad to get home. He knew the war was lost before it started. He says he remembers being at a briefing in Saigon where Secretary of Defense Robert McNamara suggested that the United States collect all its junk cars, ship them to South Vietnam, and pile them up along the northern border. *Enough of this bullshit*, Martin thought. It was time for family and a regular job—a normal life.

But when he got home to Long Beach, California, his wife and kids were gone. No note, nothing. Just gone. His wife had always been a runner, that he knew. But to leave him with an empty house— The way his knock had echoed; he will never forget the wrenching hollowness of that sound. "She left me at a time when I really needed her. I was coming home from war, I was determined that we were going to make a go of it. I was looking forward to being part of a family again. It was all gone. I lost twelve years of marriage, my home, my wife, my children, my car, my clothes. Everything. It was worse than losing a leg.

"I don't know why, but as I was standing there in the empty living room, the first thought that came into my mind was that I wanted to go back to Southeast Asia. Maybe I had a death wish. I didn't think about it. I re-enlisted."

Martin went back to Vietnam, and then to Texas and to Hawaii. In 1973, he was assigned to Rammasson Air Force Base, a huge facility in Udonthani, Thailand, from which a great proportion of the heavy air strikes of the Vietnam war had originated. By this time, Martin had been in the service since 1953, when he'd run away from his doting mother and the family's resort lodge in upstate New York. Now he'd done his twenty. He was ready to go back to the States, maybe find a new wife, start a new family—try again.

Then his house girl announced she was pregnant. Martin was suspicious of the timing, but he decided to marry her anyway. Sumlee cooked pretty well, she didn't talk back, she kept the apartment clean. She *seemed* to be in love with him. He was forty and she was twenty, a good-looking girl for a middle-aged man. Why go home and start searching? He decided to stay in Thailand.

Udon in 1974 was bustling. Thirty thousand Americans, cheap outdoor restaurants on every sidewalk. There must have been 200 bars and clubs catering to GIs, and scores of hotels, with names like the 69 and the Coconut, which had vibrating beds and fountains and mirrored ceilings in every room. An American could have anything he wanted in Udon, from a ten-year-old virgin to a hamburger pizza. At its peak, GIs were said to be spending upwards of $400,000 a day in Udon, and some small part of that cash was going to Doug Martin, who was walking door to door in his brand new civilian suit, selling *Encyclopedia Britannica*.

Soon, Martin moved into Chryslers. He sold the cars to GIs, whitewalls gratis, ready for pickup from the factory as soon they got back stateside. When the Americans pulled out of Vietnam in 1975, Martin's business went with them. Next he tried a catalog export business, only to be bilked by his partner, who turned out to be a "gay crook," Martin recalls. He wandered through some consulting jobs and more crooked partners. In Bangkok he set up a travel agency in the back of a bar. His partner was a guy the Patpong regulars remember as Nick, a retired army master sergeant who'd enlisted during World War II in lieu of serving a murder sentence. Martin and Nick did well, specializing in discount airline tickets, illegal tiger hunts in India, visa extensions, things like that. Then the business was lost. Martin is vague on the details. Around Patpong, they say it had to do with the law.

Today, Martin farms ten acres of rice paddy in a tiny village called Nongkhai, his wife's ancestral home, about eight hours northeast of Bangkok. He is a graceful, kindly man with polished fingernails—imagine Felix Unger gone native, wearing a straw hat and drawstring pajama pants. He lives with his family in a green cinder-block house with a tin roof and a porcelain hole in the floor for a toilet, on a narrow lane of deep sand, rutted with ox-cart tracks, shaded by tall palms. During the day, children laugh and play everywhere in the village—there go four of them now, all under ten years old, riding together on the back of a water buffalo, a pair of pre-teens attending. Chickens and ducks are everywhere underfoot.

By night, the air outside his house is cool, alive with the chirps of bugs and the stirrings of the family's animals. A musical kite flies from the Buddhist temple, a talisman against lurking spirits. Inside Martin's house, the village's only refrigerator is humming, its only twenty-six inch television is blazing Technicolor. A dozen women have gathered at the threshold of the open first-floor of the house to watch the latest installment of their favorite Thai soap opera. The three Martin children play Monopoly with some neighbors in the middle of the cement floor. All the villagers call Martin "Daddy." He has big plans for them—if they'd only listen; they're kind of set in their stone-age ways. For instance, he's trying to convince the other farmers to grow hay instead of having to climb trees and hack up shrubs for livestock feed. He's trying to teach them to plant their rice in straight rows for a bigger yield, to use factory fertilizer, to buy cows for the milk, a scarce commodity in Thailand. An elected member of the village council, he has convinced the elders to buy xylophones and harmoniums for the children's marching brigade. He is respected by the villagers, liked by most. They all know that he receives his pension check during the second week of the month. And they all know that when they run out of rice just before the harvest, he will share what he has with them.

On this night, Daddy Martin is sitting off to one side of the throng, the only one occupying a chair—squatting as the locals do hurts his back.

He asks them in Thai to please turn down the volume of the television. He has enjoyed his life in Thailand, he says, his English a little rusty. He speaks with enthusiasm of his experimental garden by the side of the house. He has imported exotic seeds from catalogs. Unfortunately, the village kids like to take bites out of his guavas while they're still on the tree; the neighbors' ducks love the taste of the Italian basil his mother sent from the States. But his bananas and his mint are growing pretty well, and that gives him a solid feeling of accomplishment. The water buffalo are another problem. He's never been able to solve that one. Why won't they pull the plow for him? He's tried everything; even gone so far as to sell the old buffalos and buy two new ones—but those wouldn't plow for him, either. The village elders say it's the fish sauce—the traditional Thai fish sauce that everyone here uses like ketchup on everything. Fish sauce is made by burying a fish in the ground and leaving it there for several weeks to rot and ferment, a notion that is totally disgusting to Martin. Because he doesn't eat fish sauce, the elders say, he doesn't sweat fish sauce. Hence, the buffalo all think he smells bad. Or so they say. It could be they're fucking with him, but the upshot is this: His wife has to plow the paddies—and she's not one bit happy about it. She lets him know it in many ways, large and small. He has learned to endure. It all comes down to one thing, he says. "No matter what I do, I'll never be one of them."

Such is the nature of the expat life: Nothing's the same as home. Martin's imported tomatoes won't grow in the sandy soil. He misses pizza and golf. He has to take the bus eight hours to Bangkok to call his mother. When he listens to his music on his boom box—Frank Sinatra, Bing Crosby, Jo Stafford, Elvis—his head tips back and his eyes get misty. Village children are told that if they misbehave, they will be turned over to Daddy Martin, who will eat them. He doesn't really like Thai food; his wife still refuses to eat with him. In fact, Sumlee scarcely even *talks* to him—another confounding custom of Thai wives. During my unannounced, two-day visit, he welcomes me like a long-lost brother, talking nonstop from early morning to late at night, seeming to savor our English and male conversation the way he savors a tin of sardines I offhandedly gifted him one afternoon, a favorite from home that he hasn't tasted in years. Long after the TV has been turned off, the children put to bed, the bottle of whisky drained to half, Martin unburdens himself:

"If I had the money, if I had something more than my $600 pension to live on, I'd pick up everyone right now and go build a new life in the States. There wouldn't be a minute's hesitation. My feeling right now is that I've just got to get out of here. I am drying up mentally. I'm a man who likes to use his brain. It's much easier to use brain than brawn. I have a couple of books I would love to write. I just can't get anything going here. There's a mental factor involved about living here. Like the ducks that are eating my basil. Ordinarily, you'd just put up a fence. But if I did that, it would mean, in an offhand way, that I was complaining about my neighbors' ducks, and then they'd lose face.

"I have no role here. I can never be equal. No matter whether I speak the language like they do or farm the land like they do, I am still a permanent outsider. I am still a *farang*."

VFW Post 10249 is housed in the Golden Mountain Bar, in a suburb of Udonthani, four hours northwest of Martin's village.

The Golden Mountain is an oasis of Americana—*Sports Illustrated* posters on the walls, a library of English paperbacks on the shelves, a menu of burgers and hash browns and creamed chipped beef on toast. The soundtrack is Jimi Hendrix, Ella Fitzgerald, and Earth, Wind and Fire. Abraham Lincoln stares down from behind the bar.

The veterans gather here each noon to order up pint bottles of Mekong beer and pass the idle time of retirement, to fight against what post member Leroy Wilson likes to call "the one thing over here that will eventually kill us all—boredom."

Wilson is a retired air force environmental engineer. He is sitting at the bar with John Pough, retired air force technician. Harry Reid, the owner of the Golden Mountain and also the Post commander, has just finished wiping down the bar. Now he's organizing the cigarette display. Kenneth Wilson, also retired air force, has just walked in carrying a *Better Homes and Gardens* cookbook he borrowed from the library. The mailman can be seen through the patio service window, headed toward the bar.

"Here comes your check now, Harry," Leroy Wilson says, upbeat.

"That's funny," Reid says. "I'm not due to get it till tomorrow."

"Well, I got *mine* this morning."

"Really? Maybe this is it, then."

"Maybe it is."

The postman hands over the mail; Reid thumbs through. "Guess it didn't come."

"You'll probably get it this afternoon," Wilson offers.

"Do you generally get yours in the morning or in the afternoon?" Kenneth Wilson asks Leroy Wilson.

"Sometimes in the morning. Sometimes in the afternoon. It varies, I guess you could say."

The music plays. The men sip drinks and look out the window into the dusty street. They light cigarettes.

Reid pulls out a knife and a cutting board. He begins slicing limes. "I hear Sammy up in Korat had a heart attack," he says.

Pough looks up from a four-year-old issue of *Newsweek*. "I didn't think he was *that* old."

"He's been drawing social security for some time," Reid says.

"No," corrects Leroy Wilson, "I think he's been collecting *disability*, not social security."

"I know he's older than Woodie," Reid says, referring to another member of the post. "Woodie's been getting *his* social for two years."

Reid begins restocking the beer cooler, pulling long neck bottles from a box. After living overseas for most of his twenty-five years in the service, going home to Columbus, Ohio, seemed "kind of dull," he says. "I'd go over to somebody's house, and all they could talk about was stuff like, this one just had a baby, the baby's got a rash, they need this toy. Or they talked about how this football team or that baseball team was going to win this or that game. And here I am; I'm international. I've been all over the world. I'm talking about this country here and that country there, and all they can do is nod their heads. It's just too dull back at home. You don't have anything in common. You just aren't comfortable there anymore."

If Reid and the boys aren't comfortable at home, they aren't quite comfortable in Thailand either. Reid doesn't drink the water or eat Thai food. He doesn't speak the language. He doesn't really even like Thai people. "I think all of us Americans who stay here feel that we don't really want to get involved with the people here," says Reid, a sleepy-eyed man with a molasses-slow delivery. "You don't get involved with their politics, and you don't get involved with their conversations. As friendly as they are, to a certain extent, they don't really like Americans. After a few drinks, they can get abusive. They resent us. They resent the things that we can do and have that they can't.

"I don't really like their ways, but I condone them. A person has to fit into his environment, 'cause that's the main way of survival. But that's also why we have the VFW Post. Sometimes you just want to be around Americans."

Leroy Wilson laughs and takes another swig. "Sometimes you just want to be around other people who don't have anything else to do, neither. It gets awful tiring sitting around the house, watching yourself get old. Your knees start knitting together, your arms break out at the elbows from leaning on the bar."

"Man, you *are* old!" says Kenneth Wilson.

"Find him a wheelchair," says Reid.

"Find him a *plot*," says Pough.

"Guys, I'm just kidding!" Leroy Wilson says. "It's not really *that* bad. I have four beautiful kids. I spend a lot of time cooking and cleaning and taking care of them. I could have a maid do it, but I like to do it myself. Sometimes I find myself just waiting for the kids to come home so I have something to do."

"Yeah," says Reid, restocking the display rack with bags of pretzels and chips. "No matter where you live, you gotta stay busy. Otherwise you're just wastin' precious time."

"Time you don't get back," says Leroy Wilson.

"Amen to that, brother," says Kenneth Wilson, holding up his beer bottle, offering a toast all around.

###

The Prince of Peace Seminary sits back from the road, next to a place that used to be called Kiddie Land, a combination amusement park, brothel, and gambling house before its Thai owner was ambushed by gangsters with M-16s.

The seminary building is constructed of brick—a long, low Western-inspired structure that stands in stark contrast to the primitive wood and cinderblock huts and houses that dot the nearby countryside. Inside the seminary it is cool and peaceful and empty. The walls are hung with needlepoint maps of Southeast Asia, religious oil paintings, a large framed photograph of the local Bishop meeting with the Pope in Rome. At the foot of a teak stairway are two pairs of rubber flip flops.

Father John Tabor descends the steps—a beefy guy in an olive drab undershirt—rubbing his eyes like he's just awoken. He steps into his flip-flops and walks outside into the sunlight, working his neck, looking more like an ironworker just off a binge than a Catholic priest who spent years working in refugee camps along the Thai-Laotian-Cambodian border.

There is an odd, uncomfortable look on his face, as if he's not sure exactly where he is, or if he's where he's supposed to be. His eyeballs track here and there. "Are you sweaty?" he asks me. "Are your palms sweaty? Are you cold? When I woke up, everybody said it was cold, but I didn't feel it at all. I just felt the headache. What's that in that tree?" He points to a fruit tree fifty yards away.

"It looks like a kite," I say.

He looks at me long and hard. He blinks a few times, as if trying to clear his vision. "Are you me?" he asks.

I stare him in the eyes, remain calm. "I don't think so."

Father John massages his temples for a bit, and then he digs his knuckles into the trapezius muscle at the back base of his neck. "This thing is like a rock," he says. "Maybe I need something to eat. You want something to eat? Come on inside."

Tabor turned thirty-nine yesterday. He enlisted in the Seabees after high school, an eighteen-year-old farm boy from Jaffrey, New Hampshire, who didn't want to go to college and damn sure wasn't going to collect eggs and shovel chicken shit for the rest of his life, either. He got to Danang early in the war. At that point, they were calling it a "police action." In fact, there was hardly any action at all. Mostly, he drilled water wells and partied and took it easy.

"You like frog legs?" Tabor asks. He is seated at a table in the semi-nary kitchen. He pulls a leg off a dead frog and stuffs it in his mouth. Then he puts the frog down on the plastic tablecloth, a festive red and white checkerboard. It is clear the frog is not cooked. It has not been alive for some time. There is an odor. A chunk of black decay falls out of the inside of the frog; a little red ant falls out of that. The ant scuttles across the tablecloth, past a bowl of bananas, out of sight. Tabor swigs a warm beer. "I found the frog out in the yard yesterday. It must be a gift from

God to take care of my headache. I think they use frogs for headaches in Vietnamese medicine."

"What about Vietnam?" I ask him. "What happened when you were there?"

"I don't remember much. It was a long time ago," he says. "I remember that when they told us we were going there, I didn't even know where it was. I was a choirboy. I kind of always had a calling, but I kind of didn't want to pay attention to it back then, I guess. Do you know the old name for Indonesia? It's Sumatra, I think.

"We flew in from the Philippines in a C-130. The first thing I saw was this little guy with a big helmet guarding a plane. And I thought of— what do you call those kids? From TV? The Little Rascals. I thought of them. Here was this little guy with this big helmet. Really, it was just too big for his head. It looked pitiful, you know, and I got this big feeling of superiority because we were here to train this guy. I mean, here was this little kid with a helmet as big as a bucket on his head, and a gun, and baggy old clothes, and he was out on this runway guarding a plane. Clearly he needed my help. I don't know—there was something about him. Something about the sight of him. What I felt, heaven knows. But I felt something, because at that time, at that moment, it was so attractive and so moving, it hit me like a ton of bricks. I don't know if I could analyze it, exactly. Was it the hand of God? I don't know. But that was the moment. That was when I decided to stay in Vietnam, the first minute I arrived."

Tabor finished his tour and then volunteered for a second. When that was up, he wrote to the secretary of the navy, requesting permission to stay in Vietnam to study for the priesthood with missionaries there. His request was granted. He stayed in Vietnam after the United States pulled out its troops, continuing his work. In 1978, following his ordination, Father Tabor was arrested by the ruling Vietnamese communists and tried by a people's court. After the trial, he was loaded onto a flatbed truck, handcuffed to prostitutes and criminals, paraded around the village, and then taken away to serve six months in a prison camp. Upon his release, he fled to Thailand, where he used his fluent Vietnamese and Laotian to work with refugees.

"I guess Vietnam was where I realized my calling," Tabor says. "God didn't appear to me in a vision or talk to me in a big voice. I didn't hear any voices—not back then. Sometimes I do hear voices now. I don't know who they are. I try to communicate with them, but they don't answer. I guess some of them are good voices and some are bad. They just talk to me when they want to. They told me to drown myself when I was in Rome this year. You know how hard it is to drown yourself?"

"What else do you remember about Vietnam?" I prompt, trying to keep him on track. "What did you do when you were there?"

"I remember that there was this little girl. She was something. Little Mia, I think her name was. She was like the pet for the whole little group that was drilling this well. I remember when we took her out for supper one time at this hotel in Danang. I'm trying to think of the name of it. I don't remember it too well. Somebody had made reservations, I think, and we went up there. That's where the mayor's office is now—"

Just then, the kitchen door opens. A man walks in, followed by a couple. The man is wearing a clerical collar. He looks familiar somehow. The trio wears a joint expression of extreme concern.

"Hi, Bishop," Tabor says, nonchalant.

"Hello, Father John," the Bishop says. Now I remember: He's the one with the Pope in the photograph on the wall.

"Hello, Father John," the other man and woman say in chorus. They look and sound American. "How are you feeling today?" the man asks.

"Okay, doctor," Tabor says flatly. He folds his arms across his chest, commences to rock slightly back and forth in his chair.

"John, have you packed your things?" the Bishop asks. He sounds pastoral but also slightly annoyed. "It's time for you to go."

Rolling Stone, 1984

## 9

The Sharpton Strategy

"No justice! No peace!"

"No justice! No peace!"

Oh no! Here he comes again, churning through Wall Street at high noon like a big black tug—shoulders back, arms pumping, hair luffing, flesh roiling and slushing beneath the silky nylon of his teal-blue jogging suit, his trademark, size XXL. Al Sharpton, Al Charlatan, the Reverend Soundbite, the Minister of Hate—a tribal chief leading a militant horde straight up the asphalt seam of America's silk stocking, hollering for justice, threatening the peace.

Lunchtime in New York City, at the business end of the dagger-shaped island of Manhattan. The air is gray, the streets are jammed, the Dow is down forty. The usual cacophony of urban disharmonics has been lifted to a crescendo this afternoon by the dozens of dump trucks and heavy machines that are hugging the curb two deep around City Hall park, air horns blaring solidarity with the large group of black construction workers who are protesting, a demand for more jobs.

A few minutes ago, Sharpton penetrated borough limits in a white Pontiac Grand Am. He hoisted himself out of the passenger seat, trundled across three lanes of traffic, and entered the park, where he was swallowed in a chanting, teeming mass, twelve busloads of followers, gathered as planned under the camouflage of the protest permit issued to the construction workers.

Now they head south, Sharpton and six hundred marchers, led by a phalanx of police attended by a gaggle of press.

Along the sidewalks, the usual lunchtime crowd has frozen. WASPs and Jews, Italians and Asians—all of them stare grimly, eyes glazed with hate and fear and incredulity, mouths open, beef franks and spoonfuls of yogurt suspended en route. It's him, they say to one another. *Him!* Called Jesse Jackson a limp dick. Called Mayor David Dinkins an Uncle Tom. Took over the Brooklyn Bridge. Indicted on sixty-seven counts of fraud. Implicated as an FBI informant. Defended the Central Park jogger wolf pack. Spends $2,000 a year on his hairdo!

The marchers chant in the tones and rhythms of a chain gang, a war party—six across, one hundred rows deep, a coalition of blacks and Latinos, jobless and homeless, gays and leftists. They are marking the anniversary, twenty-seven years ago today, of the historic civil rights march on Washington, D.C. After Montgomery, after the bombings, the dogs, and the fire hoses, 250,000 people from all over America gathered at the Lincoln Memorial. Fresh from a jail stint, the Rev. Martin Luther King Jr. told the country about his dream of racial harmony—his most famous speech. Today, in New York City, Al Sharpton's marchers carry Xeroxed pictures of Dr. King. Their signs ask, "What happened to the dream?" Their message is . . .

It's not altogether clear yet what the message is.

Something to do with Martin Luther King. Something to do with justice and peace.

They march swiftly, ranks tight, heels scuffing, sweat mingling, fists and pickets jabbing the air, a polyglot sampling of the nation's under-classes—hobo rags and cheap, three-piece suits, African prints, blue work shirts with names in bubbles over breast pockets—all of them here because Sharpton has called, none of them even slightly aware of the very secret stunt he has planned for later.

They turn off Broadway and enter Battery Park, a living mass, a village on a hike. They gather in front of a makeshift stage—huddling, milling, hitting up the lunch crowd for spare change. Cameras roll. Police take positions around the green.

Sharpton pulls up behind the stage, rests his hands on his ample hips. He surveys the crowd, the police. He checks the sky. Then, casually, he swivels his head to the left, puts his eyes on the prize.

Out there, across the harbor.

The Statue of Liberty.

TUESDAY MORNING, 7:30, one week earlier.

We are in Sharpton's apartment in Park Slope, Brooklyn, his living room/office. A video tape of a speech by Nation of Islam leader Louis Farrakhan is playing on the TV; a reporter from a black-owned radio station is sitting on a sofa covered with cat hair, waiting his turn for an interview. Above his head is a framed poster of Malcolm X—he looks defiantly out a window, an M-I carbine rifle in his hands. "By any means necessary," it says at the bottom.

Sharpton is wearing black socks, print boxers, and a yellow wife beater. He is pacing back and forth across the shag carpet, thundering into a telephone, using his pulpit voice for an interview with another reporter. "This town is closer to exploding than ever!" he exclaims, his typical church hyperbole. Sharpton is thirty-five. His allergies keep his nose stuffy; his gravelly voice makes you think of James Brown with a cold.

Sharpton's apartment is clean but cluttered—a walk-up above a machine shop, $1,000 a month. He lives here with his wife, Kathy Jordan Sharpton, a former backup singer for Brown (more on him later), and his daughters, Ashley, three, and Dominique, four. All four Sharptons sleep in the one bedroom. This living room has no window. Lining the walls are the typical political grin and grabs, Sharpton with George Bush, David Dinkins, Jesse Jackson, Melba Moore.

"The violence in the minds of these kids!" Sharpton preaches into the handset of the portable phone, the whip antenna following him as he continues to pace in the limited space of the room, which is decorated with furniture that might have come from somebody's dead grandma's house. "These kids think life's a fuckin' television series. They have no fear. When I was in jail after the protest, I was two cells down from that kid—the one who shot the police officer in Jersey? He said to me, 'Rev, I told 'em we shouldn't hit that dude. The car we had was too slow.' Now, I have to tell you. That rendered me speechless for a minute. Here I was, I thought the kid was gonna tell me he had a moral problem with killing a cop. I thought he was gonna tell me he was feeling remorseful. But that wasn't his problem. His problem was merely functional. 'Rev, we needed a faster car!'"

"Excuse me, Rev. Sharpton?" It's the radio reporter.

Sharpton holds up a finger, one minute. Then the other telephone line rings. He puts both calls on hold.

"What?" he asks the radio reporter.

The front door flies open.

Sharpton wheels around. "Yo!" he calls to his driver, Carl. They've been together a long time. They spend more time together than they do with their respective wives.

Then Sharpton remembers: the phones. He punches the first line. "Call you back." He punches the second line. "Call *me* back." Then he turns to Carl. "Did you get the *Journal?*"

Handing it over: "I finally found it over at—"

"Don't matter *where* you got it, long as you got it," Sharpton says, grinning with excitement as he pages through the *Wall Street Journal.* At last he spots what he's searching for. He reads to himself, his big black eyes tracking across the columns . . .

And then he throws back his head and laughs—a loud, long, phlegm-tinged guffaw that shakes his belly. "Can you believe this?" he roars.

He reads aloud for the assembled, doing a lampoonish impression of a network news anchor, albeit one with a stuffy nose:

"A trader from the New York Stock Exchange reports the following joke: 'What do you do if you have Saddam Hussein, Muammar Qaddafi, and Al Sharpton, and in your hand is a gun with only two bullets?' Answer: 'Shoot Al Sharpton twice—to be sure he's dead.'"

"Now they're advocating my *death!*" Sharpton says, slapping his large and ashy thigh, laughing real tears. He does an impression of a cracker sheriff: "Shoot Al Sharpton *twice!*"

AL SHARPTON IS one of the most reviled men in America today.

He first showed up in the national news in 1986, seemingly out of nowhere, in the aftermath of a racial killing in Howard Beach, New York.

Since then, he's become an annoying fixture on a present day civil rights stage that seems hopelessly devoid of visible leaders. Most Americans see Sharpton as a media manipulator, a rabble-rouser, a threat, a joke. One white columnist called him "a racial ambulance chaser"; another, a "race racketeer." A poll by the New York *Daily News* found that 90 percent of whites and 73 percent of blacks believe he is harming race relations rather than helping.

Representative Major Owens, a black Democrat from New York, says Sharpton's history "shows he has no principles. He's not to be trusted." Andrew Cooper, publisher of the *City Sun*, a black newspaper in New York, says, "Most middle-class black people are embarrassed by him."

But the telephone poll can be read another way: One in four blacks *does not* think Sharpton is harming relations between the races. And that doesn't account for the Sharpton followers who couldn't be polled (many don't have telephones). To the several thousand blacks who have joined the United African Movement (UAM), to countless more across the country who have seen him in the media, Sharpton is, in the words of the *New York Times*, "an authentic, stirring leader who has challenged the city and state power structure too often to be doubted."

Rev. Timothy Mitchell, pastor of Ebenezer Baptist Church, in Queens: "He's sort of a hero here to the young people. They admire his courage." Rev. William Augustus Jones, pastor of Bethany Baptist Church, the oldest congregation in Brooklyn: "We recognize his gift. We applaud his spirit. We thank God for the fact that he has been consistently on the firing line on behalf of our people and our cause." Moses Stewart, father of Yusuf Hawkins, a black teenager who was killed by a white mob in Brooklyn: "I called Rev. in 'cause I wanted to get me some justice, and that's what Sharpton does. He stands up for black folks like me, and if some whites don't like that, I could care less."

Al Sharpton: "I wanted to build a grass-roots movement with a little pizzazz. That's what Dr. King did. He brought theater into the movement. Dr. King said, 'We will close down the bus company.' It was TV. It was theater of the street. That's how King changed America.

"Look at this country. We went from Harvard-trained Kennedy/ Camelot to made-for-TV Ronald Reagan because of the media. So why shouldn't America go from Dr. King to Rev. Al? The times call for who's going to emerge. Let's not have no deception about why I'm in the media. We're talking ratings for you, followers for me. My thing is, I'm talking to the guy from Inglewood, from Brownsville, from Harlem. I'm talking to thirty million black guys out there, guys who are just like me."

###

WEDNESDAY, 7:00 P.M., six days before the march, a strategy session at a community center in lower Manhattan.

Eight people sit in swivel chairs. They drink coffee and take notes. The center belongs to the New Alliance Party, a coalition founded by a former Marxist who made a fortune in a field called Social Therapy. The NAP pulls its members from the scattered remains of the far Left. Its causes have included the fight against the government "roundup" of black leaders in America. The Jewish Anti-Defamation League has called the group anti-Semitic. This is denied by the NAP's founder-financier, Fred Newman, who is himself a Jew.

When Sharpton got the idea for the march on Wall Street, he went directly to the NAP. First, he wanted his demonstration to be racially integrated. Second, he needed technical assistance: planning, flyers, literature, copiers, fax machines, and phones. And, of course, he needed money, something white liberals are still good for.

Sharpton has a few problems with the NAP. They're a little too academic, a little too fey. But he's realistic. There aren't many liberals left; few of them want to get involved with him.

"Okay now," Sharpton is saying, "I want to hand pick the arrest crew myself, 'cause I got to live with them in jail."

"You don't want anybody from the homeless?" asks the man from the shelter.

"If they want to. But nobody with a warrant outstanding."

"So how many people we need to get arrested?" asks Raphael. He's from the Latin community.

"I think we should keep it down to about twenty people," Sharpton says. "If you start getting into big numbers, it's harder for the police to deal with."

"Do we care what's harder for the police to deal with?" asks Lenora Fulani, the NAP's perennial candidate. A black woman with close-cropped hair and big earrings, she ran for mayor of New York in 1985, for governor of New York state in 1986 and 1990, and for president of the United States in 1998.

"*Yeah*, we care," Sharpton answers sternly. "See, you don't need two hundred people going to jail. You don't need to piss off the police—they're just doing their job. It's the symbolism that's important. This is the reclaiming, the *redefining* of the King movement. If we didn't do this, nobody would be discussing the homeless, which is the issue King wanted to discuss with the Poor People's Campaign and Resurrection City. They're going to say this is another showboat piece. But we're going to make them at least discuss the issue."

"All right," Fulani concedes.

"Right on," says Rafael.

"Okay," Sharpton says, buoyant again. "Now remember. What happens *after* we get to Battery Park is strictly confidential. *Superconfidential!* Got it? It can't get out of this room! If the police find out—" his eyes budge antically. Everyone laughs.

#

WEDNESDAY, 9:00 P.M., Bedford-Stuyvesant, Brooklyn. The Slave Theater is headquarters of the year-old UAM. A once-grand movie palace, the ceiling snows green flakes onto the mildewed, graffiti-covered seats. A large epic mural, *The Holocaust of the Black Race*, depicting the African-American experience from Africa to the Middle Passage to slavery, takes up one huge wall.

The microphone squeals. Sharpton pulls away, hikes his pants, waits for the applause to die. Though he has been called a preacher without a congregation, this theater is his church for now, rented by the UAM from the black judge who owns it. The rent on the building is paid with donations collected after rallies and services. In this way, Sharpton pays all of his expenses: his leased Grand Am; a headstone for Yusuf Hawkins; ad space in black newspapers; bail for two of the Central Park jogger defendants; food, salary, and pocket money for Sharpton and his three-person staff. There's no real budget for the UAM. Whatever they can collect, they spend. A year ago, the UAM was getting 200 people at rallies. Tonight, there is standing room only, 1,500.

Sharpton speaks from high on the stage, his voice strong and throaty, the edges tinged with a soulful rasp of phlegm. He points his finger at the audience, pans it slowly across the room, the upturned faces shining—lawyers and homeboys, welfare mothers and church ladies, all of them spellbound.

"I don't care whether you a revolutionary: bang-bang-shoot-em-up," he preaches.

"Go on!" the audience responds.

"Whether you a militant: just mad but ain't got the gun."

"Tell it!"

"Whether you a moderate: where you smile at white folks and then cuss them under your breath."

"My *Lord!*"

"Or whether you an *outright* Tom—"

Hoots and shouts!

"Whatever kind of Negro you are, whether you a fat Negro or a skinny Negro, a tall Negro or a short Negro, a brilliant Negro or a simple-headed Negro, you have to *understand.*"

"Work it, Rev!"

"Ain't no homes for the homeless. Ain't no health care for the sick. Ain't no education for the young. Ain't no housing for *nobody.* Ain't no goods and no services. And now, despite *allllllll* that, they tellin' you to go over to *Iraq* and defend a flag that never defended you." He points his finger around the room, a pause for dramatic effect. "I say, hell no, we won't go!"

"Hell *no.*"

"*Hell* no"

Shouts, applause, tambourines . . .

From the time he was four, when he preached his first sermon at the largest Pentecostal church in New York State, Alfred C. Sharpton Jr. has been moving people. He has moved them to God, to the offering plate, to musical acts, to prizefights, to strike lines.

He was raised in a ten-family building in lily-white Queens. His father owned the building, along with thirty houses in Brooklyn. Al senior was a contractor. He and his wife both drove Cadillacs. Young Alfred was their famous son, known on the New York gospel circuit as the Wonderboy Preacher.

When he was seven, his father took all the money and left. Sharpton hasn't heard from him since. His mother moved her kids to Flatbush and went to work as a maid for a rabbi. Alfred's cut from revivals went straight to the family budget.

Sharpton's earliest political mentor was civil rights pioneer Adam Clayton Powell. Young Alfred was eleven when he spied the tall, dapper U.S. congressman for the first time; he was known in the neighborhood as Big Daddy. Under his tutelage, the Wonderboy Preacher matured into the Wonderboy Activist. In 1969, at fourteen, Sharpton was named youth director of the New York chapter of Operation Breadbasket, the economic arm of Dr. King's Southern Christian Leadership Conference. He was handpicked for the job by none other than Jesse Jackson. Today, with a smirk, Sharpton recalls Jesse's marching orders: "Defy and kick ass."

Sharpton generated a core of about four hundred students. They protested alongside the grown-ups for jobs and concessions from white-owned businesses in the ghetto. Two years later, Jackson was suspended from the SCLC for financial discrepancies in his handling of a Black Expo in Chicago. Sharpton started his own group, the National Youth Movement. The NYM targeted businesses at first, then turned to politics. By 1972, several presidential candidates came seeking Sharpton's endorsement.

Meanwhile, young Sharpton was attending an all-white high school in Flatbush. He was vice president of the student council, associate editor of the *Tilden Gadfly*. Many mornings before school, he would gather his followers around him and declare a boycott du jour. They'd protest cafeteria food quality, dress codes, any issue that mattered to the students. At graduation, the principal informed all assembled that he would *not* be missing Alfred Sharpton at all.

At nineteen, Sharpton met the soul singer James Brown. In time, the Godfather of Soul, the hardest working man in show biz, came to regard Sharpton as his son—and he said so frequently in public. Sharpton toured with Brown, booked his shows, hired his band. He even hired as a backup singer the woman who would eventually become his wife. She still sings occasional solo dates at Harlem's Cotton Club. Brown also deserves credit—or blame—for Sharpton's lightning rod of a hair do; never has one hairstyle caused so much ruckus. For the record: James Brown, who famously processed, or straightened, his own hair, was the one who took Sharpton to a beauty shop and got him his first wash and set. The story goes that Brown, the mentor, made young Sharpton promise to always wear his hair that way. Your hair is your strength, he believed, perhaps drawing from the Bible's Samson. Since then, Sharpton has kept his word—some say to his own detriment. Sharpton will explain no further. Obviously it is important to him. Obviously, he is fiercely loyal. Everyone he works with says so.

When Sharpton wasn't living the high life—on the road with Brown or promoting concerts and fights with the infamous, electric-haired boxing impresario Don King—he would be back in the trenches in New York, fighting the continuing battle for justice and civil rights, registering voters, marching against crack, helping at one point to uncover a nest of bad cops who were selling drugs and fencing stolen goods.

In the mid-1980s, a series of racial incidents occurred in New York that changed everything for Al Sharpton. The shooting of four black youths in a subway by Jewish everyman Bernie Goetz. The death of a young black man in Howard Beach, Long Island, after he was chased by whites into highway traffic. The shooting death of Yusuf Hawkins in the Italian enclave of Bensonhurst, Brooklyn. As he had for years, Sharpton responded to each injustice with protest. Only this time, he took the demonstrations out of the ghetto, where he had always operated, and went straight to the offending neighborhoods. He and his followers ate pizza in all-white Howard Beach, marched through all-Italian Bensonhurst, shut down the subway and the Brooklyn Bridge. He turned up the thermostat on the bonfire of the races—and the media loved it. They played the soundbites of his most hyperbolic remarks; Sharpton began to take on nearly mythic proportions. Out of nowhere, it seemed, had come this new black leader. There was only one problem: white people didn't consider him a bona fide leader.

Detractors point to his attempted run for state senator, which was ruled illegal by a judge, who found that Sharpton was trying to represent a district where he did not live. His bid on a Con Edison garbage contract was disqualified when it was discovered that his financial backer was an organized-crime figure called Matty the Horse. There was his stint as an FBI informant, his highly publicized suit for nonpayment of rent, his multiple disorderly conduct arrests as a result of protests, and his trial on sixty-seven counts of fraud (he was acquitted on all counts).

And most egregiously, there was Tawana Brawley—a fifteen-year-old who claimed she'd been raped over a four-day period by several white men who then smeared her with excrement and left her in a garbage bag. On the advice of Sharpton and her attorneys, Brawley refused to testify before a grand jury, which in turn ruled the whole affair a hoax—a story cooked up by a teenager who was trying to avoid her parents' wrath over a curfew violation.

Of all of the incidents in his past, Brawley in particular was Sharpton's undoing.

He does not apologize. "If I'm guilty of anything, it's believing Tawana. I still do. I do not believe that a fifteen-year-old black girl knocked herself out, spread shit all over herself, drank urine, the whole nine yards, just to avoid a beating from her daddy. Whether it was six cops or two cops, she told me it was cops involved. She gave me names. She knew a license number.

"If I had any feeling that this girl was wrong, it ain't like I didn't have fifty other cases I could have represented. If I'd known, I'd have picked another. This thing so hurt me. I am willing to admit that I lost a lot of my balance arguing about it. It got very personal. But I still believe Tawana."

Tonight at the Slave Theater, Sharpton doesn't mention Tawana Brawley; none of his bad press seems to matter here anyway. He is a masterly speaker—ironic, alliterative, moving. Frequent was the occasion, in my time with him, when he raised goose bumps on my flesh; to this day only the voice of Dr. King can move me more. Sharpton's political sermon this evening covers a wide range of topics. How police shoot first at blacks and ask questions later. How black leaders are being selectively targeted for investigation. How black kids are being retarded by the schools. How a new drug from Kenya is curing AIDS, but the white press will not publicize it. How public defenders are puppets of the state. How the white man has a complex about the black man's penis.

He is either frightening or inspirational, depending upon where you stand. In a recent article in *New York* magazine, Edwin Diamond investigated what he called the "reverse reality" preached by Sharpton, Farrakhan, and the black media. In this Afrocentric view of the world, Diamond wrote, "the 'facts' no longer matter; the 'truth' is beside the point—indeed, it may impede the point . . . . The city's black media have helped construct a kind of anti-universe, a world mirroring the main-stream but where everything is reversed."

But as Diamond also pointed out, a *Newsday*/Gallup poll shows that 20 percent of black New Yorkers consider black-owned media their most important source of news and information. Wrote Diamond: "The audience for these black-media outlets seems to trust them and not the mainstream press."

"To a white mind," says Sharpton, "it's tangible wins and losses that count in the world. So you can look at it like this: I got people to invest money in black banks; I got a black person a seat on the MTA board; I got the protests at Howard Beach and Bensonhurst. Those, you could say, are tangible wins. Brawley and them others—they might be losses. But that's only to a *white* mind. To a *black* mind, I'm successful 'cause I'm still here. I'm a survivor. I carry on.

"What I've been doing is trying to use the media to talk to black people and further organize a national black movement. I haven't figured out yet how I'm gonna use the media to deal with *white* America. I will admit that publicly. I haven't figured out yet how to talk to white people. That's my next challenge."

#

Thursday morning, five days before the march, a procession of cars eases through a Brooklyn drizzle, Sharpton's Grand Am in the lead. Carl is driving, Rev. Al is riding shotgun. In the backseat, behind Sharpton, are his assistant, Jennifer Josephs, and Moses Stewart.

A year ago today, Moses' son, Yusuf Hawkins, went to Bensonhurst to look at a used car. He was surrounded by a mob of Italian kids and gunned down. This morning, the family is laying a headstone. Sharpton is officiating. (He also paid for the headstone.)

Carl enters Evergreen Cemetery and pulls up to a dirt-covered grave. Reporters and cameramen are already there. Waiting with them, flanked by cops, is Charles Hynes, the Brooklyn district attorney, one of Sharpton's political arch-enemies.

Spying Hynes through the gloom, Sharpton bangs his hand on the dash with glee. "That cracker! Look at him, standing out in the rain. He couldn't show his face at the *trial*, but now he's here to get his picture took!" He twists around in his seat. "Jennifer, go over to Hynes and tell him that if he says one word to the press, we're gonna put him in one of these open graves."

Jennifer is nearly six feet tall. She speaks quietly to Hynes. He nods curtly.

The next day, *Newsday* reports: "The only official at the brief ceremony was Brooklyn district attorney Charles Hynes, who said he was invited by the family."

MONDAY NIGHT, lower Manhattan, NAP Headquarters, the last strategy meeting before the Wall Street protest.

"We need to sing 'We Shall Overcome,'" Sharpton is saying. "There's a certain segment of white America that really responds to that song."

"I agree one hundred percent," Fulani says.

"And we need to get a big picture of Dr. King," Sharpton says.

"We have one," the NAP woman says.

"That's the drama!" Sharpton explains. "Bring us your tired, your poor! Bring us your *homeless*. Right at the foot of Lady Liberty!"

"What if they don't let the press on the island?" Raphael asks.

"They will," Sharpton assures him.

"They may *not*," Fulani agrees.

"Don't worry about it," Sharpton says dismissively, a cockeyed grin on his face. "I've already thought of that."

"NO SANDWICHES! No peace!"

"No sandwiches! No peace!"

Al Sharpton is sitting like a big black Buddha in the grass on Liberty Island, listening to talk radio through headphones. Behind him, a large orange sign eddies and shudders in the harbor breeze. It says MARTIN LUTHER KING JR. CITY. Looming above the sign is the Statue of Liberty.

After the march down Wall Street, after the speeches in Battery Park, the secret plan unfolded. Sharpton announced that he was going over to

Liberty Island to lay a proclamation. He said he'd be right back. Then his assistants quickly handed out ferry tickets to one hundred of the marchers.

And lo and behold . . . It worked!

Al Sharpton's army has seized control of the Statue of Liberty!

Now they have been here for two hours. NAP members work furiously, erecting tents. The homeless are restless. They cut up, pose for pictures with tourists, beg for money. They complain about the shortage of bologna and cheese sandwiches. They begin a new chant: "No sandwiches! No peace!"

Sharpton sees the humor in the moment. All in all, things are going well. He has engineered a beautiful telegenic panorama: the tents, the King sign, the Statue of Liberty, the harbor, the blue sky. He is proud of himself, the clever way he has managed to meld the enduring images of King's Resurrection City with the Statue of Liberty—Lady Liberty's promise, King's dream, and one hundred people of color, many of them homeless. King's dream revisited, twenty-seven years later. Masterful.

Unfortunately, there are no cameras on the island.

Just a radio reporter and two print journalists.

Time passes. Sharpton makes a few calls on a cell phone. A park ranger walks over. He offers a piece of paperwork for Sharpton's perusal.

"We issued a permit for a public assembly," the ranger says, "but you've got to be at the flagpole."

Before Sharpton can speak, he is joined by a short, fierce black woman in a business suit, the NAP's lawyer. She steps forward and snatches the paper from the ranger. She studies it for a moment, thrusts it back.

"This is not us," she says dismissively. "You don't have the name right. We're the New Alliance Party, not the National Alliance Party."

"In that case, I'd be happy to issue you a new permit."

"We don't *want* a permit."

"Then I'm going to have to shut this island down."

"You do what you have to do," she says, crossing her arms.

The ranger turns and leaves. The three reporters press close to Sharpton for a comment.

"I'm gonna stay," Sharpton tells them. "The last one off this island in handcuffs will be me."

Sharpton stretches himself a little, takes a look around. The ferries have stopped running, he can see that from here. No doubt the cops are on the way. He hopes they just fine and release him. He's got a lot on his plate right now. He doesn't really have time to molder in jail. There's the appeal for the Central Park jogger defendants, Tawana's book, a fundraiser for an old Movement hand in Cairo, Illinois, who's up on an arson beef. He wants to see an agent about getting a speaking tour going, and he's working on a deal to make a record with James Brown and an all-star team of rappers—a rap against illiteracy. There are also plans for a UAM chicken franchise, a grocery store too. Economic self-determination is one of Sharpton's new big themes. And in his future, who knows. Mainstream politics, perhaps? Privately, he jokes about running for president. "Just kidding—" Is that statement ever really true? (He will do so in 2004.)

Whatever he does, he knows he's going to piss off a lot more people before he's through. He knows his disapproval rating will always remain high. Maybe he just likes it that way. Maybe that's just his style. Maybe he likes to be the one who shakes everyone up.

"What I'm sayin' needs to be said. I ain't makin' no apologies. I ain't puttin' on no Brooks Brothers suit. This is how we are. But we can still deal. We can negotiate on any level you want to negotiate on. But I'm still gonna be the same Al—Big Al from Brownsville. I didn't come out here to Liberty Island to be liked. I got plenty of home-boys that'll like me just because I'm me, and I'm more comfortable with them anyway. I like it at the Slave Theater. I like it on Fulton and Bedford Streets. It's cool. It's where I been all my life. I know that crowd. And I'm gonna make sure they get the best shot, 'cause they been good to me. It's what's right."

Now the ranger is back. He informs Sharpton and the lawyer that the island is officially closed. "The last ferry leaves in twenty minutes," he says.

"What about the press?" asks the lawyer. "They have a right to gather news."

"Be gone or be arrested," the ranger says.

With that, the press and most of the demonstrators walk over to the ferry and board. As it pulls away from the island, a police boat ties off at the docks. Three dozen cops, nightsticks drawn, file onto the island.

Over on the grass, beneath the orange sign invoking Dr. King, beneath the Statue of Liberty, Al Sharpton and thirteen volunteers circle up and hold hands. There is no press left on the island; no cameras bear witness. Just Big Al from Brownsville and his people, waiting to be arrested, wondering what happened to the dream.

They sing another chorus of "We Shall Overcome."

###

EPILOGUE: "We've been saying serious things this week. But the press puts us on the Style page. Not the black press, the *other* press. The white press puts us on the Style page while we're talking about our *humanity.*"

It is a month after the Liberty Island takeover. The speaker is Congressman Ron Dellums, the august black leader with the long, salt-and-pepper beard, from Oakland, California. The occasion is the twentieth annual gathering of the Congressional Black Caucus in Washington, D.C.—the biggest mainstream black political event of the year. This is the gala of the weekend, the awards dinner. Three thousand people are in attendance—every black luminary in America, from Jesse Jackson to Quincy Jones, from Farrakhan to Miss Black USA. Dinner is tournedos with béarnaise and salmon, $10,000 a table.

Yesterday, the caucus officially convened meetings on the "systematic harassment" of black public and elected officials. A gathering of hundreds heard stories of surveillance, wiretaps, videotaping, attempted bribes, and trumped-up indictments.

"The President is threatening to veto the civil rights bill twenty-six years after the first one," Dellums says forcefully, banging a hand on the podium. "Is that progress?"

"No!" yells the crowd.

"The world is rushing toward democracy and we're running to fascism!"

"Yes we are!"

"How long can we put up with this?"

"How long?"

"Not one minute longer."

Cheers, applause, shouts!

Over in the corner, at a donated table with Jennifer and Carl and some others, Al Sharpton listens, hands resting peacefully on his belly. His mouth is shut. He is smiling.

Esquire, 1991

10
Death in Venice

L IL' SLEEPER AND MARGARITA are hanging out at Yogi's, all three sitting on his bed. The room is dark, narrow, smoky. A towel is jammed against the bottom of the door.

"I forgot to tell you," Yogi says. "Sleeper called."

"Yeah?" asks Lil' Sleeper.

"He asked what have we done to pay back Culver City."

"Pay 'em back for what?"

"You know, man. The drive-by at the park. Those *vatos* who shot at us. Remember, *ese?*"

Lil' Sleeper chews his thumb and thinks for a minute. The TV flickers, the radio plays rap, a table fan moves air back and forth. He turns to Margarita, his girlfriend. "When this happen?"

Margarita's eyes pan slowly toward his face. They've been dating for a year. She is wearing a black miniskirt and a necklace of hickeys, a pair of three-inch heels she bought two weeks ago on her fourteenth birthday. Her hair is shoulder length, crowned at the front with a stiff pompadour—a four-inch tiara of bangs combed skyward and encased in Aqua Net hairspray. She blinks. She shrugs. She don't remember, either. One day be like the next.

Lil' Sleeper chews his thumb some more. The skin at the tip, just below the nail, is burned and crusty, a condition the homeboys call Bic Thumb. Like Yogi, he is nineteen. He is wearing a nylon sweat suit and high-top Adidas. His hair is black as tar, clipped short and oiled straight back from a widow's peak. His lashes are long and curly, his eyes are bloodshot, one of his front teeth is missing. The first time he was arrested he was six years old; he stole a TV from his grammar school. Last year, he was arrested eleven times for being under the influence of heroin and two times for being under the influence of PCP, a drug he likes because "when you do it, it be hard for you to walk and think."

As days in the neighborhood go, this one started off pretty well. At 10:00 this morning, Lil' Sleeper and Margarita ran into a crack dealer they know. He kicked down some love, gave them some free drugs, the dregs of last night's stash—a couple of five- and ten-dollar rocks and a bunch of crumbs. The pair went immediately to Yogi's place and smoked it all in fifteen minutes. Now they need more.

Sitting on the edge of the bed, Lil' Sleeper is a ramrod. His mouth is pulled back in a tight grimace. Above his lip, among the faint stirrings of a mustache, are little drops of sweat. His teeth are clenched; you can see the strain in the muscles of his jaw and in the cords of his neck, upon which is tattooed, in big blue letters, the logo of his gang, V-13.

He plucks an ice cube from his glass, holds it up, regards it in the light. "Wouldn't you like a rock this size?" He sounds like a kid wishing for a pony for his birthday—which in fact he did when he was ten.

"*Yea-ah!*" Yogi enthuses.

"How big would you say this was, a fifty?" Lil' Sleeper asks.

"A righteous five-oh," Yogi opines.

Lil' Sleeper loses himself in his daydream; hope pops like a flashbulb in his eyes, and then the light recedes. His attention drifts to the carpet. There are lots of little white pieces of paper and lint and cloth and cigarette ash down there. To him, each piece looks like a rock. Could be a rock. He has an urge to reach down with his index finger and feel around for *pedasos*, little pieces of crack cocaine. That he *knows* there are no *pedasos* on the carpet, that he's way too methodical to have dropped anything, doesn't matter at all, because something strong makes him want to get down on his hands and knees on the filthy rug in the dark, musky, narrow room and touch each little piece of paper and lint and cloth and ash and test its composition. There are no crumbs. He knows that. It doesn't matter. A few minutes ago, he tried to smoke a sesame seed. It tasted like burnt toast when he fired it up in his pipe, which is really a piece of broken-off car antenna stuffed with Choir-boy brand copper scouring sponge—the kind without the soap. A recent letter in a local weekly paper complained about the recent epidemic of broken car antennas. Now you know.

"So what are we going to do about Culver City?" Yogi asks. "Sleeper say that if we down for the neighborhood, we gotta pay them back."

Lil' Sleeper looks up from the floor. He and Yogi are members of the Venice Gang, among the oldest and most proud of the 400 gangs in Los Angeles. For more than thirty years, Chicano homeboys have claimed this neighborhood, one square mile of palm trees and poverty in the middle of Venice, California, a little piece of ghetto encrusted in the heart of the California lifestyle like plaque in an artery—long established, nearly impossible to dislodge. Ten years ago, when Yogi and Lil' Sleeper were still playing with toys, war was raging in the neighborhood; V-13 was locked in epic battles with all the gangs that surrounded it—Santa Monica, Culver City, the Shoreline Crips, the black gang with whom they share Oakwood, the official name for the section of Venice in which they live. At the time, the *Los Angeles Times* devoted a special section to the unrest. "DEATH, DAILY VIOLENCE BECOME WAY OF LIFE FOR NEIGHBORHOOD," said the lead headline, one of twelve screamers in the twelve-page pullout. The Los Angeles police department's now-infamous CRASH unit (Community Resources Against Street Hoodlums) cut its teeth in Venice; the National Guard walked the streets for a period, too. A whole generation of Venice homeboys went to jail, became addicted to heroin, or died.

These days, Venice still gets its CRASH sweeps: low-key Tuesday and Thursday night affairs. The *pop pop pop* of automatic-weapons fire is still part of the everyday soundtrack of squealing tires, cursing homeboys, laughing children, and thumping rap. But aside from Popo—a homeboy who lost his cool during a burglary and slit the throat of L.A. city councilwoman Ruth Galanter—Venice hasn't been in the news at all lately. South-central Los Angeles is where the action is now. There, black gangs have adopted the gangsta lifestyle pioneered by the Mexican *cholos* of yore; they have begun a reign of entrepreneurial terror that has turned the L.A. gang culture inside out. For generations, the poor and the powerless of Southern California—as in every urban center across the world—banded together to form neighborhood self-protection societies. They fought for the safety of their streets and for some measure of self-respect. Back in the day, in Los Angeles, the Chicanos were ascendant. Gangs like V-13 were strong and proud.

Today, gangs are no longer about turf and respect. Instead, they are about drugs and money. Crack has done to V-13 what the police and the National Guard and other gangs have been trying to do for years.

Now, in Yogi's room, Lil' Sleeper grinds his teeth some more. He looks beseechingly at his homie: "You think you can get twenty bucks from your moms?"

"*My* moms?" asks Yogi. "What about yours?"

"I asked her yesterday, *ese*."

They both look at Margarita.

###

THE DRIVE-BY happened two nights ago.

Yogi, Lil' Sleeper, and Margarita were there, and so were Wormy, Linda, and a couple more *vatos* and *heinas*, dudes and chicks. They were kickin' it on a grassy field behind Broadway Elementary, hunkered in the middle of their own neighborhood, their home turf. Someone had brought a couple *pistos*, big bottles of Colt 45 malt liquor. Someone had some *yeska*, Mexican marijuana, ditch weed. Four of the homies were *shermed*, high on *frios*, which are menthol cigarettes dipped in a bottle of liquid PCP—two of them were crawling around on all fours, unable to walk. Yogi, Lil' Sleeper, Panther, and a white guy named Mike, your reporter, were taking turns crouching behind a wall, doing blasts, taking hits of crack.

Right around midnight, Wormy was smoking another *frio*. Loud and grandiose, he was telling everyone about the time in jail he was stabbed in the head. After that, he began talking about his father, a white man who had abandoned his mom. When the *frio* was finished, he got very quiet. His face assumed a strange, tortured expression.

And then he went *off.*

He smashed a bottle on the sidewalk, uttered incantations to the devil, danced around in the grass. He locked his focus on the white guy, stood over me and shook his fists. "Prejudice!" he bellowed, over and over. I tried to remain calm and still. At last, Yogi and Lil' Sleeper tackled him. No matter how fucked up they were, during the six weeks I was with them, my boys always had my back.

After a few minutes, things got mellow again. Everybody was chillin', smokin' out, drinkin', having a laugh.

And then, out of the darkness came a souped-up, '65 Chevy, white on blue with mag wheels. It squealed around the corner. Shots rang out: quick loud pops from a semi-automatic. From the sound of it, a .22-caliber.

The rounds sizzled the air above our heads. Small bullets can do a lot of damage; they get inside your body and ping around, tearing up organs. Yogi rolled on top of Linda. Margarita rolled on top of Lil' Sleeper. Everyone else hit the dirt.

And then it was over. A single tail light receded from their territory. In the nighttime stillness, you could hear hoots of laughter coming from the car.

"There go those motherfuckers from Culver City," somebody said.

"Cheese eaters!" Yogi yelled.

"*Putos!*"

Margarita pointed in the opposite direction across the field.

It was Sleeper. He did not look pleased.

Twenty-seven years old, Sleeper is an OG, an original gangsta, one of the leaders in the 'hood. There are no elected officials in V-13; in a gang, a leader makes himself. Rank is bestowed naturally, over the course of time, by dint of service, reputation, and personality. Sleeper has a thick scar across his cheek, two bullet holes in his side, another in his shoulder. To this day, he carries a shotgun pellet in his penis. He calls it his Mexican tickler. "What the fuck was that?" he screamed at his young homies.

"Just some of those cheese eaters from Culver City," Yogi said matter-of-factly.

"*Those* motherfuckers? Again?"

Nobody said a word. The two who had earlier been nonambulatory were now passed out on the grass.

Sleeper shook his head sadly. Lately, he thinks, everything is fucked up in the neighborhood. Everything has changed. These younger homeboys know as well as he does that if someone disrespects you—if he calls you a name, if he mad-dogs you, if he owes you money, if he shoots at you, if he talks shit about your old lady, if he makes you angry about anything at all—there is only one thing you're supposed to do. You go get your gun out of its hiding place, you hunt him down, you cap him, you bust a grape. Or, if you can't find *him*, you cap one of his homeboys. You don't drive by—that's for cheese eaters, something else new in the picture. For years the homies from Venice and Culver City have been shooting each other, but it was always done face to face. That was always the rule. Yes, there were rules. A code of honor if you will: You don't shoot from a car. You don't shoot at a house. You don't do things to jeopardize innocent children or family members. A few years ago, one of the Venice homeboys took a shot at a rival gang member who was standing outside a church. A mother and her child were killed. As soon as they heard what happened, the Venice homeboys beat up their own *vato*. He was banished from the neighborhood.

Sleeper looked off in the direction the Chevy had retreated. He hocked a fat lugie on the ground. "Somebody better do something soon— or *all* y'all gonna have to deal with *me*."

#

SINCE 1900, when "Venice of America" was built, complete with canals, as a sort of residential theme park by the Pacific Ocean, the Oakwood section, just adjacent, has been poor and predominantly nonwhite, a little patch of blight along the pricey Southern California coast. The older families date back four or five generations, though the notion of generations can be deceptive here. Many of the women become pregnant at fifteen or sixteen; thirty year old grandmothers are not difficult to find.

The neighborhood claimed by V-13 is a ramshackle collection of bungalows with front and back yards. Invariably, there will be one or more older-model Chevrolets around the properties, in various states of repair, and maybe an old stove in the back yard. Women who work outside the neighborhood tend to drive small Japanese imports. The walls of all the buildings and fences are covered with graffiti, riotous scrawlings that identify the gang and its members by their street names—each gang and each man has, in effect, his own logo.

Inside, the houses are tidy and clean; the furnishings and knickknacks are inexpensive but lovingly kept. Wedding, graduation, and post–boot camp military portraits of family members are displayed high on the walls, above the typical sightline, lending the pictures an iconic air. The television burns twenty-four/seven; the electronic hearth is always on. Typically, there is a large living room with lots of sofas and chairs. The seating is plush and comfortable—in general, the dwellers are a substantial lot, owing to a diet heavy with lard and tortillas and sweets; in the eat-in kitchen, there is always an iron skillet of beans on the stove, fresh tortillas on the table. Every other room, including the back porch, is used as a bedroom. People will also sleep at night in the living room.

Typically, four or five generations of relatives live in one house. Great-grandma shares a bedroom with auntie. Grandma and an orphaned great-niece will share another. A high-ranking daughter—often the one with the best job—will have a room to herself. A young couple will also have a room. If they have a small child, the child will sleep with the ranking female. The females of the clan share an elaborate network of responsibilities. Everyone cooks, cleans, and takes care of the kids. Young couples have the fewest responsibilities. They are encouraged to sleep late, to make more babies. The older children take care of the younger children. They grow up taking care of one another. One sixteen-year-old mother, when told about the notion of "unwed motherhood" knit her brows in puzzlement. "I been taking care of babies since I was five or six," she giggled. "I love babies. I don't see it as a *bad* thing."

The women run the household with a loving but firm hand. Grandma or Great-grandma holds the lease; all the women work in some fashion or another, some off the books so they can still collect from the government. Because the homeboys live at the pleasure of their wives' or girlfriends' mother or grandmother, and because many have no job and no prospects, they are low in the family pecking order—treated not so differently from the children. Not much is expected of them, either.

Until recently, the word *gang* wasn't used in connection with V-13. Gang was something the police called them, something the newspapers called them. To themselves, they were, and have always been, simply a *neighborhood*: people who live in a place where they've lived all their lives, where their parents have lived all *their* lives. To the Chicanos of Oakwood, this one square mile is their village, their home, their world, a society within society. Everyone knows everyone, and they have known each other since they were born. When somebody disrespects the neighborhood—when somebody from Culver City hits Lutie's mom on the head with a bumper jack, or takes a knife to Beaver, or a bat to Tavo, or shoots Gato in the back—the neighborhood is supposed to make sure that somebody from Culver City is bumper-jacked or knifed or clubbed or shot. It is the job of the men to protect the honor of the neighborhood. This is the meaning of the expression "down for the 'hood." Either you is or you ain't.

Lately the youngbloods of V-13 have been eatin' cheese. Three times over the past ten days, gang members from Culver City, Chicanos from the projects in the town next door to Venice, have driven through the neighborhood and taken potshots at Venice people. Unfortunately, Yogi and Lil' Sleeper and the rest have been too fucked up on crack to continue their four-generation cycle of violence. Even the social workers have begun to notice.

"I remember the Venice from when I was gang banging," says Marianne Diaz, 29, a former member of the Compadres, another Chicano gang in Los Angeles. She is now an outreach worker with Community Youth Gang Services.

"Venice is such a big, old gang," she says. "Even back in the day they had, like, maybe a thousand homeboys. They were down. People respected them. Venice, Lennox, South Los, and Eighteenth Street. Those were your four big gangs. Everyone has heard of Venice. I mean, if you got busted, you were gonna see twenty or thirty of them down in the pen, and they were the ones running things. Just about every older Venice homeboy I meet is a *veterano*," an ex-con.

In Venice, she says, a high percentage of the males over fifteen have been to jail or to juvenile. "He figures the system is against him, that no one wants to give him a chance. And he also figures there's a good chance he will die tomorrow. It is a very live-for-today society." In his nineteen years, Lil' Sleeper has done a total of four years behind bars; Yogi is about to go off and serve a one-year sentence. He says he's innocent of the actual crime for which he was found guilty, but he's taking it like a man: "I figured I'd already done about thirty or forty *other* burglaries. They had to get me for one of them."

Being respected in the neighborhood for being an ex-con is only one aspect of a curious system of beliefs in Venice. Take the Gonzales family.

On a typical Saturday night in the living room there is popcorn and a video, adults and kids. Three people in the room, of varying ages, are nodding out from heroin. A joint of *yeska* is being passed around. The daughter's boyfriend and two of his friends are bustling in and out from the back yard, smoking crack. At one point, Great-grandma looks up from the movie. "Oh, Thumper, I *know* you are doing that shit again." She laughs heartily, setting her chins ajiggle. "You are sprunger than a motherfucker!" Everybody in the room guffaws.

Over the years, one homeboy's father, a $22,000-a-year city employee, has borrowed a total of $40,000 to bail out and defend his son for various crimes. Another's father took a week off from work to help his son kick his heroin habit. "I just love my boy," the father says. "What would you do?"

By the time gang members reach the age of twenty-five—if they live that long—they usually move toward a more settled life. Many work in city sanitation and maintenance. Delivery services are another good shot for ex-cons. Almost all of them have children; their culture puts a high value on the young; they want to see their *niños* grow up. War is a young man's game. The OGs rest on their laurels.

"The older homeboys are saying that the younger guys, all they care about is getting high," says Diaz. "They're telling them, 'You like to wear Venice on your hat, you like to write your name on the walls and throw up a hand sign and get tattoos all over your body, but you won't bust a grape on nobody.'"

Back in the 1940s and 1950s, says Diaz, the Chicano gangs that emerged in Southern California were "more or less derived from the Hispanic culture." Descendants of the Mexican *banditos*, and later of the zoot suiters, they inherited a macho culture dedicated to the preservation of territory and respect.

"Now," says Diaz, "things are changing. The rock cocaine has come in, and the blacks have taken over the gang thing. My partner, who is black, he always tells me, 'My people took your idea of gangs and totally bent it and turned it around and took away any of the pride or the respect.' I think that's true. It's like before, in the old days, the leader of a gang was the homeboy who was downest. Now it's the homeboy who is richest. In Venice, nobody's got nothing anymore. It's all about getting high."

#

LIL' SLEEPER AND YOGI are back in the room, both of them sitting on the bed. It's morning. Or maybe it's afternoon. They've been smoking a few rocks.

"*Psssssst. Pssssssst!*"

Yogi starts. His eyes go wide. "What was that?" he whispers.

"Wha?" asks Lil' Sleeper. He looks up from the carpet, where he's been searching for crumbs.

"That noise," Yogi says. He turns down the radio, switches off the fan, cocks an ear.

"What noise?" Lil' Sleeper repeats.

"Hey, *Yogi!* Lemme in, *ese!*"

Yogi pulls back the curtain on the window over his bed. Outside there is daylight. The palms rustle in the breeze. Into the room waft the scents of salty sea, pink hydrangeas, refried beans, blue exhaust from souped-up cars. It is Panther. He holds up a dove, a twenty-dollar rock, about the size of a marble.

Yogi's bedroom is the unofficial clubhouse for the members of the Little Banditos, a twelve-member *cliqua* within the V-13 gang, which numbers roughly 300. A *cliqua* is an age-affinity group of homies who were all jumped into the gang at the same time—sort of like a pledge class in a fraternity. Like a soccer or basketball club, the Venice gang has a number of *cliquas* for different age groups, ranging from early teens to late twenties. There are the Banditos, the Little Banditos, the Tiny Banditos, the Midget Banditos. Likewise, within the gang, there are *cliquas* of Locos, Winos, Chucos, and Dukes, all of them with subgroups ranging from Midgets to Bigs.

Whenever the Little Banditos come by Yogi's crib, they follow the same procedure. They check first with Yogi at the window, then they go around to the front of the house and knock politely at the door. Permitted entrance, they exchange pleasantries in the front room—like so many brown-skinned Eddie Haskels, talkin' polite shit to Yogi's mom, his grandfather, and his little sister. Then they walk down the hallway to the back room, Yogi's crib. His mom thinks they're watching television and videos all day long. Or maybe she doesn't. Over the past month, since he got his tax-refund check (he worked for his uncle's landscaping company last summer), Yogi has not been away from his room for longer than an hour. The more crack you do, the harder it is to leave the pipe and sally forth.

"First hit!" Yogi calls, in the same manner he calls "shotgun" if you're driving him somewhere.

"It's *my* rock," Panther protests.

"Yeah, but it's my *room.*" There is nothing worse than having a rock and nowhere to smoke it. You need somewhere cool and quiet. Somewhere nobody will bother you. If you don't pay attention, you can fuck off your high, which means you don't take advantage of the rush. It's only there for a little while. You can easily miss it. And then, all you're left with is the jittery need for more.

Panther hands over the rock. Yogi slices it with a razor blade, puts a piece the size of a small aquarium stone into his car-antenna-pipe. He melts it some with a Bic lighter, blows out all the air in his lungs, takes a blast. You can't hit it too hard or the hit will liquefy and you'll lose it; later you'll have to scrape it out of the pipe. The resin is like the mint after dessert. As soon as Yogi finishes his hit, Lil' Sleeper snatches the pipe from his hand; he and Panther begin to argue over who's next. Yogi sits back and closes his eyes. Finally he exhales—a light, clean smoke that smells of ether. Upon his next intake of fresh air, there is a supercharge effect—an instant explosion of pleasure inside his head, an orgasmic body rush. It drills a hole from the top of his scalp down to his groin, and then it drills another between his ears—an ecstatic, physical, electric sign of the cross. The music from the radio comes flooding into his head. His brain buzzes. He smiles cherubically, slightly crosseyed.

Then the smile recedes, the feeling starts to fade, like the light when you turn off the TV, the long white line that dissolves into a dot, then disappears. He begins thinking about the next hit.

One more hit. That's *all* he can think about, all he cares about. His teeth are clenched, his jaw muscles stand, his throat tightens. Everything inside tightens. His veins constrict, his dick shrivels, his heart pounds. He lights another cigarette.

With each subsequent hit, the rush is less intense, but the desire is *more* intense. With heroin, you have a twice-a-day obligation. You fix morning and night and forget about it. Crack is moment to moment. You do a hit, feel the rush, start obsessing immediately about the next hit. About getting more. More. One more hit. If you could stop thinking about it for thirty minutes, the urge would pass. You'd be jittery and speedy, but you could ride it out. But you can't *not* think about it. Your every thought is focused on the next hit.

But the next hit is never as good.

You don't care. You keep going.

You are *sprung*.

#

"So what are we gonna do?" Yogi asks. He is sitting on the bed in his narrow room. It is noon on another day. The drugs are gone, again. Lil' Sleeper is here, as usual. Panther is out trying to get some money some *vato* owes him.

"Let's go get a rock," Lil' Sleeper says, as if it's a new idea.

"You got any *fedia*?"

"No."

"You do *so*."

"I do not."

"Don't bullshit me, *ese*."

The way you find rock in the neighborhood is this: You walk outside of your house.

Day or night, rock is always for sale. You can buy it from men or women, boys or girls. You can buy it on corners, in alleys, though windows, inside apartment buildings. The dealers here don't even bother with packaging—no glassine envelopes, no vials. They sell the *pedasos* loose. The rocks are hard, white, crystalline, irregular. Cooked down from powder cocaine, using baking soda to trigger the chemical changes, they are pure and insoluble. The dealers stash the *pedasos* in their socks, in baggies, in pockets, beneath their tongues—a place the cops haven't yet learned to look; it won't be long. In the coming years, to frustrate the chain-of-custody considerations of the law, a more elaborate sales system will have to be developed: one guy to take the money, one guy to monitor a stash that nobody physically possesses, an underage kid to deliver the actual rock. For now, though, things are simple. The dealer has the rocks. He works the curb. He *slings*.

There is constant commerce. There are businesslike slickers with theme raps ("I'm Billy D./Stick with me"). There are hot babes, cold gangstas, skinny rock dawgs—by five in the morning, they are scrapping and arguing like extras from the set of *Night of the Living Dead*, trying to sell another rock to go score more. Besides the members of V-13 and their families—one night I partied with a group of women in their thirties and forties, all of whom were gainfully employed; they smoked *way* more crack than the homies could ever even afford—the customers are a steady stream of *gavachos*, white people in nice cars, residents of nearby Marina Del Ray, Santa Monica, and Beverly Hills. The dealers rush aggressively into the street, surrounding the cars, sticking their hands inside, jockeying and fending for position . . . vibrating, clenching, exhorting, "Take mine!" "Me!" "I got you!"

Most of the dealers are *miatas*, derogatory Chicano slang for African-American—in this case members of the Shoreline Crips, whose families have coexisted with the Chicanos in Oakwood for years. Lately, there has been peace between the two gangs. The Shorelines have no beef with the *vatos* smoking up all the product they can sell.

Sleeper remembers the days when things were different. "Nineteen seventy-seven was the first I remember somebody getting killed that I actually knew," he says. "And then, *bang*, all of a sudden there were like ten shootings a week. Homies were dropping left and right on both sides. It was all out war. When we walked down the street, we carried a gun. We wore the whole outfit, the khakis and the Pendletons, the hairnets, the bandannas, the hats, the overcoats, the whole bit. We was clean, five creases in every shirt, and we ironed them ourselves. Between me, my brother and my father, we used to go through two cans of spray starch a week.

"I sometimes carried a twelve-gauge shotgun under my overcoat. It was like the Wild West, man. You'd have homeboys on the roof, homeboys behind the trees, guns everywhere. For a while, when the National Guard had the streets barricaded, you could only get in by police escort. If a house got burned, the fire department wouldn't go in until sunrise. It was up to you to put it out. We was down, homeboy, wasn't nobody meaner."

In 1979, the media discovered the gang problem by the sea. The *Los Angeles Times* published their special report—an entire section. There were stories of stray bullets, innocent victims, grieving mothers, shattered lives, midnight death.

"THE TROUBLE IN OAKWOOD," read a subhead on the front page. "Swept by smog-free ocean breezes, bordered on the south by the affluent playground called Marina del Rey," the text read, "Oakwood is a strangely incongruous center of poverty and tragedy. While crime and gang violence tear at the community from within, mounting coastal real-estate values threaten to crush it from without."

At that time, the drugs of choice in the neighborhood were *chiva* and PCP. *Chiva* is Mexican slang for "goat". In this case, it's also slang for black tar heroin imported from Mexico. When *chiva* was the thing, the Chicanos ruled the L.A. drug trade. They had the cars and the money and the guns. They sold the heroin to the *miatas* and reaped the profits.

Since crack came to the 'hood, the *miatas* have been in control. The struggle to stay high is a difficult job. The homeboys beg their mothers or their wives or girlfriends for five or ten dollars. They say they have to get a new driver's license, or they find some other official-sounding excuse. They say they need a new asthma inhaler or another small, expensive thing that they can rip off from a drug store and produce later to back up their story. Scam done, they buy a couple hits and smoke. Then they start all over again, scamming to get more. Many have sold their tools and their father's tools. There are amazing deals floating around Venice at three in the morning—whole automotive tune-up kits for under fifty dollars, VCRs for twenty-five. Many in Venice have also sold their guns, which is probably another reason the Venice homeboys have been unable to muster the manpower to pay back Culver City. Lil' Sleeper, for one, sold his shotgun about a month ago. One night, someone offered me a .22-caliber semiautomatic Ruger rifle for the price of a twenty-dollar rock. Absent something of value to sell, the homeboys will do a robbery or burglary, though when you're sprung, that sort of business takes way too long. And then there's the business of fencing the goods—gratification too long delayed.

"The worst thing," says Joe Alarcon, a former Lennox gang member who now works for Youth Gang Services, "is that at this point we don't have much to offer Venice. The problems are even bigger in South Central. Down there we're getting, like, five homicides a week. The black areas are really bad. On a daily basis, something like 85 to 90 percent of all crimes in Los Angles are being committed by Bloods and Crips. Those guys are crazy; they just don't care. Because our resources are limited, we've had to concentrate on the areas that are the worst. We've kind of let Venice fall through the cracks, I'm afraid."

#

ANOTHER DAY in Yogi's room. Yogi, Lil' Sleeper, and Margarita are on the bed.

Lil' Sleeper: "How much *fedia* you got?"

Yogi: "Two dollars, homes."

"I got two, too," says Lil' Sleeper. Really, he has five. He turns to Margarita. "You got *fedia*?"

Margarita's eyes are large, brown, empty. She looks like a beautiful, underage zombie model. One at a time, she works three crumpled dollar bills out of the front pocket of her super-tight denim mini-skirt. Finished at last, she holds the bills aloft like a prize.

"That's six," Lil' Sleeper announces. He snatches the bills from her hand.

"Seven," Yogi contradicts.

"Wha'?"

"Two and two plus three equals *seven*."

And then: A series of hard knocks on the door—*bang bang bang*. Everybody ramrods. Eyes like saucers. *What the fuck, ese?*

Yogi turns down the radio and the fan. He calls out, innocently, musically: "Who's theeeeere?"

"Me, motherfucker! Open up!"

Yogi and Margarita trade looks. Lil' Sleeper's eyes bulge. He looks like he's about to throw up.

Five years ago, when Lil' Sleeper was still known as David and was about to be jumped into the gang, he went to Sleeper and asked him could he have his name. It is a common tradition, like adoption in reverse. Sleeper was honored. And he was willing. But there was a problem— another homeboy was *already* calling himself Lil' Sleeper. The thing was, that Lil' Sleeper had turned out to be a cheese eater. Sleeper was sorry he'd ever said yes to that *vato*. So if David wanted the handle for himself, Sleeper told him, he could have it. But first, he would have to beat up the other Lil' Sleeper and take the name away from him.

The fight was bloody but short. David became Lil' Sleeper. Thereafter, he owed his allegiance to Sleeper.

Now Lil' Sleeper chews on his thumb, trying to think. "Open the door," he says at last.

Sleeper is hype. And he's even more pissed for being made to wait outside Yogi's bedroom door like some, like some . . . . *What the fuck, ese?* His jaw is clenched. The veins in his neck are tight. He points a dirty calloused finger at his namesake. "What have you done to pay back Culver City?" he demands.

Lil' Sleeper looks up at him defiantly. "We ain't gonna do *nothing*," he says.

"We ain't gonna do *nothing*," Yogi repeats. He's got his homey's back. Little Banditos 4-ever.

"You got shot at the other day in your own neighborhood, homeboy! You got shot at *three times* in one week!"

Lil' Sleeper shrugs. "Why's it up to *me* to do something? There's other people who live here, too."

Sleeper stares at him in disbelief. *Can you believe this punk?* Then his eyes drift down to the carpet. There are lots of little white pieces of paper and lint and cloth and cigarette ash down there. To him, each piece looks like a rock. Could be a rock. He wants to reach down and . . .

"Gimme a blast," Sleeper demands. His lips are pulled back in a tight grimace.

"We was just going to get a ten from Binky," Yogi says.

"A ten?" Sleeper chews his thumb, considering.

Yogi brightens. "Maybe we could get him to kick us down a little more."

"Hand me that pipe," Sleeper says. "Is there any residue in there?"

"What about Culver City?" asks Margarita.

"We'll get them later," Sleeper says.

Rolling Stone, 1988

## 11

Hunting Marlon Brando

From the start it sounded ridiculous.

Go to Tahiti and find Marlon Brando.

Yeah? And then what?

You'll know.

I'll know?

Hmmm.

What else was I going to do? It was December. It was cold. There was promise of little: exorbitant heating bills, dirty melting snow. Christmas was coming; I didn't have a date for New Year's. There's a reason they call it suicide season. I needed something else to focus on. I needed a mission—a real, choice mission, a quest.

Yeah, that's what I needed: A quest.

I needed to learn something; it was time. Thirty years old, divorce pending. Ready now to turn the page for the big buildup. You have to dare to be bad in this world of ours, you have to try stuff you might have to fail. One thing is certain: If you do what you always do, it's guaranteed to turn out the same. After ten years of stories, I'd learned a lot about other people, and a little about myself, but not nearly so much as I'd have liked. This time, I wanted more than a story. I wanted to bring something back in first person, to write about a difference in my life.

As it was, they suggested a hunt for Marlon Brando, the most elusive actor of our time.

I took the job. Wouldn't you?

So now I'm in Papeete, the capital of Tahiti, searching for Marlon Brando, walking around in the rain—no one had bothered to mention monsoon season. It is rain like I've never seen before: a thick, pulsing mist against a white-gray sky, a tin rhythm on a rusty roof, steady, maddening . . . .

I arrived four days ago, flying from just before dusk at Dulles until just after dawn at Faaa. How many hours it took, I cannot say. Across the continent, across the equator, halfway around the world, counterclockwise. Snotty stews, grainy light, a fat man reclining his seat into my lap. Time running backward as I flew forward, yesterday arriving tomorrow, brisket and succotash arriving cold.

Since then, since landing and checking in, setting out for Marlon, everything has taken on the quality of a weird, suffocating, narcotic dream. My bones feel soft. My underwear is damp. I'm looking for a man who doesn't want to be found. I feel like I'm in a movie.

I haven't located Marlon, not exactly, not yet. But there are traces of him everywhere. Down the street, across the Boulevard Pomare, is a bar called Chaplin's. It's named for Charlie Chaplin, who directed Marlon in *A Countess From Hong Kong*. There is a famous photo of Marlon on the wall. He's astride a motorcycle, Johnny in *The Wild One*. "What are you against?" the bobby-soxer asks him. "What have you got?" Marlon sneers.

Marlon's in the bookstore down the street, too. Pieces of his life, anyway. On one shelf are eight copies of *Mutiny on the Bounty*, by Charles Nordhoff and James Norman Hall, and six copies of *The Arrangement*, by Elia Kazan. *Mutiny* you know about: Marlon, then the world, discovers Tahiti. Kazan was Marlon's greatest director: *A Streetcar Named Desire*, *On the Waterfront*, *Viva Zapata!*

Even in my room, there are signs of Marlon, reminders of him. I turned on the cable TV and found Humphrey Bogart in *The African Queen*. Bogart won the Oscar for *Queen*, beating out Marlon in *Streetcar*. Later this evening, *Catch-22* is airing. Martin Sheen is in that. Sheen was also in *Apocalypse Now*, playing another guy who goes hunting for Marlon, another guy who has no idea what he'd do if he finds him.

It's been like this for some time now. Everywhere I look, I see Marlon. His pictures, his movies, his legacy. In a way, I guess, I did this to myself, cooked up the mania and smoked it like a drug, inhaled his spirit into my body, his thoughts into my head.

After I took the job—which believe me, I really *did* think about; other than the trip, what was the upside? Marlon hadn't granted an interview in over a decade—I set out to study Marlon in depth. I bought a VCR, one of the first on my street. I collected every single one of Marlon's movies, no small feat: Have *you* ever seen *A Countess from Hong Kong?* Night after night, for four solid weeks, I darkened the lights and thumbed the remote, and old moments from Hollywood returned. Marlon moved across the screen in many guises, inhabiting first my Sony monitor and, later, the screen inside my brain. He was Napoleon, Fletcher Christian, the Godfather, Julius Caesar, Sky Masterson, Jor-El, an eyeball in a cave. Turned-down lips, carved jaw, high cheekbones, almond eyes, tousled hair. A brute, a fop, a dandy. A statesman, a queer, a killer. A don, a Nip, a crip, a Kraut . . . .

I got kind of obsessed; I stopped going out. Maybe I was doing too much cocaine, staying up too many nights without sleep. I xeroxed his pictures and taped them on the walls, I read every article ever written about him, every single book listed in the Library of Congress. I transcribed every line he said in every movie. I dropped down deep, very deep, into my own kind of Method—in his wife I saw an old girlfriend, in his divorce I saw my old wife, in his art I found a meaning, in his vision I saw purpose, too. I watched a snail crawl along the edge of a straight razor, crawl along the edge of a straight razor and survive. That was my dream. That was my nightmare. That and the others, gray and half formed, fitful and flickering in the hours before dawn.

And then one day it hit me. Marlon was James Dean before James Dean, De Niro before De Niro, Newman before Newman, Penn before Penn. He was all of it before anyone. Marlon was the template for two generations of actors—for two generations of men. He wore jeans, he did his own thing, he succeeded in what he tried. He was tough and sensitive, gifted and crude; he spoke French; he used words like *ain't*. He was talented, he made a lot of money, he gave to the world, he used the world for his own whims. So much of what we do today is Marlon. The way he puts on his sunglasses in *The Wild One.* The way he smells his lapel rose in *The Godfather.* The way he cries for Stella in *Streetcar.* The way he boycotted the Oscars to promote Native American rights, sending a beautiful young Indian woman in his place.

Marlon led the way, and then he disappeared, split from the whole program. The more I began to understand, the more I admired him. A tough mother. An original. He could have been head of the Screen Actors Guild, a politician, the occupant of whatever pedestal this hero-hungry world would have gladly offered. Instead, he bailed out. He chose his own route.

I started to think that it wouldn't be a bad idea to actually find Marlon Brando, to ask him for some guidance on the world's behalf—to ask him what he thinks, where we should be going, what we should be doing, what is supposed to come next. Look around. Everywhere on the planet things seem so bleak. War. Famine. Disease. Diminishing natural resources. The vanishing middle class. Our sorry excuses of elected leaders. Maybe Marlon had some answers. Maybe Marlon could show us the way.

All I need to do is find him.

#

I FIGURE I'LL START by consulting a local journalist. The resident colleague—always a good bet. Surely he knows stuff about Marlon—where he lives, where he eats, where he cats around, stuff like that.

I find the headquarters of *Le Nouveau Journal* and approach the reception desk. Because I speak neither French nor Tahitian, I have a hard time making myself understood; I resort to mime. I type on an imaginary typewriter. I do a Godfather imitation, complete with out-thrust lower jaw. Finally, I say the only thing I know in French: "*Parlez-vous anglais?*"

The receptionist picks up the phone. In due course, Dany Weus appears.

Weus is an ultra-thin, sunburned guy with a pointed face like a mongoose. He leads me through a courtyard, up some stairs, into a room with three desks. He sits down and offers me a chair.

I light his cigarette and then one for myself. I lean close to confide: "I've been sent by the *Washington Post* to find Marlon Brando. You think you could give me any help?"

Weus's eyes bulge. He nearly chokes on his cigarette. "Watergate!" he coughs. "*Washington Post!* Bob Woodward! You know Bob Woodward?"

He takes out a pad and a pen. "How do you spell your name?" he asks.

I began spelling. M . . . I . . . K . . . and then it hits me. "*Waitaminute!* What are you doing?"

"We make the story of you searching for Marlon Brando!" Weus is very excited, still coughing and choking. "We make picture of you, *everything.*"

Whoa. Not exactly what I need at this point—Marlon picking up the local newspaper and reading about my hunt for him. One thing I know well about Marlon: He hates publicity. He loathes journalists. The last time he was interviewed was more than a decade ago for a *Playboy* Q&A. Marlon granted the interview, he said, to "pay a debt, so to speak" to the magazine's founder, Hugh Hefner, who several years earlier had posted bond when American Indian Movement leader Russell Means was arrested.

After agreeing to the interview, Marlon kept the *Playboy* reporter on hold for seventeen months. He canceled three times before they finally met. In five sessions over ten days, Brando did his best to evade any subject that did not concern the plight of the Native American. Just prior to that, Marlon hijacked a live-TV interview with Dick Cavett. Brought to the studio to promote the movie *Superman*, Marlon talked for ninety minutes about Native American issues. At the BBC it was the same. The interviewer would ask, "Was it difficult to get into your costume for *Superman*?" and Marlon would answer, "In 1873, Wounded Knee took place. It was a travesty for our nation."

"I've regretted most interviews," Marlon told *Playboy*.

In 1946, Marlon dictated the following biography. It appeared in the playbill for his second Broadway play, *Truckline Cafe.*

"Born in Bangkok, Siam, the son of an entymologist now affiliated with the Field Museum in Chicago, Mr. Brando passed his early years in Calcutta, Indochina, the Mongolian Desert, and Ceylon. His formal education began in Switzerland and ended in Minnesota, where he found the rigid restriction of military school too confining. After a period in which he saw himself as a potential tympanic maestro, he came to New York and studied acting."

Since 1950, when he appeared as a paraplegic war vet in *The Men*, the first of his 31 movies, journalists have called Marlon "The Brilliant Brat," "The Walking Hormone Factory," "The Valentino of the Bop

Generation," "World's Highest-Paid Geek." They have pictured him racing around New York on a motorcycle, living like a beatnik in a flat with Wally Cox, living like a recluse, living like a Hollywood star. They have reported such tantalizing details as these: He wore blue jeans in public; he switched from blue jeans to suits and ties; he fathered at least six children by at least four different women; he was seen in a restaurant holding a piece of bread and buttering his sleeve.

Journalists have approached him at parties with lines like, "You seem pretty normal," only to have Marlon walk quietly to a corner and stand on his head. They have talked him into doing interviews, only to have Marlon sit catatonic for 30 minutes, then get up and leave. They've written that he was personally responsible for $6 million of the $21 million cost overrun in the filming of *Mutiny on the Bounty*. They've said he demanded that his lines be written on Maria Schneider's ass during the filming of *Last Tango in Paris*. (All of his lines for that movie were written on cue cards placed all over the set; that is what he's doing when he's looking everywhere but at his scene partner.) They've said he dogged roles, tyrannized directors, threw temper tantrums. They have cycled and recycled the story of his youth: Marlon Brando Jr., Bud to his family, born April 3, 1924, in Libertyville, Illinois. A cherubic child, the only boy, the youngest. His father was a womanizing limestone products salesman. His mom had been an amateur actress. She had a fondness for alcohol. There was the time Marlon set his sweater on fire in an elevator in a department store; the time, during the Depression, that he brought home a derelict woman he'd met along the road; the time he stole the clapper from the bell at military school.

Journalists have quoted his grandmother saying that as a youth, "Bud was always falling for the cross-eyed girls." An unnamed actress was once quoted as saying: "If he's Don Juan, he's done them all." Journalists have uncovered nude paintings of his first fiancée, Josanne Mariani-Berenger, daughter of a French fisherman. They have traveled around the world chasing rumors that his first wife was not, in reality, Anna Kashfi, a Hindu from Calcutta, but rather Joan O'Callaghan, the daughter of a Welsh factory worker. They have hinted that the reason he married Mexican actress Movita was so their son would have a last name; that the reason he stayed with Movita was so their daughter would have a last name.

They have updated the public on every new twist in his 14-year court battle over the custody of his son by Kashfi/O'Callaghan; on every new romance; on Rita Moreno's overdose of sleeping pills at his Hollywood home; on a Philippine woman's paternity suit; on France Nuyen's inability to play Suzie Wong on the screen because of her depression after he dumped her. They have called him a genius and a slob. They have written stories called "Brando: An Explosive Young Man's Fight to Be Himself," "Brando—The Real Story," "My Friend Brando," "Idealism Is a Snare for Citizen Brando," "Brando in Search of Himself." Said the *New York Times Magazine*: "Brando's riddled with paradoxes. And conflicts. And inner problems. An extraordinarily complicated Joe trying to understand himself, to come to terms with himself, to uncover his own identity."

In 1977, Marlon told *Playboy*, "I'm not going to lay myself at the feet of the American public and invite them into my soul. My soul is a private place . . . . People believe what they will believe . . . . People will like you who never met you . . . and then people also will hate you, for reasons that have nothing to do with any real experience with you. People don't want to lose their enemies . . . . Why should I talk to anyone?"

No! *Merci*, no! I tell the journalist from *Le Nouveau Journal*, backing away slowly. Sorry Dan, my man. No story today, thanks for your interest. I promise to call him on Friday and keep him abreast of my plans.

I didn't say Friday of what year.

#

I'M IN THE TERRACE BAR at the Ibis Hotel, paging through a book entitled *Brando for Breakfast*, written by Anna Kashfi Brando, one of Marlon's two ex-wives. It says here on page 120 that Marlon once fucked a duck in Paris. Literally. According to the book, it happened at an establishment just off Montmartre named Le Canard Bleu, which was near the site of Le Sphinx, the famed World War II brothel well known among American GIs for its motto: "You can put what you want where you want it." Apparently, the duck has an odd anatomy; its sexual organ, the cloaca, is a combination vagina and rectum. Presumably in a back room of the establishment, the duck would be immobilized in a type of stock, with its head in a guillotine, its rear exposed to the customer. The customer would penetrate the cloaca. As he was nearing climax, he would signal an attendant; the duck would be decapitated. The death spasms were said to generate "waves of ecstasy."

The rain has finally stopped; the sun pounds the pavement, raising steam. Ants swarm, mosquitoes buzz; I get this feeling that within the wall of plants skirting the terrace a savage spirit has awakened, and he is causing buds to form and stalks to shoot and flowers to explode. The air is very humid. It is hard to breathe.

Beyond the terrace, a South Seas city hunkers beside the concrete docks and the lava rock shoreline. Traffic swirls beneath rows of palm trees, a third-world motor-drone of scooter burps and diesel hums that mixes with the smells of rain and earth and flowers and lies close to the asphalt, pinioned between the thick clouds and the high green mountains that flank the city. Mini-cars line the narrow streets, side wheels parked up on curbs. Sullen French women with hair under their arms sit in sidewalk cafes, drinking Campari and writing post cards. American retirees off the cruise ship *Liberté* deliberate in small groups, deciding which tour to take. Two men on a bench share red slices of a freshly caught fish—sushi straight out of the ocean. The fish sits between them on a piece of newspaper, eyes staring outward, flesh exposed. A pimp named Louis—a brown bulldog of a man with thick lips, broad brow, and bowed legs—paces nervously beneath an awning, three packs of cigarettes in his hand, waiting for his girl.

And, forty miles due north from my table, out the harbor and through the clouds, Marlon Brando's private island, Tetiaroa, sits basking in the sun. I've got my ticket booked.

I'd been walking down Boulevard Pomare, through the rain and the crowds, trying to figure out how the hell I was going to find Marlon, what I was going to say once I did, what everybody would say if I didn't. Before I left Washington, I'd had ideas. One involved getting to Marlon's place, sitting cross-legged on his beach in a saffron robe, making him curious enough to come to me. Another involved a commando raid. I'd swim ashore under a canopy of darkness—a hired speedboat, black clothes, my camera and tape recorder and extra tapes and batteries secured in the waterproof scuba bag I'd gone ahead and bought at Hudson Trail Outfitters in Gaithersburg before I'd left. When I bought the bag, I'd also considered buying one of those cool and deadly survival knives. For all I knew, when I found Marlon, he would be living in a cave up a river with an army of stoned Polynesians guarding the landing with blowguns. All I knew for certain was what the commanding general told Martin Sheen before his mission in *Apocalypse Now*: "You see, Capt. Willard, things get confused out there. Power, ideals, morality . . . there's conflict in every human heart between the rational and the irrational, between good and evil. Every man has got a breaking point. You and I do. Walter Kurtz has reached his. Very obviously he has gone insane."

So this is what I'd been thinking as I was walking in the rain on the Boulevard Pomare. Part of me was afraid of what I'd find, what I'd do once I got there. I knew the risks, or imagined I knew them. But the thing I felt the most, much stronger than fear, was the desire to confront him.

And then I saw the poster.

Right there, in the window of a travel agency.

Three beautiful Tahitians—two girls and a boy—in native dress on a white sand beach beneath a blue sky. Their hands were outstretched, letting go a sea bird.

Visit Hotel Tetiaroa
Marlon Brando's Private Atoll

Hotel Tetiaroa!

Why hadn't anybody told me?

I pushed open the door, fairly threw it open, and the woman started babbling at me in French, but as you know I don't speak French, so I started tapping on the window, pointing at the poster—"Can go? Can go? Marlon Brando?"—tapping furiously with my fingernail, *tap tap tap!*, and I was sure that at any moment a crack would form and spread and the glass would shatter into puddles on the sidewalk, and my hand would bleed and maybe music would play, just like what happened to Capt. Willard in the first scene of *Apocalypse Now*, but I couldn't stop tapping— "Can go? Can go? Marlon Brando?"—because I couldn't fucking believe it: A travel poster for Marlon Brando's private atoll. *Marlon's running a tourist trap!*

"No problem," the woman said, switching easily to English. "Cash, check, or Visa?"

#

BENJI'S IN EXILE. He used to be a captain in the Philippine army. His uncle was a general. The general didn't get along with Ferdinand Marcos, so the whole family had to flee to Tahiti. Now, the general runs a grocery. Benji works at the Ibis Hotel. He arranges cars, recommends restaurants, chats up American women and sends them on the Circle Island tour to see the Blowhole of Arahoho. He looks like someone who can get you what you need.

What I need, I tell him, is a translator. Someone who speaks English, French, and Tahitian. Someone to go with me to Marlon's island. Someone who can leave right away.

"And for this someone," Benji asks, "you want girl or boy?"

"I think a girl would be best," I say, innocently enough.

"I see." Benji raises an eyebrow.

"If I go with a woman," I explain, "it would be a good cover for me, don't you think? You know, me there with a woman. Of course we'd have *separate* accommodations. I'm looking for a translator, you understand. Simply a *translator.*"

"I understand."

"And, I'm just thinking out loud here," I continue, "but it probably wouldn't hurt to have a *beautiful* woman. Marlon loves beautiful, exotic women. Maybe, when I meet him, if *I'm* with a . . . ."

#

ANGELINA ARRIVES at the Ibis bar an hour late. I know she thinks I'm insane. When we first spoke on the telephone, I told her I needed help finding Marlon Brando. She was silent for a beat. And then she said, in her musical Tahitian-French accent, "Marlon Brando: He is lost?"

She shakes my hand tentatively, sits at the table with her knees together like a Catholic schoolgirl, her purse balanced primly in her lap. She wears a flower behind her ear, and a *pareu*, a native length of cloth, tied in such a way that it looks like a gown. She wears it with an easy elegance, a languor, a certain . . . needless to say, Benji has done me solid.

She tells me a bit of her story. She learned English in New Caledonia, where her family had to move when her father was stricken with gout.

Later her father's visa ran out and they were forced to return to Tahiti. To help support her family, Angelina had to drop out of school. Now she works in a nearby hotel. One day, she continues, an Italian checked into the hotel. Instantly, he fell in love with her—a deep, unrequited love. He left Tahiti but returned, hoping to win her affections. He stayed for several months. Each night, he'd play solitaire in the lobby while she worked behind the desk. Sometimes they talked, sometimes they did not. Once she played gin rummy with him. Repeatedly, he asked her to dinner. Repeatedly she refused. Finally, on the eve of his departure, she accepted his invitation. Upon hearing her affirmative response, so long awaited, he broke down and cried.

Touched, she fell in love with him.

More recently, Angelina continues, she has had serious gynecological surgery. She's recovering now. (I needed to know this why?) When she is better, the plan goes, her Italian friend will send for her and they'll get married; she'll be able to finish her university education in Italy. Meantime, she needs money. And so she is here.

It's hard to know what she is thinking as I tell her of my plans for hunting Marlon Brando. The true language of Tahiti is a silent one, conveyed with a downcast glance, a lifted chin, a raised eyebrow. She smiles now and then in the velvet shadows of the sunset; she pouts, she giggles, she breaks my heart with the bright whites of her eyes. She seems willing enough to go on a trip and make some money. She seems to trust me— sort of. One last thing, she asks. "Why it is again that you are hunting Marlon Brando?"

I try to explain without seeming like a psychotic stalker. Assuming a scholarly tone, keeping my vocabulary simple, I tell Angelina about Marlon's career, about his movies, about his influence on men, his legacy. I tell her how this whole thing started out as an assignment, a way to get out of the cold winter weather, a way to distance myself from my failed marriage. (The four months of cohabitation ended up costing me an $18,000 cash settlement, not including lawyers' fees. I did the math and figured out that I could have spent about $150 a day on hookers for four months—or $600 a day for one month—and it would have cost me the exact same amount.) And I tell her how, after all this research I've done, all those hours and all these miles, this has become much more than just a story to me. I tell her how I value Marlon Brando. How important it is that we find him. How he may well be the key to a happy and prosperous future for all people around the world.

And then I tell her I've got reservations for two on Marlon's luxury island, separate rooms, of course. I offer her U.S. $150 a day plus all she can eat.

"We fly tomorrow," I say, looking intensely into her wide, brown, little bear eyes. "Are you in?"

THE TWIN-ENGINE, twelve-seater breaks cloud cover five minutes out of Tahiti, and thereafter the sky is clear, the ocean a vast cloth of wrinkled blue, curved at the horizon. After twenty minutes in the air, the plane makes its approach, a full circuit of Marlon's sunny atoll, then lands on the airstrip, a patch of packed sand and concrete scissored like an off-center part through five square miles of jungle.

A dozen smiling Tahitians dressed in *pareus* and Hawaiian surfer shorts meet the plane. The only other passengers are four members of a French film crew who'd just finished shooting a mini-series version of *Mutiny*. An older woman named Simone leads us to our bungalows, rustic dwellings of ancient design spaced randomly among a forest of coconut, pandanus, breadfruit, and ironwood trees. Set upon concrete slabs, the walls of the bungalows are made of woven pandanus fronds, decorated with artfully composed driftwood sculptures. The furniture is fashioned of coconut wood, cloth, and twine. There are authentic giant clam shells for sinks. The beds have mosquito netting and ample supplies of green incense coils to burn against the prodigious numbers of bugs. It never occurred to me, but of course it makes sense—the deeper you get into nature, the worse the bugs: Imagine the welts on Adam and Eve. There is electricity, but only at certain times of the day, Simone explains, and only until 10:00 at night.

Angelina and I follow along on the little tour. I can't believe we're here. I am positively enraptured. I know this is going to work out well. I can just feel it. Before we boarded the plane, I'd explained the plan to Angelina. We'd get to the island, to the hotel. We'd get our rooms, lay back, play it cool. We'd figure out the lay of the land first, then formulate a plan. Above all, we didn't want to act like journalists because Marlon hated journalists. Subtlety: that was the key.

As Simone leads us from bungalow to bungalow—spaced for privacy a good bit apart—our little group dwindles. Angelina and I are last. Standing in front of Angelina's place, my loyal translator starts speaking rapidly to Simone. Pointing at me, she says a few more paragraphs. Simone turns and studies me. She turns back and has her own say. They both giggle. Uproariously. And then Angelina says something else.

A woeful expression overcomes Simone's previously sunny face. Shaking her head clearly and firmly—*No way! No good!*—she launches into a long diatribe, the tone of which sounds rather scolding. Angelina looks mortified.

"What's she saying?" I demand.

"She say Marlon Brando not here."

I look at her with incredulity. Surely she had understood me when I explained the plan. Who is the journalist here? Who is the boss? Who's paying whom? She had outright defied me.

I smile a big smile, and shrug my shoulders, palms up, my best imitation of Alfred E. Neuman from *Mad* magazine. *What, me worry?* Okay, so things didn't exactly start out the way I planned. The measure of a man is what he does in a crisis, how he acts when things don't go as envisioned. All you can do is forge ahead.

After Simone leaves me at my bungalow, I walk back and have a little chat with Angelina, reinforcing the idea that she is working for me, that we are a team, and that she needs to follow the goddam game plan. She seems to understand.

Like any couple after a spat, we go our separate ways for a few hours, then reconnoiter. Between us, we discover that there are seventeen employees. In addition, about ten of their children are visiting for the Christmas holidays. The Hotel Tetiaroa itself consists of fifteen guest bungalows, which are rarely full all at once. There's a reception area, a dining room, a gift shop (T-shirts that say "Marlon Brando's Private Atoll"), a thatched lobby with a TV and a VCR, a bar on the beach called Dirty Old Bob's Bar. (Dirty Old Bob, I'd heard in Papeete, is a ham radio operator in Honolulu. Marlon was a ham radio enthusiast for a time. At some point, they'd become great pals.)

In the late afternoon, Angelina and I drift over to Dirty Old Bob's. While I talk to some of the French TV *Mutiny* cast, Angelina goes over to the picnic table nearby where the off duty staff and some of their family members are drinking beer and joking around. They look to be having a marvelous time. Angelina sits down and joins right in. After a little while, I amble over. Angelina acts like she likes me again. She invites me to sit, introduces me all around.

The conversation is lively. Without language to fall back on, I smile a lot and try to look cool and agreeable. I buy some drinks, offer my menthol cigarettes all around. Angelina translates some of the conversation for me. As the time passes, I start piecing things together.

The old lady with the frizzy afro is called Grandmere. She comes from Bora Bora. Her job is taking care of Marlon when he is here. She's been with him for twenty years. She remembers once she had to take Cheyenne, Marlon's daughter by Tarita—his *Mutiny* co-star and the boss lady of the atoll—to Aspen, Colorado, for a reunion of some of Marlon's kids. It was so cold she thought she would die. Popi is white-haired and grizzled, a native of New Guinea. He wears five shark teeth around his neck. His real name is John. He was given the name Popi by Christian Devi Brando, Marlon's son by Anna Kashfi. Popi says that he and Devi were working to clear the airstrip one day when Devi suddenly hugged him and said, "From now on, you're my Popi."

Charles and Suzanna are from Vanuatu. They are first cousins; they are in love; they live together. Suzanna used to be a radio announcer on Vanuatu, but Charles got tired of fishing and making copra, the work of his father and his father before that. They came here five years ago, work a few hours a day—Suzanna runs the bar, Charles does odd jobs with the other men. They make about $500 a month each. Their rent is free. A small amount is taken out of their paychecks for food. They are planning a family. They say they want to live here forever.

Matahi is from Morea. Round-bellied and missing half of his teeth, he is married to an American woman who lives in Papeete. He speaks English, but not so well considering he lived in the San Fernando Valley for twenty years. When *Mutiny* was being filmed, Matahi was hired as a carpenter. He helped build all the sets. After the movie, he moved to California, got married, and toured the country with a Tahitian song and dance troupe. He remembers going to a party once at Marlon's house in Hollywood. There was no address given on the invitation. The instructions were to drive to a certain place and then follow the *pareus* that had been hung from bamboo poles.

As you might expect, there are several people here from Tarita's home island, Bora Bora. Tarita is the mother of two of Marlon's six kids. She spends half her time on Tetiaroa, the other half in a house Marlon built in Papeete. Marlon also has three houses in Bora Bora. Tarita is on the island with her three daughters—Cheyenne (by Marlon), Miamiti (named by Marlon for Tarita's character in *Bounty*), and Reatua.

And then there is Teri'i. He's twenty-three and has been here two years. He got the job on Tetiaroa after meeting Tehotu—Marlon and Tarita's son—in the bars in Papeete. Tehotu usually runs the hotel, but he is presently in California, helping Marlon. At twenty-six, he is roughly the same age as three of Marlon's four other sons. He loves to party, Teri'i says. A good surfer, slick with the ladies, he prefers to be known by his mother's family name, Teriipaia, rather than his father's.

I can tell that Angelina has the hots for Teri'i. I have to admit that he is a fine specimen—sculpted muscles, crafted cheekbones, a parrot tattooed on his shoulder. As the sun drops low on the horizon, Teri'i invites Angelina for a walk on the beach. I go too, though I'm pretty sure I'm not invited. No matter. By this time we all have a pretty good buzz.

As he sure-foots along the sand, Teri'i carries his fishing spear, six feet long with three rusty iron prongs. A few hundred yards down the beach, he wades out into the lagoon and stands perfectly still. Like a bolt of lighting he jabs his spear into the tranquil water, comes up with something that appears to be an old flat basketball—brown and covered with spines like a porcupine. Teri'i throws it on the sand in front of us and says something. Angelina is kind enough to translate: "He say if you step on this thing, is very bad. Baddest thing in world. It can kill."

Teri'i turns the thing over with his spear. Tiny transparent appendages wriggle like worms underneath. "If you step," Angelina translates further, "you turn over like this, stick foot on wiggly things. They suck all poison gone."

Teri'i grunts, jabs the thing again. Then he throws it into the jungle. He takes Angelina's elbow, bids us to continue on.

The marijuana field is next, the plants waist high. Proudly, Teri'i picks a bud—fat, green, and sticky. He speaks English this time: "Is very good! Party! Get big stoned!"

With that, he drops his spear to the ground and jumps onto the curved bough of a coconut tree. Swift as a jungle cat, he clambers the twenty-five feet to the top, knocks down some green drinking nuts. Returning again to terra firma, he cracks one open on a rock, presents Angelina with the tender meat from the inside of the young coconut. He gives me a taste, too. It is wonderful. Funny, I've never liked coconut—that shredded stuff they put on cakes. But *this* stuff is amazing. Buoyed by our gastronomic pleasure, Teri'i walks a few feet to a stand of palm trees, breaks off a shoot from an infant plant, pulls something from the inside. "Heart of palm," Angelina translates. Utterly divine.

On the walk back to the bungalow, Angelina stops translating. She and Teri'i walk together, elbows nearly touching. I notice they've switched languages. The rolled *r*'s and throaty tones of French are replaced with the guttural singsong of Tahitian. I walk six paces behind. They seem to have forgotten me.

Back in my bungalow I sulk for a bit, then come around. Fuck it, you know? I'm not here for women. I'm here for a much bigger prize: Marlon Brando. Let Teri'i have Angelina. Maybe it will help. Maybe, after snaking my translator, he'd feel an obligation to deliver me to Marlon.

#

I wake to a clattering breeze beneath a coconut palm, a melody of fronds like wind chimes. The sand is soft ivory, warm to the touch, with a crust of coral on top like fresh ice on deep snow. Red ants skitter across a footprint, hermit crabs in painted shells motor sideways, probing with tiny claws. The vegetation is lush, a blend of vines and flowers, leaves and fruits. Coconut palms bend over the water's edge, curved and vain, ripe with green nuts. The lagoon teems with fish, feeding in bands and swirls of aquamarine and amethyst and emerald. A half-mile distant, waves break over a coral reef. Here on the beach, only a dim echo of the roar is heard. All is calm.

This is my second day on Marlon's island. It is mid-morning. I must have fallen asleep. I was up until 4:00 a.m. reading *Marlon Brando: The Only Contender*, by the same author who wrote *Doug and Mary, Lenny, Janis and Jimi: All the Stars in Heaven*. I'm still a little woozy. I rub my eyes, blink them into focus.

On the beach, five feet south, I spy . . .

An unbelievably beautiful pair of breasts. Smooth, brown, tapered in repose, they rise and fall gently with each breath. I lean back on one elbow to admire. Scraps of lust and poetry float through my mind, and I have an urge to reach out, to touch, to feel the firm softness against my palms and fingertips, the dark thimble of her breeze-swept nipple, but I cannot.

I am hunting Marlon Brando. The breasts are those of my translator, Angelina, a softly sculpted girl of 20 on an ivory beach in string bikini bottom who speaks fluent English, French, and Tahitian.

Angelina stirs.

I snap my gaze, search the blue ocean, the sea birds wheeling overhead.

Marlon discovered Tahiti in 1960, when he came here to shoot *Mutiny*. Directed by Lewis Milestone, Marlon's *Mutiny* was actually a remake of a 1935 Oscar-winning version starring Clark Gable (which itself was a remake of a 1933 film starring Errol Flynn.) More Brando kizmet: Gable's leading lady in that movie, Movita, became Marlon's second wife. When Marlon arrived in Tahiti, he stayed in an expensive bungalow, attended by beautiful *vahines*, as women are called in Tahitian. He played his conga drums with the natives, met Tarita, made the movie, knew a good thing when he'd found it. At the time, Marlon was thirty-seven. He'd been making movies for ten years. He was arguably the biggest star in Hollywood.

His success had begun on Broadway in the late 1940s with *I Remember Mama* and *A Streetcar Named Desire*. In 1949, he went to Los Angeles to film *The Men*. Next came the movie version of *Streetcar*, followed by *Viva Zapata!*, *Julius Caesar*, *The Wild One*, *On the Waterfront*, *Desirée*, *Guys and Dolls*, *The Teahouse of the August Moon*, *Sayonara*, *The Young Lions*, *The Fugitive Kind*, and *One-Eyed Jacks*.

By the time he got to Tahiti, Marlon had been nominated for an Oscar four times and had won once. On the way, he'd inspired a whole new generation of Method actors—leading men like James Dean, Paul Newman, Jack Nicholson, and Robert De Niro—who drew their craft from Brando's tentative mannerisms and untrained voice, the raw emotion and brutal reality that he brought to the screen. It is said by some that Marlon's acting helped redefine the concepts of masculine sexuality in our culture. He played men who acted one way and felt another. He reversed the old, simple, John Wayne kind of concept that a man can be judged by his actions, that he can be held responsible. Henceforth, men were free to emote.

"Because the typical Brando hero of the early Fifties was ambivalent and emotionally confused," wrote a contributing editor to *Harper's* magazine, "he could not summon the courage and maturity that had formerly been elements of a film hero's virility. Instead, he projected a kind of teenaged eroticism, intense and unfocused, which derived emotional power from an impossible passive yearning. Frustration was the bottom line of his sexuality, the frustration of a man who cannot control his fate."

Try as he might, Marlon never fit well with the Hollywood scene—the "funnies in satin Cadillacs" who lived in "the cultural boneyard." He once told James Dean that Dean was mentally unbalanced and ought to see a shrink. Of Frank Sinatra, Marlon said, "Frank is the kind of guy, when he dies, he's going to Heaven and give God a bad time for making him bald." The two biggest Hollywood gossip columnists of the day were Louella Parsons and Hedda Hopper. Marlon openly called them "The Fat One" and "The One with the Hat."

Marlon did things the way he wanted to do them. From the first, he bucked the system of studios and contract players. He was among the first modern actors to receive a percentage of gross earnings, to have script and casting approval, to start his own production company, to produce and direct his own film, *One-Eyed Jacks*, which was pretty much a disaster—something else he was among the first to discover: Most actors should leave the business end to somebody else.

As is inevitable in so many Hollywood stories, there was a turning point. By the late 1950s, Marlon's career had begun to falter. He'd made a few clunkers. He seemed mortal; his eccentricities began to feel rude instead of interesting to people around him and to the public at large. The inevitable backlash ensued. Meanwhile, his private life was in tatters. He left Movita, his pregnant second wife of several months. He was named in a paternity suit by a Philippine dancer. And his first wife was still dragging him through court. The Associated Press reported, on November 19, 1959, that Anna Kashfi "threatened Mr. Brando with a butcher knife and threw a tricycle at him. She says he beat her, threw her to the floor and terrorized her. Each says their violent battles, which included hair pulling and spanking, were the other's faults."

At work, Marlon became more and more of an attitude problem. He tyrannized directors with requests for script changes, arrived late to set, wore earplugs during takes to maintain his focus, gained so much weight during the course of production that obtuse camera angles had to be employed by the end of filming.

Soon, Marlon was heard talking about hanging it up for good. He was interested in so many other things. Long before it became popular, he began studying eastern religions and meditation, traveling to Southeast Asia, lending his image to political causes. When MGM came to him in 1960 with the idea for a remake of *Mutiny on the Bounty*, Marlon was more interested in promoting a film biography of Caryl Chessman, a rapist who had recently been executed in California. On the night Chessman had been put to death, Marlon stood outside the walls at San Quentin prison and protested.

At a meeting at his Hollywood home with producer Aaron Rosenberg and director Carol Reed, Marlon pitched Chessman's life for two hours. The men listened to his pitch and politely declined. Rosenberg proposed an alternative idea. If Marlon would agree to leave right away for Tahiti to do a remake of *Mutiny on the Bounty*, he'd be given full rein to personally cast his Polynesian leading lady.

And so it was that Marlon came to Tahiti, and so it was that he eventually bought his own atoll, thirteen islands in a pacific blue lagoon four miles across, protected by a sun-bleached coral reef. Half a world away from Hollywood and his problems, it was called Tetiaroa.

Tetia means "man standing alone." *Roa* means "far away."

It was perfect.

Now, on the beach, Angelina stirs from her mid-morning nap.

"Sleep well?" I ask, eyes averted, staring out into the middle distance.

"Yes, thank you." Her tone is businesslike. She re-affixes her bikini top. "Did you find Marlon Brando yet?"

"Ha ha," I say. "How come you like so much making fun of me?" I have taken to speaking with a Tahitian-French accent, too. It seems to make things easier.

"I not make fun. I ask question."

"How about I ask you question? What happened to *you* last night. You disappear after dinner."

"I not disappear," she says coyly. "I tired."

Tired out, I think, but I don't say it. No sense getting mad. Or jealous. I hired her to help infiltrate Marlon's people. I just didn't envision her doing it in quite this manner.

#

COME ON, MARLON, *I know you're here. Show yourself . . .*

I am hacking through the jungle on Marlon's island, beating back brush with a driftwood machete. I have a pack on my back, I'm wrapped tight, walking a step at a time on the balls of my feet, chanting under my breath to Marlon. He's close, real close. I can feel him sucking me in, repelling me even as I move closer. Something rustles in the brush. I freeze.

The jungle is all strangeness and sounds—a thick, primitive, evil thing, lewdly fertile and engorged. Plants with eight-foot leaves, vines like arms, roots like legs; a coconut falls twenty feet away and my heart stops. I picture heads.

I was too young for Vietnam, but this is what it must have been like, just like *Apocalypse Now*—a mission through the jungle, a quarry I cannot see, a reason that has become too confused to understand. Like war, like love, the desire within me is strong; it burns in my head like the midday sun. There are no odds anymore. I'm on point, I'm close, walking a path that snakes through the days and weeks of my mission like a main circuit cable plugged straight into Marlon. I want him. I need him. I have to see him and I will. That is my vow to myself: if he is here, I will find him.

I set out two hours ago. Past the last tourist bungalow, past the beachfront huts where Marlon's people live, across the flaming airstrip in the heat of day, into the breathless jungle. I followed a set of tractor treads and I found the landfill, and then I found an empty pit dug in the sand, and then the cement foundation of a big house that seems to have been started and abandoned. I found an electrical wire on a tree and I followed it a mile further into the brush, tree to tree, until it stopped, ran down to the ground and connected to a transformer in the middle of a clearing. The ground was soft, but it didn't seem like anything was buried underneath. I made a note to come back later with a shovel. Underground complex?

Just before entering the jungle I'd found a large work shed near the bungalows. Inside was stored a generator, some old bicycles, an old trail bike, a backhoe. At the rear of the work area was a set of double doors. I jimmied the lock with a screwdriver, the metal made flimsy over the years by exposure to the salt air. There were a couple of bedrooms, unoccupied.

A bathroom. A book shelf. There was no doubt in my mind that this stuff belonged to Marlon.

In the early days, when he first lived here, Marlon had been brimming with revolutionary plans for his island. He told people he wanted to bring new-age technology to Tahiti, to find ways to help modern men blend with the environment, primitive men coexist with it. In the end, few of his plans were realized. No doubt they cost too much. During his Tahiti years, the 1960s, he made one clunker after another: *The Ugly American, Bedtime Story, Morituri, The Chase, The Appaloosa, A Countess From Hong Kong, The Night of the Following Day, Candy*. Today, it is nearly impossible to find any of them on video. "I need money, I make a film," Marlon said during that period. It was obvious.

The books in particular were a dead giveaway—a carefully chosen canon, his answer to the old question: What books to take to your very own deserted island? *The Encyclopedia Americana. How to Be Rich*, by J. Paul Getty. *A Sioux Chronicle*, by George E. Hyde. *Tao, The Three Treasures*, by Bhagwan Shree Rajneesh, *Ham Antenna Construction Projects*. Manuals on everything from hydroponics to solar energy, refrigeration to birds. And audio cassettes: "Stress Management Training Program," "Biofeedback Relaxation Training."

Now, in the jungle, two hours into my search, following yet another trail, I come upon the ruins of a *marae*, a Polynesian place of worship, an outdoor temple for offerings, dances, and rituals. All that remains are a group of old stones arranged in a rectangle, ten feet long and three feet wide. In antiquity, Tetiaroa was owned by a Tahitian royal family, the Pomares. It was a summer residence, the site of religious festivals, a fashionable party spot for chiefs from the north end of Tahiti. They would arrive by sailing canoe, repair to shady groves, eat lightly of fish and coconut, have their way with the most beautiful of the beautiful. Some say virgins were sacrificed in *maraes* like this one; some say it was people who broke taboo who were the victims. Some say there was cannibalism; some say the cannibalism was limited to the eating of an enemy's eye. Whatever. There is a strange, weird feeling about the place, a palpable force, a vibration. I push on.

At last the jungle breaks on the far side of the island. I have been hiking for nearly three hours. My skin burns, my whole body throbs with welts and bites. To my left is a peaceful inlet. A house.

On closer inspection, it is really a series of houses, a network of vaguely Japanese pavilions with a crude boardwalk connecting and unifying the pavilions into a large rectangular compound. A cool breeze blows through the ironwood trees planted all around; the fine long needles whisper and sway. Out in the distance, in the lagoon, I can see Tarita and her girls, fishing from their canoe.

The pavilions have wooden frames. The walls consist of large sheets of Plexiglas, framed with wood. There is a series of ropes and pulleys—the walls are meant to be raised when inhabited. At the moment everything is nailed shut, giving the place the feeling of an installation in a natural history museum. There is a pavilion with a stove and a sink, another with a long low table for dining, another with empty shelves—seven pavilions in all, stretching perhaps 200 feet on the long side of the rectangle. The last room, ocean-front, contains a simple coco wood bed, a mosquito net, four chairs, and a simple desk.

The frames around the windows in this pavilion are screwed, nailed, padlocked, *and* secured with two-by-fours. All the windows but one are opaque. I wipe a circle in the dirt of the other and peer inside. I see a large can of bug spray, a jar of Nescafé instant coffee, a wooden salad bowl, a refrigerator, toothpicks in a shot glass. There are tools piled on the floor, a bird cage covered with a towel, a driftwood sculpture, an African fright mask, several strings of worry beads, the bleached skull of an animal. Twin fly swatters hang from the wooden beam that supports the roof. Near the bed are a set of beat-up-looking conga drums.

Conga drums?

Holy shit!

This has got to be *Marlon's* room.

These are Marlon's things. I have found Marlon's things!

I pull out a pad and feverishly begin taking notes—marble desk top, flowered blue tablecloth, shell necklaces—hoovering each detail like a line of drug, buzzed beyond belief. I have come so long. So far. Now I am here. Separated from Marlon Brando's possessions by a quarter inch of Plexiglas. Things he has touched. Things he has used. Things that he cared about. Imagine what could be inside those two small metal file cabinets! What could be inside that desk! Petal brand facial tissue (white), forks (three), a coffee cup, *Popular Science, Scientific American, Time, Newsweek, Sports Illustrated.*

And then it registers: *the mailing labels!*

The subscriber is Marlon Brando, XXXX Mullholland Drive, Beverly Hills, CA.

I have Marlon Brando's address.

I have his *home* address in Beverly Hills!

I am overcome with joy, with adrenaline, with purpose.

I jump off the porch, race back through the jungle at a dead run, headed for the work shed. *His address, his address. I've got his address!*

And now I want more.

I run for thirty or forty minutes back through the jungle, taking a straighter line this time, back to the work shed I'd found earlier. I search the floor, the shelves, the peg board, the walk-in closet.

I find what I'm looking for in the corner of the room. Rusty, three feet long: a crowbar.

I pick it up, feel the heft of it in my hand. It feels right. I turn, ready to run back to Marlon's bungalow, ready to have my way with his stuff. The desk! Imagine what could be inside! The file cabinets!

Suddenly I am overcome by an intense wave of nausea. My knees go weak. I fall to the ground, panting.

What am I doing?

WHOA.

What in the hell am I doing?

And then, *snap.*

Something occurs to me.

Marlon isn't here.

Marlon Brando is *not* on this island.

Those magazines! From what I could see, the newest ones are more than a year old. His place is shut tight. There is nowhere else on the island for him to be. I've looked everywhere. I've searched in grids. On the way in, the plane had buzzed low over the entire atoll before landing. We were not more than fifty feet above each of the thirteen islands. The pilot made a big deal about it—or so Angelina said, half translating in what would become her usual fashion. I would have seen something if there was anything to see. A clearing, a roof, something irregular in the unrelenting tangle.

Maybe Simone was telling the truth. Maybe Marlon really isn't here. Tehotu is in California for Christmas, Teri'i had told Angelina. They're probably at Marlon's house in Beverly Hills.

And now I have the address.

#

At the bungalow, there's a note on the door, stuck between the fronds.

> Mr. Sager (Mike):
> I have taken the 3:00 plane back to Papeete.
> Good luck finding Marlon!
> Angelina.
>
> P.S. You can give my salary to Benji. He will see
> that I get it.

#

Teri'i's hut is on the beach, plywood and thatch with a millionaire's view. The music is good, too—95-Rock from Papeete on a boom box that takes six D batteries to run. And there is the homegrown, of course, green and pungent.

"Have you ever seen any of Marlon's movies, Teri'i? You know, *Apocalypse Now, Superman, Godfather*—"

"*Le Pe're!*"

"Is that French for *Godfather?*"

"Oui, *Le Pe're.*"

"Is good for you, this movie?"

"Is okay. I no like movie," Teri'i says. "Is too much bad. No good for the eyes. I like look sunset."

"The sunset *is* beautiful here, isn't it?"

"Yes. Sunset. And sky. And sea. All day color change. Is not only one sea, is many seas. Here is very good for me," he says, pressing his fist to his heart, sweeping his hand outward.

In the days that follow, I come often to Teri'i's bungalow; we become fast friends. I show up, and we sit on crates and stare at the horizon, or we giggle and try to talk trash. We smoke a little. Okay, we smoke a lot—it is an intense but short-acting strain. Mostly, we run out of vocabulary, so we sit in silence. I never speak again of Angelina, and neither does Teri'i. It doesn't seem important. It's as if she was never here, a footprint the ocean has washed away. But it still nags at me. Why did she leave? What exactly happened? Maybe Teri'i feels bad about Angelina, but I doubt it. It isn't like him to dwell. And anyway, it doesn't matter. I like him; I am nice to him. He likes me; he is nice to me. In my short experience, that is the way Tahitians are—more about heart than theory. What needn't make a difference doesn't have to. What seems right is what is.

Being with Teri'i at his bungalow, and with Charles and Popi and Serge and the others who stop by to puff and hang out, I learn to do as they do—to empty my mind completely, to forget about yesterday or tomorrow. I learn why Tahitians have no need in their language for a word of apology. I learn the deep peace of dreamless sleep, the richness of the glow of the dawn. I play bare-foot soccer on the beach with the other guys and loll in the warm lagoon afterward, floating like a hippo, the waterline just below my nose, arms out, feet touching the soft sand on the bottom. I learn how to spot a fish by the ripple of the water, how to navigate an outrigger canoe through the shallows using the depth chart of the different hues. I get very tan; with my shaved head and earring, new guests take me for an employee, another of Marlon's people. They approach me tentatively, as tourists do, and ask, "Where's the good fishing?" I tell them like Teri'i had told me. "Good fish everywhere, just throw in line."

At night, when the generator is off and the guests are asleep, there are a million stars. Marlon's people sit around the picnic table and sing. Matahi teaches me the chords on guitar and I sit in, strumming and singing. I feel part of something warm, something old, some-thing very right. I find myself saying, "Here is very good," and then nodding my head yes, pressing my fist to my heart, sweeping my hand outward.

I even meet Tarita, the mistress of the atoll. I tell her my first name, greet her not as Marlon's wife, not as a movie star, not as a subject of a story, but as one human to another. I ask no questions. I try not to act at all like a journalist. I do find myself watching her very closely from afar, admiring her still-beautiful face, her still-lithe figure. There is a scene in *Mutiny* when she dances so sensuously for Marlon. I confess: Before I'd come, I'd rewound it a time or two.

Tarita was a waitress when she was picked from a group of sixteen native girls to audition for the part of Maimiti, the daughter of the chief, future wife of Mr. Christian. After arriving in Tahiti to choose his leading lady, as he'd been promised, Marlon set up shop in a hotel in Papeete. He brought each of the sixteen prescreened candidates into his second-story room and promptly threatened to jump out the window. Tarita got the part because she giggled the least when he threatened.

Tarita's acting career started and finished with *Mutiny*; afterwards, thanks to Marlon, she was able to resume the simple life of her youth. On Tetiaroa, she spends much of her time gardening. She fishes a lot, too, usually with her mother and sometimes with all three of her daughters. The eldest daughter, Cheyenne, is golden-skinned with dark blonde hair, an absolute stunner—a female version of the beautiful young Marlon. The first time I catch a glimpse of her, she is wearing a skimpy bikini, driving a large tractor out of the jungle at about thirty miles an hour, her long hair streaming behind like some kind of tropical, post-modern vision, Lady Godiva meets Soviet farmworker. The fishing trips are another highlight: five females from three generations in an outrigger canoe, all of them topless except Tarita's mother, throwing hooks baited with squid over the side, pulling up huge fish. I get in the habit of watching for their (fully clothed) return. When the boat beached, I'd be there, coincidentally, to help drag the boat and the catch ashore. The second time I helped, Tarita smiled and told me I was nice, "Not like other guest." One night she invites me to dinner at her bungalow. I am one of ten at a family-style meal. There is little English spoken. I don't remember what we ate. That night, stretched out beneath my mosquito netting, the green coils smoking all around the room, the jungle loud with its eerie nocturnal energy, I feel as if I've entered a state of earthly Nirvana.

I think a lot about meeting Marlon, about how the two of us will get along once we meet. If his atoll is any reflection of the man, I know I'll like him. Perhaps he'll like me, too. Maybe, I muse, we'll collaborate on his biography. He'll set me up on my own island. There's one right across the lagoon that seems to be totally empty. I could paddle over every morning to interview him for the book.

I haven't found Marlon, not exactly, not yet, but I have found something of him, an important something. A man who would do all this—buy an atoll, people it with gentle natives, shelter them with goodness, create a small peaceful nation in the middle of the widest of oceans—this is truly a man worth finding.

#

I leave Tetiaroa in a shower of hugs and kisses; Matahi even plays me a song and everyone claps. I know that someday I'll be back—maybe even in the company of Marlon.

The next day, in Papeete, I visit Cynthia at the Bureau de Tetiaroa, at Faaa Airport. Cynthia is a former airline stewardess, originally from Maui, Hawaii. She runs all of Marlon's Tahitian interests. It is said she is in constant telephonic contact with Marlon. According to Teri'i, she has just returned from Los Angeles, where she had a meeting with Marlon and stayed at his compound on Mullholland Drive.

"What can we do for you Mr. Sager?"

I sit down in the chair in front of her desk, hand her my card.

"You're a journalist?" The tone in her voice—such grave disappointment. She might have said, "You're a child molester?"

"Listen," I plead. "I'm not here to ask you any questions."

"Good, because I can't answer any."

"I just want to tell you something. Is that okay? Could you please just listen?"

And so it is that I deliver the most impassioned speech in a lifetime of impassioned speeches, starting with: "I am not a scoop slob running around looking to hurt someone with a quote. I don't give a damn about actors or movies. . . ."

I tell Cynthia about my assignment, my preparation, my obsession (well, I tread a little lightly on that part). I tell her about watching all of Marlon's movies, transcribing all the dialogs, reading all the books and magazines. I tell her about hiring Angelina, going to Tetiaroa, helping Tarita with her fishing and her gardening, feeling how Marlon felt.

"Going to Marlon's island, reading about him, learning about his life—I have come to think of Marlon as a visionary," I continue. "A *visionary*, Cynthia. He was one of the first actors to produce and direct. He was one of the first to get percentage of gross. He was one of the first to study eastern religion. He went to Southeast Asia before anybody even knew about the war. He gave up a starring role in *Butch Cassidy and the Sundance Kid* because he was too grief-stricken over the death of Martin Luther King Jr. Did you know that, Cynthia? He cared so much about civil rights. When King died he was too broken up to work.

"Marlon bought an island. He established his own little utopian paradise. The United Islands of Brando. Here he can be himself, the man standing alone, far away. I've seen his books and magazines. I've sat under his favorite tree. I know that Marlon has ideas. He has foresight. He's ahead of the curve. Let me put it this way, Cynthia: America needs Marlon. I have been sent by one of the great newspapers of the land to seek his advice. the *Washington Post* is seeking advice from Marlon Brando. We need to ask him: What comes next?"

Cynthia's eyes are wide. She is with me one hundred percent, nodding her head, a member of the choir. Of course she thinks Marlon is a visionary. She's been working for him for fifteen years. The funny thing is this: I'm starting to believe it, too.

"I know that Marlon is in Los Angeles. I know that you were just staying at his house. *Please*, Cynthia, I need to see Marlon. I'll fly tomorrow. I'll see him for five minutes or five hours. I'll listen for as long as he wants to talk. I'll print *exactly* what he wants me to print. Tell him that, Cynthia. Please. Tell him—"

The phone rings, interrupting my flow.

Cynthia speaks in French. A few paragraphs in, my name is mentioned. She looks at me.

Hanging up, Cynthia fairly beams. "That was Tarita," she says. "She was calling about something else, but I told her you were here. She said you were a really nice person. She couldn't believe you were *really* a journalist! Isn't that funny? 'He was *soooo nice*'" she said, doing her best Tahitian singsong.

"She said I should call Marlon for you. When are you leaving for L.A.?"

#

I PULL INTO the driveway off Mullholland and stop before the ten-foot fence that guards the entrance to Marlon's compound.

"Package for Mr. Brando," I say into the intercom, trying to look nonchalant, waving at the three different cameras focused on my rented Suzuki Sidekick.

If it could be said, along the way, that I have felt as if my mission closely paralleled the one undertaken by Martin Sheen in *Apocalypse Now* (let us not forget Conrad's *Heart of Darkness*; we are imitators all), at this point in the story I have reached the Kno Long bridge, Francis Ford Coppola's Dante-like vision of the last civilized outpost Capt. Willard passes on his way up the river to find Kurtz. Remember the scene? The flares and weird lights, the psychedelic music, the stoned-out soldiers. Too much happening at once, no one in charge.

That's Los Angeles for you. Obscenely expensive cars, palm trees with no coconuts. Valet parking available at the McDonalds on Sunset in West Hollywood. It is cold for LA LA Land, fifty degrees, and it is raining, of all things. Can I not catch a break with this rain? The sky is brown at the edges. Because I've blown through my expense account, I am staying with the parents of a photographer I know. The dad is a clinical psychologist, which seems a good fit for me at the moment. For his thesis, he studied Maori tribesman in New Zealand. He has this great wooden hot tub in his back yard in Sherman Oaks. I'd never been in one before. At night, when it is chilly outside, being in the tub feels like being under a warm blanket with your face exposed.

Upon my arrival in Los Angeles, the first thing I did, as Cynthia had instructed, was call Marlon's personal assistant, Pat Quinn.

Pat is a retired actress. She played Alice in *Alice's Restaurant*. She's been with Marlon for twenty years. After I got her on the phone, I did my speech again. She was so glad I loved Marlon's island. She'd heard *all* about me from Cynthia. She'd talk to Marlon today, she said, tomorrow at the latest. She'd set things up. It didn't feel like a problem to her.

For the next three days, each ring of the phone at my buddy's parents' house was another needle in my brain. I lay on the bed in the guest room flipping the channels.

Each day after lunch I drove up into the hills and went past Marlon's house. It was perched atop Mulholland Drive, which snakes along the summit of the Mullholland Mountains. Marlon's place has a view of Benedict Canyon, the valley to the east, the mountains to the north. I looked longingly at the gate, the concertina wire wrapped around the top. *Come on, Marlon. Call.*

Then I hurried back. I didn't want to miss the call. Yes kiddies, this was a time before cell phones.

On day four and day five, I left several messages for Pat.

On day six, she answered the phone herself.

"I can't converse with you!" she said abruptly.

"What about the interview? What about—"

"I'm sorry, Mr. Sager. I am not at liberty to converse with you in any fashion."

The line went dead.

I am not at liberty to converse with you in any fashion? What the hell was that? It sounded like legal boilerplate. Like a direct order. What was going on?

Over the next few days, I tried every avenue I could think of. I called Marlon's other assistant, Aiko. I called a woman in Los Angeles I'd met on Tetiaroa. She used to work for Quincy Jones. Quincy had been to Tetiaroa. He is friends with Marlon. No go. A friend's father knew someone who knew someone who once had Marlon to dinner. He worked that angle. I called Marlon's bookkeepers, Brown and Kraft. I called Cynthia. She sounded glad to hear from me. I told her what had happened with Pat. She acted surprised. She said she didn't know what to think. Then she paused a moment, as if deliberating whether to tell me a bit of truth or not. "Marlon's got a lot of problems right now," she said at last. "All the new tax laws, that stuff, he's been meeting with accountants day and night, trying to solve a few serious tax problems. That's why Tehotu is there. He's helping Marlon get some other things done that have been bothering him."

I thanked Cynthia. She wished me luck, a dubious tone.

But I wasn't giving up. Not yet.

I was offering Marlon a golden opportunity to speak his mind. If taxes and accounting had him down, certainly politics would get him going. It would be good therapy for him. The salve for his wounds. We could work together, write a good story about something important, something that mattered to Marlon. Okay, so maybe our collaboration on his biography would have to wait. Obviously, he wasn't in the mood for that. No matter. Right now, all that mattered was meeting Marlon. Seeing him. Completing my mission. I wanted to look him in the eye, to hear his voice, to see him walk across a room toward me, to shake my hand, still tanned from the warm sun over his atoll. Maybe I'd play a few Tahitian tunes for him on the guitar. At this point, I'd settle for anything.

I went to Radio Shack and bought a small tape recorder, then drove up to Mulholland, parked overlooking Marlon's canyon. I lit a cigarette, put a tape of Tahitian songs in the deck, turned it down kind of low, for background music. Then I started the tape recorder. I felt breathless, as if I'd been running. My voice quavered a little bit.

"Marlon Brando," I began. "Please forgive this further intrusion. In the two months I have spent learning about you, visiting Tetiaroa, meeting your extended family, I have become involved, fascinated, and respectful. I flatter only the facts in concluding that you are a man with great vision.

"What I am offering is this: A 10,000-word article in the *Washington Post Sunday Magazine*. One million copies of the magazine are distributed each week. You can direct the subject matter. Any cause or concern. The choice is yours.

"I know you've gotten reports from your people concerning my handling of this assignment. As you know, I took no pictures of your family. I did not intrude. I didn't act like a typical journalist—I tried to be a decent human being. I tried to treat people as I'd want to be treated myself.

"I know that you want to be left alone. But I also know that you care about the world and about doing good. I know that you are an idealist—or at least you were at one time. Together, I think, we can do a little good for the world. The choice is up to you. I await your answer."

When I finished, I put the tape recorder, along with some clips of my past stories, things I thought he would like—a piece about the Great Peace March for Global Nuclear Disarmament, one about urine testing, another about the proliferation of nonsmoking areas, another about a Native American icon named Princess Pale Moon—into a large Ziploc baggie. I used the baggie because I could seal it, and because Marlon could easily see that there wasn't a bomb inside. I hoped it would make him curious, this little dog-and-pony show in a Ziploc. Maybe he would open it. Maybe he would listen.

# # #

So NOW I'M AT Marlon's gate with the package.

After an interval, a voice on the intercom: "Drive slowly and stay to the left."

The gate creaks open. There's a red sign advertising "Armed Response."

Marlon's compound is dense with foliage. There's a fenced-in area 100 feet up the driveway. As I roll slowly past, two giant dogs throw themselves at the gate and howl.

The road forks, I stay left. Down the right fork, I understand, is the home of Marlon's good bud, the actor Jack Nicholson. At the end of Marlon's driveway, a line of shrubs blocks further entrance. Then some of the shrubs turn out to be a gate. The gate swings inward on an asphalt parking area. I pull in. There are three separate little houses—low-slung, stucco, painted an orangey-brown—with a common area in between; a layout reminiscent of the house I found on Tetiaroa. A sign in the driveway advises: "Stay in Car. Attack Dogs on Premises."

In due time, a young man appears. He has a Doberman on a leash. Handsome, well-muscled, he's wearing a white T-shirt.

Oh. My. God.

It's Stanley Kowalski—*Stella!* It's Terry Malloy—*I coulda been a contenda.* It's the vision of the Marlon that I've lived with in my mind, asleep and awake, for six long weeks. Here. Right before me. Turned-down lips, sleek jaw, high cheekbones, almond eyes, tousled hair. He is Marlon—okay, Marlon with a deep tan. A young Marlon in his prime, when he was turning Hollywood upside down, long before all the wives and the press and the bullshit that drove him away from the world.

I call out as if greeting a long lost friend: "Tehotu! What's happening!"

He looks at me like I'm some kid of psycho.

I back up a few steps and introduce myself.

He cracks a big smile: "Cynthia said you might be coming."

I am overwhelmed with joy. I feel like I've returned home. "Teri'i told me to say hello," I say. "He wants to know when you're coming back. The plants are ready to harvest. Oh, and I'm supposed to tell you that Charles says . . . ."

I am yammering away like a fool, but I can't help it. *Jesus Christ, this kid looks exactly like Marlon.* I struggle to regain my composure, to shut my mouth. Still sitting in my car, I smile abashedly and hand Tehotu the baggie with the tape recorder and the clips. "Listen," I say. "Please tell your dad (*your DAD!*) that if he thinks I'm a jerk or whatever and he doesn't want to talk to me, it's cool, I'll go away. But ask him please just to think about it. And to answer. If he'll just say yes or no, I'll go from there. If he doesn't want to talk, I'll stop bugging him. I'll fly home. Just let me know, okay?"

Tehotu smiles again. I think of the beach and the stars and the lagoon.

"My dad is out right now but he'll be back soon. I'm sure he won't think you're a jerk."

#

THREE MORE DAYS. No word from Marlon—yet.

There is more rain. (I thought it never rained in sunny California.) More cable TV. More hot tubbing. I'm afraid to leave the house, thinking He might call.

Day four, I wake up in a complete and utter state of self-loathing. What the hell am I doing? This entire hopeless charade has turned out to be an even worse idea than my first marriage. I am a total JERK! I am fucking delusional. I will never make anything of myself. I suck. I should have stayed in law school, I'd be rich by now.

To hell with Marlon Brando. To hell with *hunting* Marlon Brando. He doesn't deserve a story. He doesn't deserve my time and obsession. Who the fuck cares about his opinion? What could he possibly have to say of any relevance at all? He's nothing but an actor. A fucking *actor*. Who cares?

I swing my feet to the floor, take stock of my surroundings. A sewing machine sits on top of the desk—a basket of mending occupies the chair. There is a Barbie Club House stored on one side of the room, blocking entrance to the closet. Yesterday, after sneaking into the back yard with the remnants of Marlon's marijuana, I had ventured inside the pink plastic structure—built to a kindergarten scale—and sat on a little chair for what felt like a very long time, staring at my distorted face in the faux glass mirror that was hanging over the faux fireplace. Maybe this whole thing has gone on long enough. I've already exceeded my expense account and spent most of my fee. At this point, I won't be making any money on this story at all—and I still have to write the sucker. (Not to mention the mortgage!)

But wait a minute.

You have to dare to be bad, right? You have to try things you might fail. If you do what you always do, it's guaranteed to turn out the same. After ten years of stories, I've learned a lot about other people and a little about myself—but not nearly enough. This time, I wanted more than a story. I wanted to bring something back in first person, to write about a difference in my life.

As it was, they suggested a hunt for Marlon Brando, the most elusive actor of our time.

I took the job. Wouldn't you?

(And hey, for better or for worse, I've just spent the entire month in Tahiti, Hawaii, and California!)

Now I have to finish what I started.

I get up and get dressed, take a fresh razor to my head. Someday, every schmo on the street will look like me—they'll have a shaved head, a beard, and an earring. But right now, during this winter of 1987, I feel pretty darn unique, just me and R&B singer Isaac Hayes share this look, and I don't think he has an earring. I buy some bagels, some coffee, two newspapers, a pair of binoculars. I make my way to Mulholland Drive. I park at a curve overlooking Marlon's compound.

I didn't want to have to do this. This is exactly what I've tried not to be—a journalist on a stakeout, a scoop slob looking for a quote, some tidbit to put in the first paragraph of a regurgitated story about Marlon Brando's life. A doggie bag to warm in the media microwave.

But I accepted the job. I've traveled 18,000 miles. I've spent a shitload of money. (For the record, this story is part of a two-story deal. I've yet to go to the Marshall Islands for the second piece, about the refugees from the Bikini Atoll.) Everyone I'd consulted had advised me to turn down this assignment—too risky, they all said, you're going to fail, it's a can't-win situation. When I get home, I'm going to have to look them in their faces. And even more important, when I get home, I'm going to have to figure out something to write. In *Last Tango in Paris* Marlon says that in order to live your life, you have to look first into the maw of death. I feel like I understand.

The sky is gray and cloudy. Predatory hawks soar over the canyon, hunting for rats and snakes and other small critters. Mercedes-Benzes and Jaguars and BMWs screech around the curves on Mulholland. People stare into the window of my red Suzuki. They see a guy with a black Nikon cap and sunglasses and binoculars on a stakeout. I know what they're thinking. I'm thinking it about myself, too.

Four hours pass. I listen to tapes of Tahitian music. I think about Teri'i and the other folks. I wish I had a little more of Marlon's weed.

Then, I detect some movement.

Up there, through the break in the trees, three hundred yards away, on a deck in Marlon's compound.

I raise the binoculars.

It's Tehotu. He's carrying a saw and a long board, probably a two-by-six.

And walking behind him is . . .

Marlon Brando.

I spin the little wheel, focus.

Marlon is fat. *Fat.* He's wearing a blue bathrobe. He looks tired and worried. He is bald on top with a tangled fringe of white hair around the sides. He points here, points there. He appears distracted.

It's been thirteen years since he made *Godfather* and earned his second Oscar, which he refused to accept, and about $21 million in salary and back end percentages, which he did accept. After that came *Last Tango, The Missouri Breaks, Superman, Apocalypse Now,* and *The Formula.* For the last three, he made more than $10 million each for less than 30 minutes onscreen.

Through the binoculars, I can see Marlon pretty clearly. He looks nothing like the Brat, the Slob, the Valentino of the Bop Generation, the Walking Hormone Factory, the man standing alone far away, the visionary. I see nothing of Terry Malloy, Stanley Kowalski, Fletcher Christian. Not to be too gay, but *holy shit,* Marlon was a beautiful man. And what an actor. Watch his death scene in the *Young Lions.* He was good enough to change Hollywood forever. Go to the movies now and you see his influence. Newman, Redford, Nicholson, Pacino, Hoffman, Penn . . . before all of them, there was Brando.

And now, here he is.

An old guy. Fat, bald, blue bathrobe. Directing some repairs to his deck.

I key the Suzuki; it putters to life. I drive down the hill, around the curve.

For six weeks now I've been hunting Marlon. I xeroxed his pictures and taped them to my walls. I read every book and every article, watched every movie several times; I even transcribed the dialogue on my laptop computer (a lot of it is quoted throughout this text, incorporated into the narrative). I dropped down deep, very deep, into my own kind of Method—in his wife I saw an old girlfriend; in his divorce I saw an old wife; in his art I found a meaning; in his vision I saw one, too. I saw a snail crawl along the edge of a straight razor, crawl along the edge of a straight razor and survive. That was my dream. That was my nightmare. I walked his ivory beaches and floated like a hippo in his blue lagoon. I picked out the site to build my own bungalow on his lonely atoll in the middle of the South Pacific. I knew beyond a doubt that someday I'd return.

Over the weeks I realized that Marlon was the template for the modern version of the American man. He'd shown us how to be young, how to be hip and cool and vulnerable all at the same time. And then he'd split the whole program, left us on our own. In the ensuing years, the world has clearly gone down the shitter. I started to think that maybe it wouldn't be a bad idea at all, on behalf of the entire world, to go find Marlon—to hunt him down, to ask him what he thinks. Where should we be going, Marlon? What should we be doing? Clearly, the world is in a sorry state. *We need you, Marlon Brando.* That's how it formed in my mind. *We need you before it's too late.*

I pull into Marlon's driveway, stop at the imposing gate he shares with his buddy, Jack. I edge up even with the little intercom box. There's a button. One button to Marlon Brando.

As I stick my hand out the window, a car comes into view on the other side of the gate, rounding the bend, descending the hill from Marlon's compound. A four-door Toyota. It pulls to a stop on the other side of the gate, mirroring my position. A hand reaches out of the window and pushes a button on a box on the other side. The gate opens.

A woman emerges from the car. She's fortyish, Japanese. I know instantly who it is—Aiko, Marlon's other personal assistant. After Pat had told me she "couldn't converse," I'd called Aiko. I spoke to her once. She declined to return any of my subsequent thirteen calls.

Aiko walks through the gate, toward the mailbox. Though I am sitting right there, behind the wheel of the Suzuki, she ignores me—pretends I'm not there, the way polite people do. Standing twenty feet away from me, she sifts through the mail.

I roll down my passenger-side window. "Aiko?"

She turns in my direction.

"I'm Mike Sager."

She gets a look on her face, as if to say, *Gosh, I was so lost in thought, I didn't even notice you sitting there in your red SUV.* "How are you today?" she asks.

How are you today? How do you fucking think? "I was wondering—"

"We received your package," she says, a saccharin smile on her face. "We forwarded it to Marlon. To his *next* stop, wherever he's going. I'm afraid we're not allowed to know! I'm sure he'll get back to you on the matter very soon. We heard very nice things about you. I'm sure it will all work out."

Her lips are moving, but I'm not hearing the sound.

The bitch is lying to my face.

I have just seen Marlon Brando. He is fat and bald, wearing a blue bathrobe. He's up there on his deck. I have traveled 18,000 miles. Give me a fucking break.

I look at Aiko, twenty feet away. And then I look through my windshield, toward the gate. It is open. Her car is in front of mine, sort of. There is room for my little Suzuki to squeeze past. If I so choose, I could floor it. I could be in Marlon's compound in a few seconds. It's right up that hill. I've been there before. I could get to Marlon. If someone called the police, it would probably take them fifteen minutes to get here. By then I could get a quote, at least. By then I would have an ending to my story. I could get *arrested!* That would be an *excellent* ending.

Or maybe it would just be the beginning—the beginning of a friendship with Marlon. Maybe he'd be impressed with my monumental efforts. My dedication. Such *ballsy* moves.

Maybe, before the cops got here, we'd have time to become acquainted a bit. Time to become—dare I say? *Friends.* Hadn't I carried Tarita's fish? Hadn't I refrained from taking pictures of Cheyenne as she sped through the jungle on that huge tractor? Did I mention how beautiful she was? Did I mention that she'd been topless? No, I said she was wearing a bikini because I wanted to be respectful of Marlon's daughter's beautiful breasts. I'd been nice to the natives; I'd jammed with the help. I'd even refrained from crow-barring open Marlon's private residence—and I could have, so easily; I could have been inside his desk and his file cabinets and everything. What secrets I turned down

I will never know. Surely, I'd shown myself, over the course of my hunt, to be much more than a journalist—I'd comported myself like a decent human being.

In *Apocalypse Now*, before Capt. Willard goes up the river, the general tries to prepare him for his mission, for the horror he is likely to find. "You see, Willard," the general says, "things get confused out there. Power, ideals, morality . . . there's a conflict in every human heart between the rational and the irrational, between good and evil."

Capt. Willard, of course, was a soldier. A hired gun, an assassin. He had a job to do. He did it.

Me, I'm a journalist. It's a strange profession, not unlike Willard's, though I don't kill anyone. What I do is maneuver myself behind the lines of people's lives and personalities. I take scrapings of their insides, samples of their deepest inner thoughts and feelings, and then I display it all for everyone to see. I do all this under the banner of the First Amendment to the U.S. Constitution. Under the banner of The People's Right To Know. I dog, I posture, I say what they want to hear. I do what I have to do to get my story, just like Willard has to do to get his man.

This time I'd wanted it to be different.

I figured I could show myself to Marlon as a man worthy of meeting. But somewhere along the line, things got confused. Like some zany hypnotist who has hypnotized himself by accident, I started believing my own con.

Marlon knows better, of course. He knows me better than I know myself. All the dog-and-pony shows in all the Ziploc baggies in the world are not going to change his mind. I thought I was being a real person, a good human being. And in a way, I have been. But Marlon knows the *whole* truth. No matter how you cut it, I'm still just another journalist trying to cook up a story.

Aiko knows this, too. That's why she's lying to my face. And that's why she feels justified in doing so. And maybe that's also why she seems to be enjoying herself so much. Because to her, my face isn't just my face. It is the face of all journalists, of all the scoop slobs who have hunted Marlon for thirty years.

From the start it sounded ridiculous. *Go to Tahiti and find Marlon Brando.*

And then what?

You'll know.

Hmmm.

I take measure of the distance between the fender of Aiko's Toyota and the gate-pole, gun the Suzuki's tinny little engine.

And then I put it in reverse and back out of Marlon's driveway.

I take the next plane home.

The Washington Post Sunday Magazine, 1987

Acknowledgments

\# \# \#

John Radziewicz, Lissa Warren, David Granger, Peter Griffin, Tyler Cabot, Buddy Kite, Carolyn White, David Rosenthal, Jann Wenner, Don Graham, Jay Lovinger, Bill Hamilton, Bob Love, Bob Wallace, Robert Vare, Terry McDonell, David Hirshey, Bill Tonelli, Art Cooper, Lisa Henricksson, Sandy Dijkstra, Mollie Glick, Will Balliett, Mark Corsey.

Bob Greene, Walt Harrington, Sam Freedman, Henry Schuster, Hunter S. Thompson, Richard Ben Cramer, Kurt Andersen, Morgan Entrekin, George Pelecanos, Jamison Stoltz, Deb Seager, Matt Koreiwo, Barry Siegel, Patricia Pierson, William Pereira, Robert Boynton, John H. Richardson, John Fennell, Clay Ezell, Elizabeth Fishman, Lisa Keller, Ben Yagoda, Brad T. Seibel, Denise Jones, Elizabeth Leik, Patsy Sims, Kelly Justice, Rene Martin, Brandon Reynolds, Kia Bowman, Kinsee Morlan, David Rolland, Angela Carone, Tom Fudge, David Gessner, Jackie Bullard, Sheila Tefft, Frank Reiss, Patrick Beach, David Lee Simmons, Thomas Bell, Ken Edelstein, Neil Henry, Dierdre English, Richard Karpel, Michael Tisserand, Warwick's Bookstore, Susan McBeth, Bill Zehme, Peter Mehlman, Steve Jones, Steve Cohen, Lee Cohen, Hesh Beker, Al Baverman, Scott Goldstein, Nate Braverman, Steven Sulcov, Mike Elizondo, David Kelley, Geoff Diner, Marshall Keys, Federico Gonzalez

Peña, Jim Brogan, Terrell Lamb, Chris Janney, Bill Regardie, Jack Limpert, Ken Ringle, Herb Denton.

Miles Sager, Rebekah Sager, Beverly and Marvin Sager, Wendy Sager, William H. Sager, Larry Alfred.

To my students: Your trust helps to quiet the noise of my own self doubts.

Permissions

#

Hunting Marlon Brando" was first published in a different form in the *Washington Post Sunday Magazine,* July 5, 1987.

The following stories were first published in a different form in *Rolling Stone*:
"Thailand's Home for Wayward Vets" May 10, 1984; "A Boy and His Dog in Hell" July 2, 1987; "Death in Venice" September 22, 1988; "The Ice Age" February 8, 1990.

The following stories were first published in a different form in *GQ*: "Big" June 1995; "Generation H" September 1995.

The following stories were first published in a different form in *Esquire*: "The Sharpton Strategy" January 1991; "The Smartest Man in America" November, 1999; "Kobe Bryant Doesn't Want Your Love" November 2007; "Wounded Warriors" (published as "Wounded Battalion") December 2007.

About the Author

#

Mike Sager quit law school after three weeks to work the graveyard shift as a copy boy at the *Washington Post*. Eleven months later, he was promoted to staff writer by then Metro Editor Bob Woodward. He left the *Post* after six years to pursue a career in magazines. For the past decade, he has been a writer-at-large for *Esquire*. His first two collections of journalism, *Scary Monsters and Super Freaks* and *Revenge of the Donut Boys*, were *Los Angeles Times* bestsellers. His first novel, *Deviant Behavior*, was published by Grove/Atlantic's Black Cat. He is at work on a second.

Sager is a former contributing editor of *Rolling Stone* and writer-at-large for *GQ*. He has also written for *Vibe, Spy, Interview, Playboy, Washingtonian,* and *Regardies*. He has read and lectured widely; his work is included in several textbooks in use in college classrooms. Each spring, he leads a popular workshop at the University of California-Irvine, where he is a Pereira Visiting Writer. Many of his stories have been optioned for film. A graduate of Emory University, he lives with his wife and son in La Jolla, California.

For more information, please see www.MikeSager.com.